JANE AUSTEN

A GUIDE TO
Jane Austen

―――

MICHAEL HARDWICK

CHARLES SCRIBNER'S SONS
NEW YORK

1 3 5 7 9 11 13 15 17 19 I/C 20 18 16 14 12 10 8 6 4 2

Printed in Great Britain
Library of Congress Catalog Card Number 73-21143
ISBN 0 684 13824 7

Contents

Introduction

LIKE its companion volumes, this work sets out to provide an introduction to its subject for those readers who have little or no acquaintance with it; to serve as a quick-reference guide for anyone wishing to recall or check a point of character, plot or date (and this can involve much delving when no single-volume *aide-memoire* exists); and, for the seasoned lover of Jane Austen's books, to evoke well-remembered scenes and people, and perhaps prompt a reappraisal of a work which is not yet appreciated.

In a public library recently I heard an old lady asking that question so familiar to librarians: 'Can you recommend me a good novel for the weekend?', adding, 'I hadn't anything last week, so I read *Emma* again. I always go back to *Emma* when there's nothing else.' I would hope that, if she chances to browse through this present volume, she might emerge to expect almost as much delight awaiting her in one or two of Jane Austen's other books which, as yet, have not won such deep affection from her.

Following the pattern of the other titles in this series, a brief assessment of Jane Austen and an outline of her life comes first, followed by a 'who's who' of characters, on this occasion restricted to those who take a significant part – though sometimes small – in the story: servants, background figures and people from reported events are omitted, to make room for reasonably substantial descriptive quotations which I feel would lose something essential if truncated. Then follow plots of the six main novels and four other pieces, embodying longer quotations pertinent to the story or to something markedly characteristic of Jane Austen's writing.

There is no discography this time. Little of Jane Austen's work has found its way into recordings, though there are two current issues worth mentioning. One is of a series of extracts from the stories and the letters, with brief biographical material, spoken by Dorothy Reynolds and Angus Mackay in a recital at the National Portrait Gallery, London. The other is in the first part of the Royal Shakespeare Company's recording of 'The Hollow Crown', an entertainment devised by John Barton, in which Dorothy Tutin reads extracts from Jane's *History of England*, 'by a partial, prejudiced, & ignorant Historian'.

The order in which to consider Jane's works has always posed problems, since it is not certain when some of them were written, and their publication occurred in anything but their sequence of composition. I have led off with the most complete and rewarding of the juvenile pieces, *Love and Freindship* [*sic*], followed by two more written before she became established as a novelist, the fragment *The Watsons* and the perfunctorily completed *Lady Susan*. The six novels follow these, followed by *Sanditon*, the fragment of the novel on which Jane was working as a fatal disease approached its terminal stage. I have not included the rest of the *Juvenilia*, nor considered the *Letters* as a work. They are, of course, indispensable reading for anyone who really wants to get to know Jane Austen, and are easily accessible in *Jane Austen's Letters*, a single-volume edition, collected and edited by the late R. W. Chapman (Oxford University Press). Dr Chapman, the pre-eminent figure in the study of Jane Austen, was also responsible for the best editions of her works, and for *The Oxford Illustrated Jane Austen*, the only complete one, with many comments and illustrations, revised in 1965–7 by Mary Lascelles from Dr Chapman's earlier versions and his notes.

I do not propose to offer an extensive bibliography. As an excellent general-purpose biography I would recommend *Jane Austen* by Elizabeth Jenkins, first published by Gollancz in 1938 and now obtainable in paperback from Sphere Books. I have also referred elsewhere to *The Double Life of Jane Austen* by Jane Aiken Hodge: this was published by Hodder & Stoughton in 1972. Three other, more academic studies, might be mentioned:

Jane Austen and her Art by Mary Lascelles (Clarendon Press, 1939); *The Novels of Jane Austen* by Robert Liddell (Longmans, 1963); and *Jane Austen: The Six Novels* by W. A. Craik (Methuen, 1965). Any of these will in turn point the way to other works of detailed scholarship. The study closest in time to Jane herself is *A Memoir of Jane Austen* by her nephew James Edward Austen-Leigh, first published in 1870. A *Life and Letters* by two later Austen-Leigh descendants brought together much interesting material for the first time in 1913. Unfortunately, too late for me to benefit by it in compiling my own book, which is being printed as I interpolate this sentence, there has appeared in 1973 *A Jane Austen Companion* by F. B. Pinion (Macmillan); a work of exhaustive scholarship which, had it appeared earlier, would not have deterred me from continuing with this less academically-intentioned guide, but would, through its wealth of detail, have afforded me several valuable short-cuts.

Inevitably, Jane Austen has a place in that admirable series *The Critical Heritage* (Routledge & Kegan Paul), whose selections from criticism of the time makes fascinating reading. In Jane's case, however, as B. C. Southam, the editor of the volume devoted to her, points out, only twelve reviews are known to exist which appeared in her lifetime; she wrote anonymously, and her fame developed gradually only after her death. Mr Southam has supplemented these twelve reviews with many later ones, and his volume loses nothing in comparison with others in the series; but this same paucity of contemporary material is the reason why I have omitted references to critical reception from my pre-ambles to the plots.

As to the passages of Jane Austen's own prose quoted in this volume, I have permitted myself a small amount of editing of punctuation, principally in *The Characters* section and largely in the interest of readers for whom English is not a first language and who might otherwise be confused and put off. I have retained Jane's own spelling, whose occasional eccentricity by today's standards adds period charm to her work.

MICHAEL HARDWICK

Jane Austen

JANE AUSTEN'S life, compared with those of many of the writers who figure in this series of *Guides*, was relatively uneventful. Nothing of great note, in the personal sense, occurred; neither adventure nor accident embroiled her in immediate drama. She did nothing much, met no one much, went nowhere much; yet she is celebrated as one of the greatest observers of human behaviour, its motives and its consequences, and her themes, limited as they are in situation, time, place and class of society, have a universality which makes them as valid today as when they were conceived in the days of George III.

Virginia Woolf said of Jane Austen, as a writer, that she was 'mistress of much deeper emotion than appears upon the surface. She stimulates us to supply what is not there.' This is pertinent, also, to her life, Many people have written fancifully of her, and few authors' works have been so relentlessly scrutinized and dissected in search of clues to confirm that there *must* have been more to the life of a woman who could so unerringly pinpoint the reactions of others, male as well as female, to the dilemmas of the sexes. But the truth would seem to be that there was not. Some sort of abortive love affair evidently took place, and there have been suggestions of a nervous breakdown; Jane Austen's fame, though, depends not at all on private infamy. Admirably studied and readably presented though Jane Aiken Hodge's *The Double Life of Jane Austen* is, the allusion to a double life – perfectly valid in her context – turns out to mean something quite other than its obvious implications.

No, it is Jane Austen's consistently perceptive and honest depiction of the people around her, with her special touch for irony, which afford her books such timeless success. 'I could no more write a romance than an epic poem,' she answered the Prince Regent's librarian, the Rev J. S. Clarke, who had un-perceptively urged her to do so. 'I could not sit seriously down to write a serious romance under any other motive than to save my life; and if it were indispensable for me to keep it up and never relax into laughing at myself or at other people, I am sure, I should be hung before I had finished the first chapter.'

This is not to suggest that nothing moved or perturbed her: that her nature was one of clinical detachment. Quite small occurrences could affect or keenly interest her to a degree we might find hard to comprehend in our own comparatively *blasé* times. But her view of life is essentially as a human comedy, with the recollection that a principal element of most comedy is catastrophe to some degree. So subtle an approach to relation-ships calls for the highest literary ability for even one success; but Jane Austen succeeded at almost every attempt. It was sheer writing skill which enabled her to assemble these impressions of hers into such compelling narratives about such extraordinarily convincing people. As to any deeply-pondered profundity which may be read into them, I think Jane would have had great fun at the expense of some of the scholarship of recent decades, devoted to seeking out elaborate symbolism which, if it is there, I am sure got there for the most part unconsciously. Because her range of acquaintance was small, and not very diverse, and she deliber-ately chose to restrict her stories to this circle and its preoccu-pations, she knew every reaction any given circumstance or utterance would, or should, provoke. She could convey an entire trait of character merely by making someone respond in a way they should or should not have done in their society and time. It is, on the whole, an unrewarding exercise to try to identify her fictional characters with those of her life, including herself. Few 'lower class' or really aristocratic figures feature in her stories. Almost all her people belong somewhere in between – country gentlemen of modest means, their wives, their marriageable daughters, their rather unsatisfactory sons, and the indispensable bachelors, heirs, officers and eligible young clergymen. They tend to speak 'correctly', as the literary requirements of Jane Austen's time dictated, yet in a way which reads perfectly easily today. It takes only a lapse or two of grammar, or a slight roughness of expression, to convey that a character is ill-bred or badly brought up, without any recourse to contemporary slang which would have dated the works markedly.

Jane Austen's recorded utterances on the craft of authorship are few, and mostly arose from her kindly and constructive criticisms of her niece Anna Lefroy's attempts to write a novel entitled *Which is the Heroine?*, which seems to have been promising enough to make us deplore its author's decision to destroy the unfinished manuscript soon after Jane's death. The most quoted passage crystallizes Jane's own approach: 'You are now collecting your People delightfully, getting them exactly in such a spot as is the delight of my life; – 3 or 4 Families in a Country Village is the very thing to work on.' She somewhere referred to 'the little bit (two inches wide) of ivory on which I work with so fine a brush as produces little effect after much labour.' Certainly, she laboured hard, revising and cutting her work with an objectivity not all authors can muster for their own productions.

She disliked any notion of celebrity, and was dismayed when her anonymity was lost. She belonged to no literary cliques, met no great contemporaries in her field, and did not wish to do so. The quiet, predictable routine of a country household was her ideal, and adds to our difficulty in understanding how she achieved the results she did. Any reader curious enough to pursue this point, and to see Jane Austen as woman and artist in the context of her circumstances and period of history could do no better, in my view, than turn to that most readable of biographies, *Jane Austen* by Elizabeth Jenkins. Meanwhile, the following is a brief summary of Jane's life, complemented to some extent in the preambles to the synopses of the works.

She was born on 16 December 1775, at the rectory of Steventon, in Hampshire, where her father, the Rev George Austen, lived the tranquil, ordered life of a scholar-parson. A classically handsome man, he had no press of duties and could spend plenty of time amongst his books and paying calls with his aristocratic-looking wife Cassandra, the daughter of a notable Master of Balliol College, Oxford. Their intellects and cultivated tastes were matched, their ironic sense of humour interplayed.

Jane had six brothers and one sister, Cassandra, her senior by almost three years. The two girls, who were to be lifelong companions and confidantes, were sent away to school together for some five years from 1782, first at Oxford and then at Reading, with a brief and almost fatal interlude for them at Southampton where they caught 'putrid sore throat' and nearly died. From about the age of twelve, Jane's education was supplied by her father, of whom one of her brothers subsequently wrote: 'Being not only a profound scholar, but possessing a most exquisite taste in every species of literature, it is not wonderful that his daughter Jane should at a very early age have become sensible to the charms of style and enthusiastic in the cultivation of her own language.' She was already writing the odds and ends which comprise her *Juvenilia*, including that delightful satirical novel *Love and Freindship* and the brief *History of England, from the reign of Henry the 4th to the death of Charles the 1st*, which she described as being by 'a partial, prejudiced and ignorant historian', a jolly romp typified by its judgement of Henry VI: 'I cannot say much for this Monarch's sense. Nor would I if I could, for he was a Lancastrian. I suppose you know all about the Wars between him and the Duke of York, who was on the right side; if you do not, you had better read some other History.'

As they moved through their late girlhood, Jane and Cassandra, according to a friend, were 'breaking hearts by the dozen'. Jane had been somewhat chubby as a child, but grew tall for a woman; very slender, elegant and pretty, with brunette colouring and rosy cheeks. But, although all but one of their brothers was to marry, neither of the girls did so. Cassandra became engaged in about 1795 to a Rev Thomas Fowle, but he was dead within two years and she remained a spinster. There is evidence of a romance in 1801 between Jane and a young man whose identity has never been discovered. It seems that he, too, soon died. One December day in 1802 she went so far as to accept an offer of marriage from a long-standing friend several years her junior, Harris Bigg Wither. She retracted the following day, and never again, so far as is known, contemplated matrimony or indulged in any romantic associations.

The Austen family were all great readers and, like most cultivated circles of their time, wrote poems, 'charades' – which we should call riddles – and sometimes more substantial pieces, to be read aloud to one another in the candle-lit evenings. When, in 1797, Jane read her three-volume novel entitled *First Impressions*, her father's own impressions of it were so favourable that he wrote to a publisher friend, offering to send the manuscript and pay the costs of producing it. Messrs Cadells' immediate reply declining even to read the work has often been cited as one of the classic cases of a publisher's folly. Unwittingly, though, the refusal did literature a great service; for had *First Impressions* been published as it stood, Jane Austen would never have re-written it, when she was several years more mature, as *Pride and Prejudice*. Meanwhile, *First Impressions* went into a drawer and *Sense and Sensibility*, at first titled *Elinor and Marianne*, began to take shape.

Up to 1801 Jane's home life had been spent at Steventon and it came as an emotional shock to her, hard to appreciate today, when her mother announced that year that they were going to leave Steventon for good and live in Bath. It was a drastic uprooting for a girl of twenty-five who had ordered her life into a placid routine that was entirely agreeable to her temperament and working needs; in fact, we are told that she fainted on hearing the news, the impact of which, together with the distress she was probably feeling at the ending of her only romance, may account for the gap in her correspondence, which has made the subsequent three years of her life a gift to scholar-detectives.

Mr Austen's declining health had precipitated the move to Bath, with its curative waters and community of physicians; but, despite these, he died there in January 1805, without having had the pleasure of seeing any of his gifted daughter's work in print.

He was unlucky not to have done so. *Northanger Abbey*, then entitled *Susan*, had been completed in 1803 and was sold for £10 to a publisher on Jane's behalf by her brother Henry, a banker living in London. But publication did not follow, and it was not to appear until after its author's own death.

On her husband's death Mrs Austen took her daughters from the house at 4 Sydney Place which had been their home for three years to lodgings in Gay Street, in another part of the city. The following year they moved again, this time to Southampton, where they took a house in Castle Square. The purpose of this was to provide a convenient visiting-place on the Naval coast for Jane's brothers, Francis and James, both of whom were pursuing successful careers in the Royal Navy. (Francis was to superintend the embarkation of Sir John Moore's retreating army at Corunna in January 1809, and later to become an Admiral of the Fleet; his younger brother reached the rank of admiral.) In 1809, however, another move was made. Jane's third brother, Edward, had been adopted in his boyhood by a Mr Thomas Knight, the childless owner of rich estates at Godmersham, near Canterbury, Kent, and Chawton, near Winchester, Hampshire. Thomas Knight had died in 1794, leaving his estates to Edward, who had taken the surname of his benefactor in accordance with contemporary custom. Edward had lost his wife in 1808, and felt it would be desirable for himself and his children, as well as for his mother and sisters, if Mrs Austen, Jane, Cassandra, and the girls' intimate friend from childhood, Martha Lloyd, who lived with the Austen family, could reside close to one or the other of his homes. Accordingly, he offered Mrs Austen the choice of two modest houses, one at Godmersham, the other at Chawton. She chose the latter, and within a few days of their moving in, Jane was writing to Captain Francis Austen:

> As for ourselves, we're very well;
> As unaffected prose will tell. –
> Cassandra's pen will paint our state,
> The many comforts that await
> Our Chawton home, how much we find

Already in it, to our mind;
And how convinced, that when complete
It will all other Houses beat
That ever have been made or mended,
With rooms concise, or rooms distended.
You'll find us very snug next year,
Perhaps with Charles & Fanny near,
For now it often does delight us
To fancy them just over-right us. –

The Chawton home was to be Jane Austen's last and most settled. It was during the nine years there that she resumed the writing which had been no more than spasmodic since the upheavals of 1801, and saw her four greatest works published. The house still stands, and may be visited by the public. It contains a number of items and copies of others associated with Jane, and the guide-leaflet published by the Jane Austen Memorial Trust, who maintain and administer the place, gives some impression of the life she and her family led there. But the interest of a visit to Chawton House, as to any home of someone famous, is enhanced enormously by a little reading beforehand, so that the visitor has a preconception of the way things were and what to look for. For this purpose, I can think of no more evocative picture than that reconstructed by Elizabeth Jenkins in the biography already mentioned:

The left-hand parlour was the larger of the two, and Jane's piano stood there; but in the right-hand one, which was the common sitting-room, was kept her mahogany writing-desk. She had, says her nephew, no separate study to retire to; there was no dressing-room here as there had been at Steventon in which she worked with no one near her but her 'other self.' She wrote now in a living-room overlooking the road, in which any caller immediately perceived her to be at home, where the children from Steventon were constantly walking in. Her sole protections against the world were, a door which creaked, whose hinges she asked might remain unattended to because they gave her warning that somebody was coming, and the blotting-paper under which she slipped her small sheets of exquisitely written manuscript when a visitor was shown in. The many long spells of quiet when the others had walked out, her mother was in the garden and she had the room to herself; or when the domestic party was assembled, sewing and reading, with nothing but the soft stir of utterly familiar sounds and no tones but the low, infrequent ones of beloved, familiar voices – these were the conditions in which she created *Mansfield Park*, *Emma* and *Persuasion*. They seem inadequate, it is true; the important novelists of today, who have their agents and their secretaries, whose establishments are run entirely for their own convenience and who give out that they must never in any circumstances be disturbed while they are at work – these have, in every respect, a superior régime to that of Jane Austen's unprofessional existence – but their books are not so good.

Hers were not conditions in which any but a mind of exceptional strength could have exerted itself to full advantage; but the shaping spirit of imagination that created human beings, whole and entire, was a force too powerful to be thrown out of gear by having to break off in a conversation or a paragraph because a child wanted to talk to her. When James's Edward, in his Winchester holidays, or the young lady Anna, or the four-year-old Caroline, or one of the tribe of Godmersham cousins, on a visit to the great house opposite, came into the right-hand parlour of the cottage, they remembered afterwards that their Aunt Jane had frequently been writing at her desk before, at their entrance, she turned to greet them with her gay, affectionate manner. Their remorse, afterwards, for the mischief they might have done was intense; it could not be otherwise, when they considered that they had interrupted her in *Mansfield Park*, or *Emma* or *Persuasion*; but they did no injury; she put the sheet under the blotting-paper with a smile.

Not that Jane never moved from Chawton. She often went to Godmersham, to stay with Edward, to enjoy (and observe) the society of his family and friends; and she was quite often in London, visiting Henry in Hans Place. Since her father's death he had been acting as her intermediary with publishers and overseeing her business in general. For all the benefits this latter relationship brought her, though, it also hastened her end. In 1815 her strength, which was less than her healthy appearance and vitality proclaimed, was heavily taxed by nursing Henry through severe illness; and the following year she underwent the strain of seeing him financially ruined and left a bankrupt. Her own health was declining, and she knew it. In January 1817 she was beginning the fragment we know as *Sanditon* with sparkling verve and humour, but by the middle of March she could do no more. An internal disease – identified in our own time by Sir Zachary Cope, surgeon and expert in diseases of the abdomen, as Addison's Disease – had been gradually sapping her resources with its debilitating symptoms. She committed herself to the care of a surgeon in Winchester, Giles King Lyford, and travelled there in Edward Knight's carriage on 24 May 1817.

Her case was hopeless. On 18 July she died in the arms of her sister Cassandra at their lodgings in College Street, a house which now bears a plaque to her memory. Two months to the day after her arrival in Winchester, she was buried there, in the Cathedral.

The inscription on her grave bears no reference to her literary achievements, and the pamphlet *Jane Austen in Winchester*, by Canon Frederick Busby, on sale in the Cathedral, tells of how one of the vergers in the middle of last century was perplexed at the number of inquiries he had to answer about the whereabouts of the grave. Was there 'anything particular about that lady?' he is recorded as having asked. It is a question many have asked since. It has been answered in most emphatic terms by a host of scholars, 'Janeites', and ordinary readers since her work came to be widely celebrated (which, incidentally, was not until late in her century). There have been equally firm detractors: people who 'cannot take' Jane Austen for a variety of reasons, chief of which are perhaps that very lack of dramatic action in her works; her indifference to the larger events of the times in which they are set, and to the widespread wretchedness of so many then living; the constantly recurring *leit-motif* of the husband-hunt; and some regard her ironic comment upon human foibles and weaknesses as an unwarranted assumption of the seat of judgement.

Whether one would sooner admire the literary architecture of *Mansfield Park*, or indulge a secret preference for the fun of *Northanger Abbey* or *Love and Freindship*, or ponder the symbolical possibilities of every last semi-colon, or merely escape into a filmed version of *Pride and Prejudice*, there is something for most of us in Jane Austen. I think of Sir Walter Scott in early 1826, harrassed, financially wrecked not two months earlier, facing years of gargantuan labour which would so contrast with Jane's easy-paced creativity, relaxing briefly with a third reading of *Pride and Prejudice*, and then opening his journal to record the tribute of an avowed professional to a determined amateur: 'That young lady had a talent for describing the involvement and feelings and characters of ordinary life which is to me the most wonderful I ever met with. The Big Bow-wow strain I can do myself like any now going, but the exquisite touch which renders ordinary commonplace things and characters interesting from the truth of the description and the sentiment is denied me. What a pity such a gifted creature died so early.'

The Characters

ALLEN, MR and MRS: Middle-aged neighbours of the Morlands who launch Catherine into Bath society. *Mrs. Allen was one of that numerous class of females, whose society can raise no other emotion than surprise at there being any men in the world who could like them well enough to marry them. She had neither beauty, genius, accomplishment, nor manner. The air of a gentlewoman, a great deal of quiet, inactive good temper, and a trifling turn of mind were all that could account for her being the choice of a sensible, intelligent man, like Mr. Allen.* (Northanger Abbey)

AUGUSTUS: A friend of Edward Lindsay, married to Sophia. He is jailed for theft and later dies with Edward in an accident. *'They had been married but a few months when our visit to them commenced during which time they had been amply supported by a considerable sum of Money which Augustus had gracefully purloined from his unworthy father's Escritoire, a few days before his union with Sophia.'* – Laura (Love and Freindship)

BATES, MRS and MISS HETTY: Widow of a former vicar of Highbury and her daughter, still living in the neighbourhood. Jane Fairfax, who arrives to stay with them, is Mrs Bates's granddaughter. *Mrs. Bates . . . was a very old lady, almost past everything but tea and quadrille. She lived with her single daughter in a very small way, and was considered with all the regard and respect which a harmless old lady, under such untoward circumstances, can excite. Her daughter enjoyed a most uncommon degree of popularity for a woman neither young, handsome, rich, nor married . . . She had never boasted either beauty or cleverness. Her youth had passed without distinction and her middle of life was devoted to the care of a failing mother, and the endeavour to make a small income go as far as possible. And yet she was a happy woman, and a woman whom no one named without good-will . . . She was a great talker upon little matters.* (*Emma*)

BENNET, CATHERINE (KITTY): The fourth daughter. She is as giddy as Lydia while they are together, but improves afterwards, though she does not marry. *She was not of so ungovernable a temper as Lydia; and, removed from Lydia's example, she became, by proper attention and management, less irritable, less ignorant, and less insipid.* (*Pride & Prejudice*)

BENNET, ELIZABETH: The second daughter. She rejects William Collins and eventually marries Darcy. *Mr. Darcy has at first scarcely allowed her to be pretty; he had looked at her without admiration at the ball; and when they next met, he looked at her only to criticise. But no sooner had he made it clear to himself and his friends that she had hardly a good feature in her face, than he began to find it was rendered uncommonly intelligent by the beautiful expression of her dark eyes. To this discovery succeeded some others equally mortifying. Though he had detected with a critical eye more than one failure of perfect symmetry in her form, he was forcing to acknowledge her figure to be light and pleasing; and in spite of his asserting that her manners were not those of the fashionable world, he was caught by their easy playfulness.* (*Pride & Prejudice*)

BENNET, JANE: The oldest daughter. She marries Charles Bingley. '*You never see a fault in anybody. All the world are good and agreeable in your eyes. I never heard you speak ill of a human being in my life.*' – Elizabeth (*Pride & Prejudice*)

BENNET, LYDIA: The youngest daughter. She elopes with, then marries, Wickham. *A stout, well-grown girl of fifteen, with a fine complexion and good-humoured countenance; a favourite with her mother, whose affection had brought her into public at an early age. She had high animal spirits and a sort of natural self-consequence, which the attention of the officers, to whom her uncle's good dinners and her own easy manners recommended her, had increased into assurance.* (*Pride & Prejudice*)

BENNET, MARY: The third daughter: she is still a spinster when the book ends. *Mary had neither genius nor taste; and though vanity had given her application, it had given her likewise a* pedantic air and conceited manner, which would have injured a higher degree of excellence that she had reached. 'While I can have my mornings to myself,' said she, 'it is enough – I think it is no sacrifice to join occasionally in evening engagements. Society has claims on us all; and I profess myself one of those who consider intervals of recreation and amusement as desirable for everybody.' (*Pride & Prejudice*)

BENNET, MRS: Bennet's wife; sister of Mrs Philips and Edward Gardiner. *She was a woman of mean understanding, little inform-ation, and uncertain temper. When she was discontented, she fancied herself nervous. The business of her life was to get her daughters married; its solace was visiting and news.* 'I tell you what, Miss Lizzy – this way, you will never get a husband at all – and I am sure I do not know who is to maintain you when your father is dead. I shall not be able to keep you – and so I warn you. I have done with you from this very day. I told you in the library, you know, that I should never speak to you again, and you will find me as good as my word. I have no pleasure in talking to undutiful children. Not that I have much pleasure, indeed, in talking to anybody. People who suffer as I do from nervous complaints can have no great inclination for talking. Nobody can tell what I suffer! But it is always so. Those who do not complain are never pitied.' (*Pride & Prejudice*)

BENNET, WILLIAM: Of Longbourne, near Meryton, Hertford-shire. Father of Jane, Elizabeth, Mary, Kitty and Lydia. *Captivated by youth and beauty, and that appearance of good humour which youth and beauty generally give, had married a woman whose weak understanding and illiberal mind had very early in their marriage put an end to all real affection for her. Respect, esteem, and confidence had vanished for ever; and all his views of domestic happiness were overthrown. But Mr. Bennet was not of a disposition to seek comfort for the disappointment which his own imprudence had brought on, in any of those pleasures which too often console the unfortunate for their folly or their vice. He was fond of the country and of books; and from these tastes had arisen his principal enjoyments. To his wife he was very little otherwise indebted, than as her ignorance and folly had contributed to his* amusement. *This is not the sort of happiness which a man would in general wish to owe to his wife; but where other powers of entertainment are wanting, the true philosopher will derive benefit from such as are given.* (*Pride & Prejudice*)

BENWICK, CAPTAIN JAMES: A friend of Wentworth and Harville, he is mourning the loss of Harville's late sister when he meets the Musgroves and ultimately falls in love with Louisa. *He had a pleasing face and a melancholy air, just as he ought to have ... He was evidently a young man of considerable taste in reading, though principally in poetry ... He repeated, with such tremulous feeling, the various lines which imaged a broken heart, or a mind destroyed by wretchedness, and looked so entirely as if he meant to be understood, that she* [Anne] *ventured to hope he did not always read only poetry: and to say that she thought it was the misfortune of poetry to be seldom safely enjoyed by those who enjoyed it completely; and that the strong feelings which alone could estimate it truly were the very feelings which ought to taste it but sparingly.* (*Persuasion*)

BERTRAM, EDMUND: The younger son. Studying for the clergy, he is protectively kind to Fanny Price. Though Mary Crawford becomes his romantic objective, it is Fanny whom he marries. *He was always true to her interests, and considerate of her feelings, trying to make her good qualities understood, and to conquer the diffidence which prevented their being more apparent.* (*Mansfield Park*)

BERTRAM, JULIA: The younger daughter. She is her sister Maria's rival for the attentions of Henry Crawford, but elopes with, and marries, his friend, the Hon John Yates. '*Though Julia fancies she prefers tragedy, I would not trust her in it. There is nothing of tragedy about her. She has not the look of it. Her features are not tragic features, and she walks too quick, and speaks too quick, and would not keep her countenance.*' – Tom Bertram (*Mansfield Park*)

BERTRAM, LADY: Wife of Sir Thomas, formerly Maria Ward, sister of Mrs Norris and Mrs Price. *She was a woman who spent her days in sitting, nicely dressed, on a sofa, doing some long piece of needlework, of little use and no beauty, thinking more of her pug than her children, but very indulgent to the latter, when it did not put herself to inconvenience.* (*Mansfield Park*)

BERTRAM, MARIA: The elder daughter. Although her preference is for Henry Crawford and her father offers her the chance to break her engagement with James Rushworth, she marries the latter, but later elopes with the former. *Mrs. Rushworth acknowledged herself very desirous that her son should marry, and declared that of all the young ladies she had ever seen, Miss Bertram seemed, by her amiable qualities and accomplishments, the best adapted to make him happy. Mrs. Norris accepted the compliment, and admired the nice discernment of character which could so well distinguish merit. Maria was indeed the pride and delight of them all – perfectly faultless – an angel.* (*Mansfield Park*)

BERTRAM, SIR THOMAS: Of Mansfield Park, Northamptonshire, husband of Maria Ward, whose niece, Fanny Price, he takes into his household, joined later by her sister Susan. His own children are Tom, Edmund, Maria and Julia. (*Mansfield Park*)

BERTRAM, TOM: The elder son. He is something of a spendthrift and gets into debt, but subsequently mends his ways. *He was just entering into life, full of spirits, and with all the liberal dispositions of an eldest son, who feels born only for expense and enjoyment.* (*Mansfield Park*)

BICKERTON, MISS: Parlour boarder at Mrs Goddard's who is with Harriet Smith when they are accosted by gipsies. *A child on the watch came towards them to beg; and Miss Bickerton, excessively frightened, gave a great scream, and calling on Harriet to follow her, ran up a steep bank, cleared a slight hedge at the top, and made the best of her way by a short cut back to Highbury.* (*Emma*)

BINGLEY, CAROLINE: See HURST, MRS. (*Pride & Prejudice*)

BINGLEY, CHARLES: The new tenant of Netherfield Park, brother of Louisa (Mrs Hurst) and Caroline. He marries Jane Bennet. *Good-looking and gentlemanlike; he had a pleasant countenance, and easy, unaffected manners.* (*Pride & Prejudice*)

BLAKE, MRS: Widowed sister of the Rev Howard, with whom

she lives. *A lively pleasant-looking little Woman of 5 or 6 & 30. Her ten-year old son Charles is 'uncommonly fond of dancing'.* (*The Watsons*)

BOURGH, ANNE DE: Daughter of Lady Catherine; betrothed to her cousin Darcy from infancy. *Pale and sickly; her features, though not plain, were insignificant; and she spoke very little, except in a low voice.* (*Pride & Prejudice*)

BOURGH, RT HON LADY CATHERINE DE: Widow of Sir Lewis de Bourgh. Sister of Darcy's late mother, and mother of Anne de Bourgh. Patroness of the Rev William Collins. *A tall, large woman, with strongly-marked features, which might once have been handsome. Her air was not conciliating, nor was her manner of receiving them such as to make her visitors forget their inferior rank. She was not rendered formidable by silence; but whatever she said was spoken in so authoritative a tone, as marked her self-importance.* (*Pride & Prejudice*)

BRANDON, COLONEL: A friend of Sir John Middleton, in love with Marianne Dashwood whom he eventually marries. He had formerly loved his childhood's sweetheart, Eliza Williams, who, however, was married off to his brother. The 'natural child' he is believed to have fathered is Eliza's by a lover. This daughter, also named Eliza, is seduced by Willoughby. Brandon fights a duel with him, without outcome, and then cares for the abandoned girl and her baby. *He was silent and grave. His appearance, however, was not unpleasing, in spite of his being, in the opinion of Marianne and Margaret, an absolute old bachelor, for he was on the wrong side of five-and-thirty; but though his face was not handsome, his countenance was sensible, and his address was particularly gentlemanlike.* (*Sense & Sensibility*)

BRERETON, CLARA: Poor cousin of Lady Denham, with whom she lives, and object of Sir Edward Denham's seductive intentions. *Charlotte thought she had never beheld a more lovely, or more interesting young Woman. – Elegantly tall, regularly handsome, with great delicacy of complexion & soft Blue eyes, a sweetly modest & yet naturally graceful Address, Charlotte could see in her only the most perfect representation of whatever Heroine might be most beautiful & most bewitching, in all the numerous vols. they had left behind them on Mrs. Whitby's shelves. Perhaps it might be partly oweing to her having just issued from a Circulating Library – but she could not separate the idea of a complete Heroine from Clara Brereton. Her situation with Lady Denham so very much in favour of it! She seemed placed with her on purpose to be ill-used. (Sanditon)*

CAMPBELL, COLONEL: Comrade of Jane Fairfax's late father. He and his wife had brought her·up, after her parents' deaths, with their only daughter, now a Mrs Dixon. *Right-minded and well-informed people. (Emma)*

CARTERET, THE HONOURABLE MISS: Daughter and constant companion of Lady Dalrymple. *So plain and so awkward that she would never have been tolerated in Camden-place but for her birth. (Persuasion)*

CHURCHILL, FRANK WESTON. Son of Mr Weston. He is brought up by his late mother's brother and his wife in Yorkshire, and given their surname. Emma Woodhouse believes him to be in love with her, but he is secretly engaged to Jane Fairfax, whom he marries after Mrs Churchill's death frees him to do so. *He was presented to her* [Emma], *and she did not think too much had been said in his praise. He was a very good-looking young man.– height, air, address, all were unexceptionable, and his countenance had a great deal of the spirit and liveliness of his father's – he looked quick and sensible. She felt immediately that she should like him; and there was a well-bred ease of manner, and a readiness to talk, which convinced her that he came intending to be acquainted with her and that acquainted they soon must be. (Emma)*

CHURCHILL, MRS: Sister-in-law of the late Mrs Weston. She and her husband take responsibility for the child, Frank Weston, on his mother's death and gave him their surname. Mrs Churchill's death frees Frank to marry the woman of his choice. *'Oh, Mrs. Churchill! everybody knows Mrs. Churchill,' replied Isabella, 'and I am sure I never think of that poor young man without the greatest compassion. To be constantly living with an ill-tempered person must be dreadful. It is what we happily have never known anything of; but it must be a life of misery. What a blessing that she never had any children! Poor little creatures, how unhappy she would have made them!'* (*Emma*)

CLAY, MRS PENELOPE: John Shepherd's daughter, mother of two children. Her marriage is over and she seems determined to capture Sir Walter Elliot, but finishes up living with William Elliot. *'She is a clever, insinuating, handsom woman, poor and plausible and altogether such in situation and manner, as to give a general idea among Sir Walter's acquaintance of her meaning to be Lady Elliot.'* – Mrs Smith (*Persuasion*)

COLES: Nouveau riche neighbours of the Woodhouses who incense Emma by not sending her an invitation she had been looking forward to refusing. *Good sort of people, friendly, liberal and unpretending; but, on the other hand, they were of low origin, in trade, and only moderately genteel. On their first coming into the country they had lived in proportion to their income, quietly, keeping little company, and that little unexpensively; but the last year or two had brought them a considerable increase in means ... The Coles were very respectable in their way, but they ought to be taught that it was not for them to arrange the terms on which the superior families would visit them. This lesson, she* [Emma], *very much feared, they would receive only from herself.* (*Emma*)

COLLINS, WILLIAM: Clergyman cousin of William Bennet and heir to the Longbourne estate. Rejected in marriage by Elizabeth Bennet, he marries Charlotte Lucas. *A tall, heavy-looking young man of five-and-twenty. His air was grave and stately, and his manners were very formal ... The deficiency of nature had been but little assisted by education or society; the greatest part of his life having been spent under the guidance of an illiterate and miserly father; and though he belonged to one of the universities, he had merely kept the necessary terms, without forming at it any useful acquaintance. The subjection in which his father had brought him up had given him originally great humility of manner; but it was now a good deal counteracted by the self-conceit of a weak head, living in retirement, and the consequential feelings of early and unexpected prosperity. A fortunate chance had recommended him to Lady Catherine de Bourgh when the living of Hunsford was vacant; and the* respect which he felt for her high rank, and his veneration for her as his patroness, mingling with a very good opinion of himself, of his authority as a clergyman, and his right as a rector, made him altogether a mixture of pride and obsequiousness, self-importance and humility. (Pride & Prejudice)

CRAWFORD, ADMIRAL: Uncle and guardian of Henry and Mary Crawford. His influence gains William Price his promotion to lieutenant. *A man of vicious conduct, who chose, instead of retaining his niece, to bring his mistress under his own roof. (Mansfield Park)*

CRAWFORD, HENRY and MARY: A brother and sister who come to stay with the Grants and become much involved with the Bertrams. Mary becomes Edmund Bertram's romantic objective, but he is disillusioned by her approval of Henry's elopement with Maria Rushworth. *Miss Crawford's beauty did her no disservice with the Miss Bertrams. They were too handsome themselves to dislike any woman for being so too, and were almost as much charmed as their brothers with her lively dark eyes clear-brown complexion, and general prettiness. Had she been tall, full formed, and fair, it might have been more of a trial: but as it was, there could be no comparison; and she was most allowably a sweet, pretty girl, while they were the finest young women in the county. Her brother was not handsome; no, when they first saw him he was absolutely plain, black and plain; but still he was the gentleman, with a pleasing address. The second meeting proved him not so very plain; he was plain, to be sure, but then he had so much countenance, and his teeth were so good, and he was so well made, that one soon forgot he was plain, and after a third interview, after dining in company with him at the Parsonage, he was no longer allowed to be called so by anybody. He was, in fact, the most agreeable young man the sisters had ever known, and they were equally delighted with him. (Mansfield Park)*

CROFT, ADMIRAL: Sir Walter Elliot's tenant of Kellynch Hall. *Sir Walter, without hesitation, declared the Admiral to be the best-looking sailor he had ever met with, and went so far as to say that if his own man might have had the arranging of his hair he should not be ashamed of being seen with him any where.* (*Persuasion*)

CROFT, MRS SOPHIA: The Admiral's wife, sister to Captain Wentworth. Mrs Croft, though neither tall nor fat, had a squareness, uprightness, and vigour of form, which gave importance to her person. *She had bright, dark eyes, good teeth, and altogether an agreeable face; though her reddened and weather-beaten complexion, the consequence of her having been almost as much at sea as her husband, made her seem to have lived some years longer in the world than her real eight and thirty. Her manners were open, easy, and decided, like one who had no distrust of herself, and no doubts of what to do; without any approach to coarseness, however, or any want of good humour.* (*Persuasion*)

DALRYMPLE, DOWAGER VISCOUNTESS: Mother of the Hon Miss Carteret. Cousin of the Elliot family, whose society in Bath flatters Sir Walter Elliot and Elizabeth. *Anne was ashamed. Had Lady Dalrymple and her daughter even been very agreeable, she would still have been ashamed of the agitation they created, but they were nothing. There was no superiority of manner, accomplishment or understanding. Lady Dalrymple had acquired the name of 'a charming woman' because she had a smile and a civil answer for every body.* (*Persuasion*)

DARCY, FITZWILLIAM: Son of the late Lady Anne Darcy; brother of Georgiana Darcy, whose guardian he is jointly with his cousin Colonel Fitzwilliam, Nephew of Lady Catherine de Bourgh, he had been betrothed in infancy to her daughter Anne, but he marries Elizabeth Bennet. *Mr. Darcy soon drew the attention of the room by his fine, tall person, handsome features, noble mien, and the report which was in general circulation within five minutes after his entrance, of his having ten thousand a year. The gentlemen pronounced him to be a fine figure of a man, the ladies declared he was much handsomer than Mr. Bingley, and he was looked at with great admiration for about half the evening, till his manners gave a disgust which turned the tide of his popularity; for he was discovered to be proud; to be above his company, and above being pleased; and not all his large estate in Derbyshire could then save him from having a most forbidding, disagreeable countenance, and being unworthy to be compared with his friend.* (*Pride & Prejudice*)

DARCY, GEORGIANA: Darcy's younger sister and ward. She goes to live with him and Elizabeth Bennet at Pemberley after their marriage. *The attachment of the sisters was exactly what Darcy had hoped to see. They were able to love each other, even as well as they intended. Georgiana had the highest opinion in the world of Elizabeth; though at first she often listened with an astonishment bordering on alarm at her lively, sportive manner of talking to her brother. He, who had always inspired in herself a respect which almost overcame her affection, she now saw the object of open pleasantry. Her mind received knowledge which had never before fallen in her way. By Elizabeth's instructions she began to comprehend that a woman may take liberties with her husband, which a brother will not allow in a sister more than ten years younger than himself.* (*Pride & Prejudice*)

DASHWOOD, ELINOR: Eldest daughter of Mrs Henry Dashwood. She marries Edward Ferrars. *This eldest daughter whose advice was so effectual, possessed a strength of understanding, and coolness of judgment, which qualified her, though only nineteen, to be the counsellor of her mother, and enabled her frequently to counteract, to the advantage of them all, that eagerness of mind in Mrs. Dashwood which must generally have led to imprudence.* (*Sense & Sensibility*)

DASHWOOD, HARRY: Only child of John and Fanny Dashwood, whose engaging ways determine Henry Dashwood's uncle to leave the Norland estate entailed to the boy. *This child who, on, occasional visits with his father and mother at Norland had so far gained on the affections of his uncle, by such attractions as are by no means unusual in children of two or three years old: an imperfect articulation, an earnest desire of having his own way, many cunning tricks, and a great deal of noise, as to outweigh all the value of all the attention which, for years, he had received from his niece and her daughters.* (*Sense & Sensibility*)

DASHWOOD, HENRY: Inheritor from an uncle of the Norland estate in Sussex. Father of John by his first marriage and of Elinor, Marianne and Margaret by his second. He dies at the beginning of the story. *His temper was cheerful and sanguine, and he might reasonably hope to live many years, and by living economically, lay by a considerable sum from the produce of an estate already large, and capable of almost immediate improvement. But the fortune which had been so tardy in coming, was his only one twelvemonth. He survived his uncle no longer; and ten thousand pounds, including the late legacies, was all that remained for his widow and daughters.* (*Sense & Sensibility*)

DASHWOOD, MRS HENRY: Widow of Henry Dashwood; mother of Elinor, Marianne and Margaret, and stepmother of John; cousin of Sir John Middleton. *In seasons of cheerfulness, no temper could be more cheerful than hers, or possess, in a greater degree, that sanguine expectation of happiness which is happiness itself. But in sorrow she must be equally carried away by her fancy, and as far beyond consolation as in pleasure she was beyond alloy.* (*Sense & Sensibility*)

DASHWOOD, JOHN: Son of the late Henry Dashwood by his first marriage. He is married to Fanny, sister of Edward and Robert Ferrars. They have one child, Harry. *He was not an ill-disposed young man, unless to be rather cold-hearted, and rather selfish, is to be ill-disposed; but he was, in general, well respected; for he conducted himself with propriety in the discharge of his ordinary duties. Had he married a more amiable woman, he might have been made still more respectable than he was; he might even have been made amiable himself: for he was very young when he married, and very fond of his wife. But Mrs. John Dashwood was a strong caricature of himself; more narrow-minded and selfish.* (*Sense & Sensibility*)

DASHWOOD, MARGARET: Youngest daughter of Mrs Henry Dashwood. *A good-humoured, well-disposed girl; but as she had already imbibed a good deal of Marianne's romance, without having much of her sense, she did not, at thirteen, bid fair to equal her sisters at a more advanced period of life.* (*Sense & Sensibility*)

DASHWOOD, MARIANNE: Second daughter of Mrs Henry Dashwood. Passionately in love with John Willoughby, she is passed over by him and ultimately marries her steady admirer,

Colonel Brandon. *She was sensible and clever, but eager in everything; her sorrows, her joys, could have no moderation. She was generous, amiable, interesting: she was everything but prudent. The resemblance between her and her mother was strikingly great. (Sense & Sensibility)*

DAVIES, DR: Escort of the Steele girls from Devonshire to London and declared by everyone except herself to be Nancy Steele's admirer. *'There now, you are going to laugh at me too. But why should not I wear pink ribbons? I do not care if it is the Doctor's favourite colour. I am sure for my part, I should never have known he did like it better than any other colour, if he had not happened to say so.'* (*Sense & Sensibility*)

DE COURCY, REGINALD: Son of Sir Reginald and Lady De Courcy, and brother of Catherine Vernon. Captivated by Lady Susan, he is at length disenchanted by proof of her disreputable ways. His sister and brother-in-law nurse him into the frame of mind to marry Lady Susan's daughter instead. *'A handsome young Man, who promises me some amusement. There is something about him that rather interests me, a sort of sauciness, of familiarity which I shall teach him to correct. He is lively & seems clever, & when I have inspired him with greater respect for me than his sister's kind offices have implanted, he may be an agreeable Flirt. There is exquisite pleasure in subduing an insolent spirit, in making a person pre-determined to dislike, acknowledge one's superiority.'* – Lady Susan (*Lady Susan*)

DE COURCY, SIR REGINALD and LADY: Of Parklands, Sussex. Parents of Reginald De Courcy and Catherine Vernon. (*Lady Susan*)

DENHAM, SIR EDWARD, BART: Nephew of Lady Denham's late husband, Sir Harry. Brother of Esther. Persistent follower of Clara Brereton. *Sir Edw.'s great object in life was to be seductive. With such personal advantages as he knew himself to possess, & such Talents as he did also give himself credit for, he regarded it as his Duty. He felt that he was formed to be a dangerous Man – quite in the line of the Lovelaces. The very name of Sir Edward he thought, carried some degree of fascination with it. To be generally gallant &*

assiduous about the fair, to make fine speeches to every pretty Girl, was but the inferior part of the Character he had to play. Miss Heywood, or any other young Woman with any pretensions to Beauty, he was entitled (according to his own views of Society) to approach with High Compliment & Rhapsody on the slightest acquaintance; but it was Clara alone on whom he had serious designs; it was Clara whom he meant to seduce. (*Sanditon*)

DENHAM, ESTHER: Sir Edward's sister. *A fine young woman, but cold & reserved, giving the idea of one who felt her consequence with Pride & her Poverty with Discontent, & who was immediately gnawed by the want of an handsomer Equipage than the simple Gig in which they travelled.* (*Sanditon*)

DENHAM, LADY: Of Sanditon House; widow of Mr Hollis of Sanditon, and Sir Harry Denham of Denham Park. Patroness of her poor cousin, Clara Brereton. *Lady D. was of middle height, stout, upright & alert in her motions, with a shrewd eye, & self-satisfied air – but not an unagreeable Countenance – & tho' her manner was rather downright & abrupt, as of a person who valued herself on being free-spoken, there was a good humour & cordiality about her. She had been too wary to put anything out of her own Power – and when on Sir Harry's Decease she returned again to her own House at Sanditon, she was said to have made this boast to a friend 'that though she had got nothing but her Title from the Family, still she had given nothing for it!'* (*Sanditon*)

DIXON, MR: Married to Colonel Campbell's daughter, though initially preferring Jane Fairfax, he is thought to be the mysterious donor of Jane's pianoforté. '*A man, a very musical man, and in love with another woman – engaged to her – on the point of marriage – yet would never ask that other woman to sit down to the instrument, if the lady in question could sit down instead – never seemed to like to hear one if he could hear the other. That I thought, in a man of known musical talent, was some proof.*' – Frank Churchill (*Emma*)

DOROTHEA, LADY: Originally engaged to Edward Lindsay, but later married to his father. '*I soon perceived that tho' Lovely and Elegant in her Person and tho' Easy and Polite in her Address, she was of that Inferior order of Beings with regard to Delicate Feeling, tender Sentiments, and refined Sensibility.'* – Laura (*Love and Freindship*)

EDWARDS, MARY: Daughter of Mr Edwards. *The daughter, a genteel looking girl of 22, with her hair in papers, seemed very naturally to have caught something of the stile of the Mother who had brought her up.* (*The Watsons*)

EDWARDS, MR: Of 'D' (presumably Dorking) in 'Surry'. Father of Mary. *'I dare say it will be a very good Ball . . . If Mr. E. does not lose his money at cards, you will stay as late as you can wish for; if he does, he will hurry you home perhaps.'*– Elizabeth Watson (*The Watsons*)

EDWARDS, MRS: Wife of the above. *Mrs. Edwards acknowledged herself too old-fashioned to approve of every modern extravagance however sanctioned – & tho' complacently viewing her daughter's good looks, would give but a qualified admiration.* (*The Watsons*)

ELLIOT, ANNE: Second daughter of Sir Walter. Once secretly engaged to Wentworth, she had been dissuaded by her father and Lady Russell; but it is Wentworth whom she eventually marries. *Anne, with an elegance of mind and sweetness of character, which must have placed her high with any people of real understanding, was nobody with either father or sister: her word had no weight; her convenience was always to give way; she was only Anne . . . A few years before, Anne Elliot had been a very pretty girl, but her bloom had vanished early; and as even in its heights, her father had found little to admire in her, (so totally different were her delicate features and mild dark eyes from his own); there could be nothing in them now that she was faded and thin to excite his esteem.* (*Persuasion*)

ELLIOT, ELIZABETH: Eldest daughter of Sir Walter. It had been hoped that she would marry Walter Elliot, but he refused her and she remains a spinster. *Thirteen years had seen her mistress of Kellynch Hall, presiding and directing with a self-possession and decision which could never have given the idea of her being younger than she was . . . She had the consciousness of being nine-and-twenty, to give her some regrets and some apprehensions. She was fully* satisfied of being still quite as handsome as ever; but she felt her approach to the years of danger, and would have rejoiced to be certain of being properly solicited by baronet-blood within the next twelvemonth or two. (*Persuasion*)

ELLIOT, MARY: See MUSGROVE, MRS CHARLES. (*Persuasion*)

ELLIOT, WILLIAM WALTER. Widowed relative of the Elliots of Kellynch and heir presumptive to Sir Walter's title and estate. He had refused to marry Elizabeth, seems to be planning to propose to Anne, but is finally left living with Mrs Clay. *Mr. Elliot was rational, discreet, polished, – but he was not open. There was never any burst of feeling, any warmth of indignation or delight, at the evil or good of others. This, to Anne, was a decided imperfection. Her early impressions were incurable. She prized the frank, the open-hearted, the eager character beyond all others. Warmth and enthusiasm did captivate her still. She felt that she could so much more depend upon the sincerity of those who sometimes looked or said a careless or hasty thing, than of those whose presence of mind never varied, whose tongue never slipped. Mr. Elliot was too generally agreeable. Various as were the tempers in her father's house, he pleased them all. He endured too well – stood too well with everybody. He had spoken to her with some degree of openness of Mrs. Clay; had appeared completely to see what Mrs. Clay was about, and to hold her in contempt; and yet Mrs. Clay found him as agreeable as anybody.* (*Persuasion*)

ELLIOT, SIR WALTER: Of Kellynch Hall, Somerset. Widowed father of Elizabeth, Anne and Mary. *Vanity was the beginning and the end of Sir Walter Elliot's character; vanity of person and of situation. He had been remarkably handsome in his youth; and, at fifty-four, was still a very fine man. Few women could think more of their personal appearance than he did; nor could the valet of any new made lord be more delighted with the place he held in society. He considered the blessing of beauty as inferior only to the blessing of a baronetcy; and the Sir Walter Elliot, who united these gifts, was the constant object of his warmest respect and devotion.* (*Persuasion*)

ELTON, REV: Clergyman at Highbury. Intended by Emma to make a match with Harriet Smith, he proposes to Emma instead, is rejected, and eventually marries Augusta Hawkins. '*I think a young man might be very safely recommended to take Mr. Elton as a model. Mr. Elton is good-humoured, cheerful, obliging, and gentle. He seems to me to be grown particularly gentle of late. I do not know whether he has any design of ingratiating himself with either of us, Harriet, by additional softness, but it strikes me that his manners are softer than they used to be. If he means anything, it must be to please you.*' (*Emma*)

He was really a very pleasing young man, a young man whom any woman not fastidious might like. He was reckoned very handsome; his person much admired in general, though not by her, there being a want of elegance of feature which she could not dispense with. (*Emma*)

ELTON, MRS AUGUSTA (*née* Hawkins): Wife of the Rev Elton. She has a sister Selina and brother-in-law, Mr Suckling, whose home, Maple Grove, she frequently cites as superior to those in the Highbury district. *Such as Mrs. Elton appeared to her [Emma] on this second interview, such she appeared whenever they met again: self-important, presuming, familiar, ignorant, and ill-bred. She had a little beauty and a little accomplishment, but so little judgment that she thought herself coming with superior knowledge of the world, to enliven and improve a country neighbourhood; and conceived Miss Hawkins to have held such a place in society as Mrs. Elton's consequence only could surpass.* (*Emma.*)

FAIRFAX, JANE: An orphan brought up by Colonel Campbell; granddaughter of Mrs Bates. Secretly engaged to Frank Churchill, she breaks it off and accepts a post as governess, but is saved from it by Frank's mother's death, which enables them to marry. Emma had earlier been jealous of her over a supposed attraction for Mr Knightly. *Jane Fairfax was very elegant ... Her height was pretty, just such as almost everybody would think tall, and nobody could think very tall; her figure particularly graceful; her size a most becoming medium, between fat and thin, though a slight appearance of ill-health seemed to point out the likeliest evil of the two. Emma could not but feel all this; and then, her face – her features – there was more beauty in them all together than she had* *remembered; it was not regular, but it was very pleasing beauty. Her eyes, a deep grey, with dark eyelashes and eyebrows, had never been denied their praise; but the skin, which she had been used to cavil at, as wanting colour, had a clearness and delicacy which really needed no fuller bloom. It was a style of beauty of which elegance was the reigning character and as such, she must, in honour, by all her principles, admire it. (Emma)*

FERRARS, EDWARD: Mrs Ferrars's elder son. Expected by his mother to marry the Hon Miss Morton, he becomes engaged to Lucy Steele, which causes his mother to disinherit him. A reconciliation follows his escape from this entanglement and he marries his original love, Elinor Dashwood, and takes Holy Orders. *He was not handsome, and his manners required intimacy to make them pleasing. He was too diffident to do justice to himself; but when his natural shyness was overcome, his behaviour gave every indication of an open, affectionate heart. His understanding was good, and his education had given it solid improvement. But he was neither fitted by abilities nor disposition to answer the wishes of his mother and sister, who longed to see him distinguished . . . All his wishes centred in domestic comfort and the quiet of private life. (Sense & Sensibility)*

FERRARS, FANNY: See DASHWOOD, JOHN. *(Sense & Sensibility)*

FERRARS, MRS: Widowed mother of Edward, Robert and Fanny (Mrs John Dashwood). *A little, thin woman, upright, even to formality, in her figure, and serious, even to sourness, in her aspect. Her complexion was sallow; and her features small, without beauty, and naturally without expression; but a lucky contraction of the brow had rescued her countenance from the disgrace of insipidity, by giving it the strong characters of pride and ill-nature. She was not a woman of many words; for, unlike people in general, she proportioned them to the number of her ideas. (Sense & Sensibility)*

FERRARS, ROBERT: Mrs Ferrars's younger son. He marries Lucy Steele, thus freeing Edward to marry Elinor Dashwood. *He was giving orders for a toothpick-case for himself, and till its size, shape, and ornaments were determined – all of which, after examining and debating for a quarter of an hour over every toothpick-case in the shop, were finally arranged by his own inventive fancy – he had no leisure to bestow any other attention on the two ladies, than what was comprised in three or four very broad stares; a kind of notice which served to imprint on Elinor the remembrance of a person and face of strong, natural, sterling insignificance, though adorned in the first style of fashion. (Sense & Sensibility)*

FERRARS, SIR ROBERT: Uncle of Edward and Robert Ferrars, who erroneously persuaded their mother to place Edward under private tuition as a boy, instead of sending him to Westminster school. (*Sense & Sensibility*)

FITZWILLIAM, COLONEL: Darcy's cousin and joint guardian with him of Georgiana Darcy; nephew of Lady de Bourgh. *About thirty, not handsome, but in person and address most truly the gentleman. (Pride & Prejudice)*

FORSTER, COLONEL and MRS: Wickham's commanding officer, with whose wife, Harriet, Lydia Bennet is staying at Brighton when she elopes with Wickham. *This invaluable friend was a very young woman, and very lately married. A resemblance in good humour and good spirits had recommended her and Lydia to each other. (Pride & Prejudice)*

GARDINER, MR and MRS EDWARD: Mrs Bennet's brother and sister-in-law, with whom Elizabeth Bennet visits Derbyshire. *Mr. Gardiner was a sensible, gentlemanlike man, greatly superior to his sister, as well by nature as education. The Netherfield ladies would have had difficulty in believing that a man who lived by trade, and within view of his own warehouses, could have been so well-bred and agreeable. Mrs. Gardiner . . . was several years younger than Mrs. Bennet. (Pride & Prejudice)*

GODDARD, MRS: Mistress of the school at which Harriet Smith has grown up from pupil to parlour boarder. She introduces her to Emma. *Mrs. Goddard was the mistress of a school – not of a seminary, or an establishment, or anything which professed, in long sentences of refined nonsense, to combine liberal acquirements with elegant morality, upon new principles and new systems – and where young ladies for enormous pay might be screwed out of health and into vanity – but a real, honest, old-fashioned boarding-school, where a reasonable quantity of accomplishments were sold at a reasonable price, and where girls might be sent to be out of the way, and scramble themselves into a little education, without any danger of coming back prodigies ... She was a plain, motherly kind of woman, who had worked hard in her youth, and now thought herself entitled to the occasional holiday of a tea-visit.* (Emma)

GRAHAM: Janetta's betrothed, from whom she is rescued by Sophia and Laura. '*They said he was sensible, well-informed, and Agreable; we did not pretend to Judge of such trifles, but as we were convinced he had no soul, that he had never read the Sorrows of Werter, and that his Hair bore not the least resemblance to auburn, we were certain that Janetta could feel no affection for him, or at least that she ought to feel none. The very circumstance of his being her father's choice too, was so much in his disfavour, that had he been deserving her, in every other respect yet that of itself ought to have been a sufficient reason in the Eyes of Janetta for rejecting him.*' – Laura (*Love and Freindship*)

GRANT, REV and MRS: The Norris's successors at Mansfield, at whose parsonage Mrs Grant's brother and sister, Henry and Mary Crawford, come to stay. *A hearty man of forty-five ... He had a wife about fifteen years his junior, but no children; and they entered the neighbourhood with the usual fair report of being very respectable, agreeable people.* (*Mansfield Park*)

GREY, SOPHIA: Ward of Mr and Mrs Ellison, married for her money by John Willoughby, who passes over Marianne Dashwood, to his occasional regret. *A very fashionable-looking young woman.* (*Sense & Sensibility*)

GUSTAVUS: See PHILANDER and GUSTAVUS. (*Love and Freindship*)

HARVILLE, CAPTAIN: Friend of Wentworth and of Benwick, who had been engaged to Harville's late sister. *Captain Harville was a tall, dark man, with a sensible, benevolent countenance; a little lame; and from strong features, and want of health, looking much older than Captain Wentworth ... His lameness prevented him from taking much exercise; but a mind of usefulness and ingenuity seemed to furnish him with constant employment within.*

He drew, he varnished, he carpentered, he glued; he made toys for the children, he fashioned new netting-needles and pins with improvements; and if every thing else was done, sat down to his large fishing net at one corner of the room. (*Persuasion*)

HARVILLE, MRS: Captain Harville's wife. *A degree less polished than her husband, seemed however to have the same good feelings.* (*Persuasion*)

HAWKINS, AUGUSTA: see ELTON, MRS. (*Emma*)

HAYTER, CHARLES: Brother of the Misses Hayter and cousin of the Musgrove brothers and sisters, in love with Henrietta and made briefly jealous by her liking for Wentworth. *The eldest of all the cousins, and a very amiable, pleasing young man, between whom and Henrietta there had been a considerable appearance of attachment previous to Captain's Wentworth's introduction. He was in orders, and having a curacy in the neighbourhood where residence was not required, lived at his father's home, only two miles from Uppercross.* (*Persuasion*)

HAYTER, MR and MRS and the MISSES: Parents and sisters of Charles Hayter. *Mrs. Musgrove and Mrs. Heyter were sisters. They had each had money, but their marriages had made a material difference in their degree of consequence. Mr. Hayter had some property of his own, but it was insignificant compared with Mr. Musgrove's; and while the Musgroves were in the first class of society in the country, the young Hayters would, from their parents' inferior, retired, and unpolished way of living, and their own defective education, have been hardly in any class at all, but for their connexion with Uppercross.* (*Persuasion*)

HEYWOOD, CHARLOTTE. Eldest of the daughters at home, taken to Şanditon by the Parkers in gratitude for the family's hospitality after their accident. *A very pleasing young woman of two and twenty. She was a very sober-minded young Lady, sufficiently well-read in Novels to supply her Imagination with amusement, but not at all unreasonably influenced by them.* (*Sanditon*)

HEYWOOD, MR and MRS: Of Willingden, Sussex. Parents of Charlotte and thirteen others; they care for Mr and Mrs Thomas Parker after their accident. *They had very pretty*

Property – enough, had their family been of reasonable Limits to have allowed them a very gentlemanlike share of Luxuries and Change – enough for them to have indulged in a new Carriage & better roads, an occasional month at Tunbridge Wells, & symptoms of the Gout and a Winter at Bath: but the maintenance, Education and fitting out of 14 Children demanded a very quiet, settled, careful course of Life & obliged them to be stationary and healthy at Willingden. What Prudence had at first enjoined, was now rendered pleasant by Habit. They never left home, & they had a gratification in saying so. (*Sanditon*)

HOWARD, REV: Clergyman of the parish encompassing Osborne Castle, Surrey, and formerly tutor to Lord Osborne; brother of Mrs Blake. *In himself, she* [Emma] *thought him as agreable as he looked; tho' chatting on the commonest topics he had a sensible, unaffected, way of expressing himself, which made them all worth hearing, & she only regretted that he had not been able to make his pupils' Manners as unexceptionable as his own.* (*The Watsons*)

HUGHES, MRS: Schoolfellow of the late Mrs Tilney, who chaperones Eleanor Tilney at Bath and introduces her to Catherine Morland. (*Northanger Abbey*)

HURST, MRS (LOUISA) and BINGLEY, CAROLINE: Charles Bingley's elder and younger sisters. *They were in fact very fine ladies; not deficient in good humour when they were pleased, nor in the power of being agreeable when they chose it, but proud and conceited. They were rather handsome, had been educated in one of the first private seminaries in town, had a fortune of twenty thousand pounds, were in the habit of spending more than they ought, and of associating with people of rank, and were therefore in every respect entitled to think well of themselves, and meanly of others. They were of a respectable family in the north of England; a circumstance more deeply impressed on their memories that than their brother's fortune and their own had been acquired by trade.* MR HURST, Louisa's husband, is described as *an indolent man, who lived only to eat, drink, and play at cards.* (*Pride & Prejudice*)

ISABEL: Mother of Marianne, to whom Isabel's friend Laura tells the story in letters. *Our freindship first commenced. Isabel was then one and twenty. Tho' pleasing both in her Person and Manners (between ourselves) she never possessed the hundredth part of my Beauty or Accomplishments. Isabel had seen the World. She had passed 2 Years at one of the first Boarding-schools in London; had spent a fortnight in Bath and had supped one night in Southampton. –* Laura (*Love and Freindship*)

JANETTA: Macdonald's fifteen-year-old daughter, betrothed to Graham but aided by Sophia and Laura to elope with Captain M'Kenzie. *Naturally well disposed, endowed with a susceptible Heart, and a simpathetic Disposition, she might, had these amiable qualities been properly encouraged, have been an ornament to human Nature; but unfortunately her Father possessed not a soul sufficiently exalted to admire so promising a Disposition, and had endeavoured by every means in his power to prevent its encreasing with her Years. He had actually so far extinguished the natural noble Sensibility of her Heart, as to prevail on her to accept an offer from a young Man of his Recommendation.* (*Love and Freindship*)

JENNINGS, MRS: Widowed mother of Lady Middleton and Charlotte Palmer and eager promoter of the romantic prospects of the Dashwood girls and others. *A good-humoured, merry, fat, elderly woman, who talked a good deal, seemed very happy, and rather vulgar. She was full of jokes and laughter, and before dinner was over had said many witty things on the subject of lovers and husbands ... She had only two daughters, both of whom she had lived to see respectably married, and she had now therefore nothing to do but to marry all the rest of the world.* (*Sense & Sensibility*)

JOHNSON, MR: Alicia Johnson's husband and guardian of Mrs Manwaring; his disapproval of Lady Susan equals hers of him. '*My dear Alicia, of what a mistake were you guilty in marrying a Man of his age! – just old enough to be formal, ungovernable & to have the gout – too old to be agreable & too young to die.*' (*Lady Susan*)

JOHNSON, MRS ALICIA: Lady Susan's London confidante who assists with her assignations until foiled by the disapproving Mr Johnson. '*Mr. Johnson leaves London next Tuesday. He is going for his health to Bath, where if the waters are favourable to his constitution & my wishes, he will be laid up with the gout many weeks. During his absence we shall be able to chuse our own society, & have true enjoyment.'* – Mrs Johnson (*Lady Susan*)

KING, MISS: Inheritor of her grandfather's fortune, to whom Wickham turns from Elizabeth Bennet. *'A man in distressed circumstances has not time for all those elegant decorums which other people may observe. If she does not object to it, why should we?'* – Elizabeth (*Pride & Prejudice*)

KNIGHTLEY, MR: Of Donwell Abbey, near Highbury, Surrey. The eldest of the Knightley brothers, he appears first attracted to Jane Fairfax, then to Harriet Smith; but it is Emma whom he loves and marries. *A sensible man about seven or eight-and-thirty, was not only a very old and intimate friend of the family, but particularly connected with it, as the elder brother of Isabella's husband. He lived about half a mile from Highbury, was a frequent visitor, and always welcome.* (*Emma*)

KNIGHTLEY, JOHN: Younger of the Knightley brothers; a lawyer married to Isabella Woodhouse. Father of Henry and John and three others. *A tall, gentlemanlike, and very clever man, rising in his profession; domestic, and respectable in his private character: but with reserved manners which prevented his being generally pleasing; and capable of being sometimes out of humour. He was not an ill-tempered man . . . but his temper was not his great perfection; and, indeed, with such a worshipping wife, it was hardly possible that any natural defects in it should not be increased. The extreme sweetness of her temper must hurt his. He had all the cleverness and quickness of mind which she wanted; and he could sometimes act an ungracious, or say a severe thing.* (*Emma*)

KNIGHTLEY, MRS JOHN. Emma Woodhouse's elder sister Isabella. She has five children. *A pretty, elegant little woman, of gentle, quiet manners, and a disposition remarkably amiable and affectionate, wrapped up in her family, a devoted wife, a doting mother, and so tenderly attached to her father and sister that, but for these higher ties, a warmer love might have seemed impossible. She could never see a fault in any of them. She was not a woman of strong understanding or any quickness; and with this resemblance of her father, she inherited also much of this constitution; was delicate in her own health, over-careful of that of her children, had many fears and many nerves.* (*Emma*)

LAURA: The writer of the letters to her friend Isabel's daughter Marianne. She is the daughter of Polydore and Claudia and granddaughter of Lord St Clair. She is fifty-five years old, the widow of Edward Lindsay. *I was once beautiful. But lovely as I was the Graces of my Person were the least of my Perfections. Of every accomplishment accustomary to my sex, I was Mistress . . . In my Mind, every Virtue that could adorn it was centered; it was the Rendez-vous of every good Quality and of every noble sentiment. A sensibility too trembling alive to every affliction of my Freinds, my Acquaintance and particularly to every affliction of my own, was my only fault, if a fault it could be called. Alas! how altered now! Tho' indeed my own Misfortunes do not make less impression on me than they ever did, yet now I never feel for those of an other. My accomplishments too, begin to fade – I can neither sing so well nor Dance so gracefully as I once did – and I have entirely forgot the Minuet Dela Cour.* (*Love and Freindship*)

LINDSAY, AUGUSTA: Daughter of Sir Edward Lindsay and sister of Edward. She marries Graham. *I found her exactly what her Brother had described her to be – of the middle size. She received me with equal surprize though not with equal Cordiality, as Philippa. There was a disagreeable Coldness and Forbidding Reserve in her reception of me which was equally Distressing and Unexpected. None of that interesting Sensibility or amiable simpathy in her manners and Address to me when we first met which should have Distinguished our introduction to each other. Her Language was neither warm, nor affectionate, her expressions of regard were neither animated nor cordial; her arms were not opened to receive me to her Heart, tho' my own were extended to press her to mine.* – Laura (*Love and Freindship*)

LINDSAY, EDWARD: Son of Sir Edward. Refusing to marry Lady Dorothea, he marries Laura, but is killed with Augustus in an accident. *The most beauteous and amiable Youth, I have ever*

*beheld ... The noble Youth informed us that his name was Lindsay –
for particular reasons however I shall conceal it under that of Talbot.
(Love and Freindship)*

LINDSAY, SIR EDWARD: Father of Edward' and Augusta. He
marries Lady Dorothea, whom his son had refused to marry.
*My father is a mean and mercenary wretch ... Never shall it be
said that I obliged my Father.* – Edward (*Love and Freindship*)

LUCAS, CHARLOTTE: Elder daughter of Sir William and Lady
Lucas and intimate friend of Elizabeth Bennet. She marries
William Collins after he has been turned down by Elizabeth.
A sensible, intelligent woman, about twenty-seven. (*Pride & Pre-
judice*)

LUCAS, MARIA: Younger sister of Charlotte. *A good-humoured
girl, but ... empty-headed.* (*Pride & Prejudice*)

LUCAS, SIR WILLIAM and LADY: Neighbours of the Bennets;
parents of Charlotte and Maria. *Sir William Lucas had been
formerly in trade in Meryton, where he had made a tolerable fortune,
and risen to the honour of knighthood by an address to the king,
during his mayoralty. The distinction had perhaps been felt too
strongly. It had given him a disgust to his own business, and to his
residence in a small market town; and, quitting them both, he had
removed with his family to a house about a mile from Meryton,
denominated from that period Lucas Lodge, where he could think with
pleasure of his own importance, and unshackled by business, occupy
himself solely in being civil to all the world. For, though elated by his
rank, it did not render him supercilious: on the contrary, he was all
attention to everybody. By nature inoffensive, friendly, and obliging,
his presentation at St. James's had made him courteous. Lady Lucas
was a very good kind of woman, not too clever to be a valuable
neighbour to Mrs. Bennet. They had several children.* (*Pride &
Prejudice*)

MACDONALD: Widowed cousin of Sophia and father of Janetta,
who invites Sophia and Laura to Macdonald Hall after the
arrest of Augustus and disappearance of Edward. *The haste with
which he came to our relief so soon after the receipt of our Note,
spoke so greatly in his favour that I hesitated not to pronounce him at*

first sight, a tender and simpathetic Freind. Alas! he little deserved the name – for though he told us that he was much concerned at our Misfortunes, yet by his own account it appeared that the perusal of them, had neither drawn from him a single sigh, nor induced him to bestow one curse on our vindictive Stars – Laura (*Love and Freindship*)

M'KENZIE, CAPTAIN: At Sophie's urging he elopes to Gretna Green with Janetta Macdonald and marries her. *The amiable M'Kenzie, whose modesty as he afterwards assured us had been the only reason of his having so long concealed the violence of his affection for Janetta.* (*Love and Freindship*)

MANWARING, MARIA: The Manwarings' daughter, detached by Lady Susan from Sir James Martin, whom she wants for her own daughter, Frederica, but eventually marries herself. *I confess that I can pity only Miss Manwaring, who coming to Town & putting herself to an expence in Cloathes, which impoverished her for two years, on purpose to secure him, was defrauded of her due by a Woman ten years older than herself.* (*Lady Susan*)

MANWARING, MR: Of Langford; Lady Susan's married lover, seduced by her during her visit to his house. *'Manwaring is so uncommonly pleasing that I was not without apprehensions myself. I remember saying to myself as I drove to the House, "I like this Man; pray Heaven no harm come of it!" But I was determined to be discreet, to bear in mind my being only four months a widow, & to be as quiet as possible, – & have been so; My dear Creature, I have admitted no one's attentions but Manwaring's'* – Lady Susan (*Lady Susan*)

MANWARING, MRS: Manwaring's wife and mother of Maria; formerly ward of Mr Johnson. She is despised by Lady Susan and her friend Alicia Johnson for her resentment of her husband's philandering. *'That detestable Mrs. Manwaring, who for your comfort, has fretted herself thinner & uglier than ever.'* – Mrs Johnson (*Lady Susan*)

MARIANNE: Daughter of Isabel and recipient of the letters in which Laura tells the story. (*Love and Freindship*)

MARTIN, SIR JAMES: Maria Manwaring's suitor, detached from

her by Lady Susan for the benefit of her own daughter, Frederica; but it is she herself who eventually marries him. *'Tho' his person & address are very well, he appears both to Mr. Vernon & me a very weak young Man.'* – Catherine Vernon (*Lady Susan*)

MARTIN, ROBERT: Young farmer brother of two former schoolfellows of Harriet Smith and tenant of Knightley. Emma believes Harriet too good for him, and tries to deter him, but he marries her in the end. *His appearance was very neat and he looked like a sensible young man, but his person had no other advantage: and when he came to be contrasted with gentlemen, she [Emma] thought he must lose all the ground he had gained in Harriet's inclination . . . Mr. Martin looked as if he did not know what manner was.* (*Emma*)

MIDDLETON, SIR JOHN: Cousin of Mrs Henry Dashwood. He provides her and her daughters with a home, Barton Cottage, near his own Barton Park, in Devonshire. *A good-looking man about forty . . . His countenance was thoroughly good-humoured; and his manners were as friendly as the style of his letter.* (*Sense & Sensibility*)

MIDDLETON, LADY: Daughter of Mrs Jennings and elder sister of Charlotte Palmer; wife of Sir John Middleton and mother of four infants, JOHN, WILLIAM, ANNAMARIA, and another. *Not more than six or seven and twenty; her face was handsome, her figure tall and striking, and her address graceful. Her manners had all the elegance which her husband's wanted. But they would have been improved by some share of his frankness and warmth; and her visit was long enough to detract something from their first admiration, by showing that, though perfectly well-bred, she was reserved, cold, and had nothing to say for herself beyond the most common-place inquiry or remark.* (*Sense & Sensibility*)

MORLAND, CATHERINE: The Morland's eldest daughter. She marries Henry Tilney. *Her heart was affectionate, her disposition cheerful and open, without conceit or affectation of any kind – her manners just removed from the awkwardness and shyness of a girl; her person pleasing, and, when in good looks, pretty – and her mind about as ignorant and uninformed as the female mind at seventeen usually is.* (Northanger Abbey)

MORLAND, JAMES: The Morland's eldest son, a clergymen. He becomes engaged to Isabella Thorpe, but she breaks it off. *Of a very amiable disposition, and sincerely attached to her* – Catherine Morland (*Northanger Abbey*)

MORLAND, REV and MRS RICHARD: Of Fullerton, Wiltshire. Parents of Catherine, James and eight other children. *Her father was a clergyman, without being neglected, or poor, and a very respectable man, though his name was Richard – and he had never been handsome. He had a considerable independence, besides two good livings – and he was not in the least addicted to locking up his daughters. Her mother was a woman of useful plain sense, with a good temper, and, what is more remarkable, with a good constitution. She had three sons before Catherine was born; and instead of dying in bringing the latter into the world, as any body might expect, she still lived on – lived to have six children more – to see them growing up around her, and to enjoy excellent health herself.* (*Northanger Abbey*)

MORTON, THE HONOURABLE MISS: Daughter of the late Lord Morton. Heiress reported by John Dashwood to be going to marry Edward Ferrars, but it does not eventuate. (*Sense & Sensibility*)

MUSGRAVE, TOM: The most renowned ladies' man in the Watson's neighbourhood. *'Perhaps Tom Musgrave may take notice of you – but I would advise you by all means not to give him any encouragement. He generally pays attention to every new girl, but he is a great flirt and never means anything serious.'* – Elizabeth Watson (*The Watsons*)

MUSGROVE, CHARLES: Husband of Mary Elliot, and brother of Henrietta and Louisa. *Charles Musgrove was civil and obedient; in sense and temper he was undoubtedly superior to his wife; but not of powers, or conversation, or grace, to make the past, as they were connected together, at all a dangerous contemplation; though, at the same time, Anne could believe, with Lady Russell, that a more equal match might have greatly improved him; and that a woman of real understanding. might have given more consequence to his character, and more usefulness, rationality, and elegance to his habits and pursuits. As it was, he did nothing with much zeal, but sport; and his time was otherwise trifled away, without benefit from books, or any thing else. He had very good spirits, which never seemed much affected by his wife's occasional lowness.* (Persuasion)

MUSGROVE, HENRIETTA and LOUISA: Charles's sisters. Henrietta marries Charles Hayter. Louisa, although apparently attached to Wentworth, marries Benwick. *Young ladies of nineteen and twenty, who had brought from a school at Exeter all the usual stock of accomplishments, and were now, like thousands of other young ladies, living to be fashionable, happy, and merry. Their dress had every advantage, their faces were rather pretty, their spirits extremely good, their manners unembarrassed and pleasant; they were of consequence at home, and favourites abroad.* (Persuasion)

MUSGROVE, MR and MRS: Parents of Charles, Henrietta, Louisa and others. *In the old English style . . . a very good sort of people; friendly and hospitable, not much educated, and not at all elegant.* (Persuasion)

MUSGROVE, MRS CHARLES: Youngest daughter of Sir Walter. She has two children, Charles and Walter. *Though better endowed than the elder sister, Mary had not Anne's understanding or temper. While well, and happy, and properly attended to, she had great good humour and excellent spirits; but any indisposition sunk her completely; she had no resources for solitude; and inheriting a considerable share of the Elliot self-importance, was very prone to add to every other distress that of fancying herself neglected and ill-used. In person she was inferior to both sisters, and had, even in her bloom, only reached the dignity of being 'a fine girl.'* (Persuasion)

MUSGROVE, RICHARD: Late brother of Charles, Henrietta and Louisa, who had served under Captain Wentworth, a connection which brings about Wentworth's introduction to the Musgrove family. *The real circumstances of this pathetic piece of family history were that the Musgroves had had the ill fortune of a very troublesome, hopeless son; and the good fortune to lose him before he reached his twentieth year; that he had been sent to sea, because he was stupid and unmanageable on shore; that he had been very little cared for at any time by his family, though quite as much as he deserved; seldom heard of, and scarcely at all regretted when the intelligence of his death abroad had worked its way to Uppercross.* (*Persuasion*)

NORRIS, MRS: Formerly Miss Ward, sister of Lady Bertram and Mrs Price. Her husband, incumbent of the living of Mansfield, dies early, leaving her childless. [She] *consoled herself for the loss of her husband by considering that she could do very well without him.* (*Mansfield Park*)

OSBORNE, LADY: Of Osborne Castle, Surrey. Mother of Lord Osborne and an unmarried daughter. *Tho' nearly 50, she was very handsome, & had all the Dignity of Rank.* (*The Watsons*)

OSBORNE, LORD: Son of the above. *A very fine young man; but there was an air of Coldness, of Carelessness, even of Awkwardness about him, which seemed to speak him out of his Element in a Ball room. He came in fact only because it was judged expedient for him to please the Borough – he was not fond of Women's company, & he never danced.*(*The Watsons*)

PALMER, MR: Husband of Mrs Jennings's daughter Charlotte. *A grave-looking young man of five or six and twenty, with an air of more fashion and sense than his wife, but of less willingness to please or be pleased. He entered the room with a look of self-consequence, slightly bowed to the ladies without speaking a word, and, after briefly surveying them and their apartments, took up a newspaper from the table and continued to read it as long as he stayed.* (*Sense & Sensibility*)

PALMER, MRS CHARLOTTE: Younger daughter of Mrs Jennings and sister of Lady Middleton, married to Palmer, whose child she bears during the story. *Mrs. Palmer was several years younger than Lady Middleton, and totally unlike her in every respect. She was short and plump, had a very pretty face, and the finest expression of good-humour in it'that could possibly be. Her manners were by no means so elegant as her sister's, but they were much more prepossessing. She came in with a smile – smiled all the time of her visit, except when she laughed, and smiled when she went away.* (*Sense & Sensibility*)

PARKER, ARTHUR: Thomas Parker's hypochondriacal brother. *She* [Charlotte] *had had considerable curiosity to see Mr. Arthur Parker; & having fancied him a very puny, delicate-looking young Man, the smallest very materially of not a robust Family, was astonished to find him quite as tall as his Brother & a great deal Stouter – Broad made & Lusty – and with no other look of an Invalide, than a sodden complexion.* (*Sanditon*)

PARKER, DIANA: One of Thomas Parker's hypochondriacal sisters. *It was not a week since Miss Diana Parker had been told by her feelings that the Sea Air would probably in her present state be the death of her, and now she was at Sanditon, intending to make some Stay, & without appearing to have the slightest recollection of having written or felt any such thing.* (*Sanditon*)

PARKER, SIDNEY: Younger brother of Thomas. *About 7 or 8 & 20, very good-looking, with a decided air of Ease & Fashion, and a lively countenance.* (*Sanditon*)

PARKER, SUSAN: One of Thomas Parker's hypochondriacal sisters. *Miss P – whom, remembering the three Teeth drawn in one day, Charlotte approached with a peculiar degree of respectful Compassion, was not very unlike her Sister in person or manner – tho' more thin & worn by Illness and Medecine, more relaxed in air, & more subdued in voice. She talked however the whole Evening as incessantly as Diana – & excepting that she sat with salts in her hand, took Drops two or three times from one out of the several Phials already at home on the Mantelpiece, – & made a great many odd faces & contortions, Charlotte could perceive no symptoms of illness which she, in the boldness of her own good health, would not have undertaken to cure, by putting out the fire, opening the Window, & disposing of the Drops & the salts by means of one or the other.* (*Sanditon*)

PARKER, THOMAS and MRS: Of Trafalgar House, Sanditon. The couple whose carriage accident brings them into contact with the Heywood family, whose daughter Charlotte they take back with them to Sanditon, which Parker is eagerly developing into a prosperous resort. They have four children. His brothers are Sidney and Arthur, and his sisters Susan and Diana. *Mr. P was evidently an amiable, family-man, fond of Wife, Children, Brothers & Sisters & generally kind-hearted; Liberal, gentlemanlike, easy to please; of a sanguine turn of mind, with more Imagination than Judgement. And Mrs. P. was as evidently a gentle, amiable, sweet tempered Woman, the properest wife in the World for a Man of strong understanding, but not of capacity to supply the cooler reflection which her own Husband sometimes needed, & so entirely waiting to be guided on every occasion, that whether he were risking his Fortune or spraining his Ancle, she remained equally useless. (Sanditon)*

PHILANDER and GUSTAVUS: Travelling players, illegitimate grandsons of Lord St Clair through his youngest daughters, Bertha and Agatha, by Philip Jones, a bricklayer, and Gregory Staves, an Edinburgh staymaker. *Philander and Gustavus, after having raised their reputation by their Performances in the Theatrical Line at Edinburgh, removed to Covent Garden, where they still Exhibit under the assumed names of Lewis and Quick. (Love and Freindship)*

PHILIPPA: Edward Lindsay's aunt, visited in Middlesex by him and Laura after their marriage. She marries a 'young and illiterate Fortune-hunter' *of whom I learned having spent all her fortune, had recourse for subsistence to the talent in which, he had always most excelled, namely, Driving, and that having every thing which belonged to them except their Coach, had converted it into a Stage and in order to be removed from any of his former Acquaintance, had driven it to Edinburgh, from whence he went to Sterling every other Day. (Love and Freindship)*

PHILIPS, MR and MRS: Mrs Bennet's brother-in-law and sister. He had been their late father's clerk, and succeeded him as attorney in Meryton. *The broad-faced, stuffy uncle Philips, breathing port wine. (Pride & Prejudice)*

PRATT, MR: Uncle of the Steele sisters, with whom Edward Ferrars lives as pupil for four years, during which time Edward becomes engaged to Lucy Steele. *(Sense & Sensibility)*

PRICE, FANNY: Eldest daughter of Lieutenant and Fanny Price, she is taken into the Bertram household as an act of benevolence and eventually marries Edmund Bertram. *Though there might not be much in her first appearance to captivate, there was at least nothing to disgust her relations. She was small for her age, with no glow of complexion, nor any other striking beauty; exceedingly timid and shy, and shrinking from notice; but her air, though awkward, was not vulgar, her voice was sweet, and when she spoke her countenance was pretty.* (*Mansfield Park*)

PRICE, MR: Father of Fanny, Susan and many more; a disabled lieutenant of marines. *He was more negligent of his family, his habits were worse, and his manners coarser, than she* [Fanny] *had been prepared for. He did not want abilities; but he had no curiosity, and no information beyond his profession: he read only the newspaper and the navy-list; he talked only of the dockyard, the harbour, Spithead, and the Motherbank; he swore and he drank, he was dirty and gross. She had never been able to recall anything approaching to tenderness in his former treatment of herself. There had remained only a general impression of roughness and loudness; and now he scarcely ever noticed her, but to make her the object of a coarse joke.* (*Mansfield Park*)

PRICE, MRS: Formerly Frances Ward, sister of Lady Bertram and Mrs Norris, she is married to a disabled lieutenant of marines and is the mother of a large family, including Fanny, Susan, Tom, Charles, Sam and Betsey. *Mrs. Price was not unkind; but, instead of gaining on her affection and confidence, and becoming more and more dear, her daughter* [Fanny] *never met with greater kindness from her than on the first day of her arrival. The instinct of nature was soon satisfied, and Mrs. Price's attachment had no other source. Her heart and her time were already quite full ... Her days were spent in a kind of slow bustle; always busy without getting on; always behind hand and lamenting it, without altering her ways.* (*Mansfield Park*)

PRICE, SUSAN: Fanny's favourite sister; she, too, is taken into the Bertram family. *Her more fearless disposition and happier nerves made everything easier to her there. With quickness in understanding the tempers of those she had to deal with, and no natural timidity to restrain any consequent wishes, she was soon welcome and useful to all; and after Fanny's removal succeeded so naturally to her influence over the hourly comfort of her aunt as gradually to become, perhaps, the most beloved of the two. (Mansfield Park)*

PRICE, WILLIAM: Eldest son of Lieutenant and Mrs Price, and Fanny's favourite brother. He joins the Royal Navy and in time is promoted, through Admiral Crawford's influence, to lieutenant. *A young man of an open, pleasant countenance, and frank, unstudied, but feeling and respectful manners. (Mansfield Park)*

REYNOLDS, MRS: Darcy's housekeeper, who shows Mr and Mrs Gardiner and Elizabeth Bennet over Pemberley House. *A respectable-looking elderly woman, much less fine, and more civil, than she had any notion of finding her. (Pride & Prejudice)*

RUSHWORTH, JAMES: Of Sotherton Court, near Mansfield Park; encouraged by the Rev Norris to court Maria Bertram, who marries him but later elopes with Henry Crawford. *He was a heavy young man, with not more than common sense; but as there was nothing disagreeable in his figure or address, the young lady was well pleased with her conquest. (Mansfield Park)*

RUSHWORTH, MRS: James's mother, with whom he lives at Sotherton Court. *A well-meaning, civil, prosing, pompous woman, who thought nothing of consequence but as it related to her own and her son's concerns. (Mansfield Park)*

RUSSELL, LADY: Friend of the late Lady Elliot and substitute mother to the three girls; responsible, with Sir Walter, for ending Anne's early association with Wentworth. *She was a woman rather of sound than of quick abilities . . . She was of strict integrity herself, with a delicate sense of honour; but she was as desirous of saving Sir Walter's feelings, as solicitous for the credit of the family, as aristocratic in her ideas of what was due to them, as any body of sense and honesty could well be. She was a benevolent, charitable, good woman, and capable of strong attachments; most correct in her conduct, strict in her notions of decorum, and with manners that were held a standard of good-breeding. She had a cultivated mind, and was, generally speaking, rational and consistent – but she had prejudices on the side of ancestry; she had a value for rank and consequence, which blinded her a little to the faults of those who possessed them. Herself the widow of only a knight, she gave the dignity of a baronet all its due.* (Persuasion)

ST CLAIR, LORD: Grandfather of Laura, Sophia, Philander and Gustavus in consequence of his liaison with an Italian opera girl, Laurina. *Following the Venerable Stranger into the Room he had been shewn to, I threw myself on my knees before him and besought him to acknowledge me as his Grand Child. He started, and after having attentively examined my features, raised me from the Ground and throwing his Grand-fatherly arms around my Neck, exclaimed, 'Acknowledge thee! Yes dear resemblance of my Laurina and Laurina's Daughter, sweet image of my Claudia and my Claudia's Mother, I do acknowledge thee as the Daughter of the one and the Granddaughter of the other.'* (Love and Freindship)

SHEPHERD, JOHN: Sir Walter Elliot's agent and father of Mrs Clay; instrumental in Sir Walter's leasing Kellynch Hall. *A civil, cautious lawyer, who, whatever might be his hold or his views on Sir Walter, would rather have the disagreeable prompted by any body else.* (Persuasion)

SMITH, HARRIET: A parlour boarder at Mrs Goddard's, of unknown parentage until the end of the story, when the father proves to be a prosperous tradesman. Emma tries to match her with the Rev Elton and with Frank Churchill, then believes that Knightley is interested in her; but it is Robert Martin whom Harriet comes to love and marry. *'What are Harriet Smith's claims, either of birth, nature, or education, to any connection higher than Robert Martin? She is the natural daughter of nobody knows whom, with probably no settled provision at all, and certainly no respectable relations. She is known only as parlour boarder at a common school. She is not a sensible girl, nor a girl of any information. She has been taught nothing useful, and is too young and too simple to have acquired anything herself. At her age she can have no experience; and, with her little wit, is not very likely ever to have any that can avail her. She is pretty, and she is good-tempered, and that is all.'* – Knightley (*Emma*)

SMITH, MRS: An older cousin of Willoughby, who expects to inherit Allenham Court from her. *The girls had, in one of their earliest walks, discovered an ancient respectable-looking mansion, which, by reminding them a little of Norland, interested their imagination, and made them wish to be better acquainted with it. But they learnt, on inquiry, that its possessor, an elderly lady of very good character, was unfortunately too infirm to mix with the world, and never stirred from home.* (*Sense & Sensibility*)

SMITH, MRS ANNE (née Hamilton): Widowed former schoolfriend of Anne Elliot, reunited with her in Bath. Her husband had been ruined by William Elliot's financial mismanagement. *Twelve years had changed Anne from the blooming, silent, unformed girl of fifteen, to the elegant little woman of seven and twenty, with every beauty except bloom, and with manners as consciously right as they were invariably gentle; and twelve years had transformed the fine-looking, well-grown Miss Hamilton, in all the glow of health and confidence of superiority, into a poor, infirm, helpless widow.* (*Persuasion*)

SOPHIA: Wife of Augustus. She becomes Laura's closest friend and it is found that she, too, is a granddaughter of Lord St Clair. She dies of galloping consumption a few days after her husband is killed. *Sophia was rather above the middle size; most elegantly formed. A soft languor spread over her lovely features, but increased their Beauty –. It was the Charectarestic of her Mind. She was all Sensibility and Feeling.* (*Love and Freindship*)

STEELE, LUCY: The younger of the Steele sisters, cousins of Sir John Middleton. Elinor Dashwood, who is in love with Edward Ferrars, becomes the confidante of Lucy, who tells her that she and Edward have been engaged for four years; but it is Robert Ferrars whom Lucy eventually marries, to Edward's and Elinor's relief. *In the other, who was not more than two or three and twenty, they acknowledged considerable beauty: her features were pretty, and she had a sharp, quick eye, and a smartness of air, which, though it did not give actual elegance or grace, gave distinction to her person. (Sense & Sensibility)*

STEELE, ANNE: The elder of the Steele sisters, cousins of Sir John Middleton. She is much teased by relatives and friends for her interest in Dr Davies. *Nearly thirty, with a very plain and not a sensible face. (Sense & Sensibility)*

SUSAN, LADY, (VERNON): Recently widowed mother of one daughter, Frederica Susanna. Sister-in-law of Charles Vernon. She wrecks the Manwarings' marriage by her association with the husband; entices Reginald De Courcy into loving her in order to spite his family; blights her daughter's life by neglect and the insistence that she marry Sir James Martin; but finishes up married to Sir James herself. *'The most accomplished Coquette in England. As a very distinguished Flirt, I have been always taught to consider her; but it has lately fallen in my way to hear some particulars of her conduct at Langford, which prove that she does not confine herself to that sort of honest flirtation which satisfies most people, but aspires to the more delicious gratification of making a whole family miserable ... but by all that I can gather, Lady Susan possesses a degree of captivating Deceit which must be pleasing to witness & detect.'* – Reginald De Courcy (*Lady Susan*)

TAYLOR, MISS: See WESTON, MRS. (*Emma*)

THORPE, ISABELLA: Mrs Thorpe's eldest daughter. She becomes infatuated with Frederick Tilney, breaks her engagement to James Morland, but is left unattached. *Miss Thorpe, however, being four years older than Miss Morland, and at least four years better informed, had a very decided advantage in discussing such points; she could compare the balls of Bath with those of Tunbridge; its fashions with the fashions of London; could rectify the opinions of her new friend in many articles of tasteful attire; could discover a flirtation between any gentleman and lady who only smiled on each other; and point out a quiz through the thickness of a crowd. These powers received due admiration from Catherine, to whom they were entirely new; and the respect which they naturally inspired might have been too great for familiarity, had not the easy gaiety of Miss Thorpe's manners, and her frequent expressions of delight on this* acquaintance with her, softened down every feeling of awe, and left nothing but tender affection. (*Northanger Abbey*)

THORPE, JOHN: Mrs Thorpe's eldest son; Oxford friend of James Morland, influential upon General Tilney's attitude towards Catherine Morland. *A stout young man of middling height, who, with a plain face and ungraceful form, seemed fearful of being too handsome unless he wore the dress of a groom, and too much like a gentleman unless he were easy where he ought to be civil, and impudent where he might be allowed to be easy.* (*Northanger Abbey*)

THORPE, MRS: Widowed ex-schoolfriend of Mrs Allen, encountered by chance at Bath. Mother of three sons and three daughters, including John and Isabella. *Mrs. Thorpe, however, had one great advantage as a talker, over Mrs. Allen, in a family of children; and when she expatiated on the talents of her sons, and the beauty of her daughters, – when she related their different situations and views, – that John was at Oxford, Edward at Merchant-Taylors', and William at sea, – and all of them more beloved and respected in their different station than any other three beings ever were, Mrs. Allen had no similar information to give, no similar triumphs to press on the unwilling and unbelieving ear of her friend, and was forced to sit and appear to listen to all these maternal effusions, consoling herself, however, with the discovery, which her keen eye soon made, that the lace on Mrs. Thorpe's pelisse was not half so handsome as that on her own.* (*Northanger Abbey*)

TILNEY, ELEANOR: Daughter of General Tilney. She marries a viscount, thereby mellowing the General's attitude towards Catherine Morland. *I know no one more entitled, by unpretending merit, or better prepared by habitual suffering, to receive and enjoy felicity. Her partiality for this gentleman was not of recent origin; and he had been long withheld only by inferiority of situation from addressing her. His unexpected accession to title and fortune had removed all his difficulties; and never had the General so loved his daughter so well in all her hours of companionship, utility, and patient endurance, as when he first hailed her, 'Your Ladyship!'* (*Northanger Abbey*)

TILNEY, CAPTAIN FREDERICK: General Tilney's eldest son. Isabella Thorpe becomes infatuated with him and breaks her engagement to James Morland, but Frederick's flirtation with her does not last. *A very fashionable-looking, handsome young man ... She* [Catherine Morland] *looked at him with great admiration, and even supposed it possible, that some people might think him handsomer than his brother, though, in her eyes, his air was more assuming, and his countenance less prepossessing. His taste and manners were beyond a doubt decidedly inferior, for, within her hearing, he not only protested against every thought of dancing himself, but even laughed openly at Henry for finding it possible. From the latter circumstance it may be presumed that, whatever might be our heroine's opinion of him, his admiration of her was not of a very dangerous kind ... He cannot be the instigator of the three villains in horsemen's great coats, by whom she will hereafter be forced into a travelling chaise and four, which will drive off with incredible speed.* (*Northanger Abbey*)

TILNEY, GENERAL: Widowed father of Frederick, Henry and Eleanor. Owner of Northanger Abbey. '*He is a fine old fellow, upon my soul! – stout, active, – looks as young as his son. I have a great regard for him, I assure you: a gentleman-like, good sort of fellow as ever lived.*' – John Thorpe (*Northanger Abbey*)

TILNEY, HENRY: Younger son of General Tilney. He marries Catherine Morland. *He seemed to be about four or five and twenty, was rather tall, had a pleasing countenance, a very intelligent and lively eye, and if not quite hadnsome, was very near it. His address was good, and Catherine felt herself in high luck.* (*Northanger Abbey*)

VERNON, MRS CATHERINE: Charles Vernon's wife; daughter of Sir Reginald and Lady De Courcy, and sister of Reginald. She and her husband take charge of Frederica Vernon after Lady Susan's re-marriage. '*She is perfectly well bred indeed, & has the air of a woman of fashion, but her Manners are not such as can persuade me of her being delighted at seeing me – I was as amiable as possible on the occasion – but all in vain – she does not like me.*' – Lady Susan (*Lady Susan*)

VERNON, CHARLES: Of Churchill, Sussex. Husband of Catherine and father of 'children in abundance'. Brother-in-law of Lady Susan and son-in-law of Sir Reginald and Lady De Courcy. '*I really have a regard for him, he is so easily imposed on!*' – Lady Susan (*Lady Susan*)

VERNON, FREDERICA SUSANNA: Only daughter of Lady Susan. Cared for by the Charles Vernons, of Churchill, after her mother's marriage to Sir James Martin, whom Lady Susan had always intended her to marry, she is eventually married to Reginald De Courcy. '*Tho' totally without accomplishment, she is by no means so ignorant as one might expect to find her, being fond of books & spending the cheif of her time in reading. Her Mother leaves her more to herself now than she did, & I have her with me as much as possible, & have taken great pains to overcome her timidity. We are very good friends, & tho' she never opens her lips before her Mother, she talks enough when alone with me, to make it clear that if properly treated by Lady Susan she would always appear to much greater advantage. There cannot be a more gentle, affectionate heart, or more obliging manners, when acting without restraint.*' – Catherine Vernon (*Lady Susan*)

VERNON, LADY SUSAN: see SUSAN, LADY, (VERNON). (*Lady Susan*)

WALLIS, COLONEL and MRS: Friends of William Elliot in Bath who convince Sir Walter Elliot that his heir's marriage had not been so discreditable as supposed. *A highly respectable man, perfectly the gentleman . . . And there was a Mrs. Wallis, at present only known to them by that description, as she was in daily expectation of her confinement.* (*Persuasion*)

WARD, MARIA, MISS and FRANCES: Huntingdonshire sisters, married respectively to Sir Thomas Bertram, the Rev Norris and Lieutenant Price. (*Mansfield Park*)

WATSON, ELIZABETH: Eldest of the Watson girls, disappointed in expectations of marriage with one Purvis. *Whose delight in a Ball was not lessened by a ten years Enjoyment.* (*The Watsons*)

WATSON, EMMA. One of the sisters, brought up away from the family by her Aunt Turner, but now reunited with them. *Not*

*more than of the middle height – well made & plump, with an air of
healthy vigour. Her skin was very brown, but clear, smooth and
glowing; which with a lively Eye, a sweet smile, & an open
Countenance, gave beauty to attract, & expression to make that
beauty improve on acquaintance.* (*The Watsons*)

WATSON, MARGARET: One of the sisters. *Margaret was not without beauty; she had a slight, pretty figure, & rather wanted Countenance than good features; but the sharp & anxious expression of
her face made her beauty in general little felt. On meeting her long-
absent Sister* [Emma], *as on every occasion of shew, her manner was
all affection & her voice all gentleness; continual smiles & a very
slow articulation being her constant resource when determined on
pleasing.* (*The Watsons*)

WATSON, MR: Of Stanton, Surrey. Widowed, invalid father of
Robert, Sam, Elizabeth, Margaret, Penelope and Emma. *Her*
[Emma's] *father, if ill, required little more than gentleness & silence
&, being a Man of Sense and Education, was if able to converse, a
welcome companion.* (*The Watsons*)

WATSON, PENELOPE: One of the Watson girls, regarded by
Elizabeth as having destroyed her chance of marrying Purvis.
'*Penelope makes light of her conduct, but I think such Treachery
very bad ... Do not trust her with any secrets of your own, take
warning by me, do not trust her; she has her good qualities, but she
has no Faith, no Honour, no Scruples, if she can promote her own
advantage.*' – Elizabeth (*The Watsons*)

WATSON, ROBERT: Brother of Sam and the Watson girls; an
attorney, married, with a daughter, Augusta. *In a good way of
Business; very well satisfied with himself for the same, & for having
married the only daughter of the Attorney to whom he had been
Clerk, with a fortune of six thousand pounds, & for being now in
possession of a very smart house in Croydon, where she gave genteel
parties, & wore fine cloathes. In her person there was nothing
remarkable; her manners were pert and conceited.* (*The Watsons*)

WATSON, SAM: Brother of Robert and the Watson girls; a
surgeon at Guildford, in love with Mary Edwards. '*He has been
very much in love with her these two years, & it is a great dis-*

appointment to him that he cannot always get away to our Balls – but Mr. Curtis won't often spare him, & just now is a sickly time at Guilford.' – Elizabeth Watson (*The Watsons*)

WENTWORTH, CAPTAIN FREDERICK: Mrs Croft's brother. Dissuaded from his engagement to Anne Elliot some years before the story begins, he marries her at its end. *Captain Wentworth had no fortune. He had been lucky in his profession, but, spending freely what had come freely, had realized nothing. But he was confident that he should soon be rich; full of life and ardour, he knew that he should soon have a ship, and soon be on a station that would lead to every thing he wanted. He had always been lucky; he knew he should be so still. Such confidence, powerful in its own warmth, and bewitching in the wit which often expressed it, must have been enough for Anne; but Lady Russell saw it very differently. His sanguine temper and fearlessness of mind operated very differently. on her. She was in it but an aggravation of the evil. It only added a dangerous character to himself. He was brilliant, he was headstrong. Lady Russell had little taste for wit; and of any thing approaching to imprudence a horror. She deprecated the connexion in every light.* (*Persuasion*)

WESTON, MR: Of Randalls, Highbury, Surrey. Father of Frank Weston Churchill by his first wife, formerly a Miss Churchill. In widowhood he marries Miss Taylor. *Mr. Weston was a native of Highbury, and born of a respectable family, which for the last two or three generations had been rising into gentility and property. He had received a good education, but, on succeeding early in life to a small independence, had become indisposed for any of the more homely pursuits in which his brothers were engaged; and had satisfied an active, cheerful mind and social temper by entering into the militia of his county. 'There is an openness, a quickness, almost a bluntness in Mr. Weston, which everybody likes in him, because there is so much good humour with it – but that would not do to be copied.'* – Emma (*Emma*)

WESTON, MRS: Formerly Miss Taylor, the Woodhouse family governess and Emma's close friend. She marries widowed Mr Weston, father of Frank Churchill, and bears him a daughter.

She had been a friend and companion such as few possessed: intelligent, well-informed, useful, gentle, knowing all the ways of the family, interested in all its concerns, and peculiarly interested in herself [Emma], *in every pleasure, every scheme of hers; one to whom she could speak every thought as it arose, and who had such an affection for her as could never find fault.* (*Emma*)

WICKHAM, GEORGE: Son of the deceased manager of Darcy's family estates, Pemberley, he is helped financially by Darcy, attempts to elope with Georgiana Darcy, goes out of his way to persuade Elizabeth Bennet of Darcy's defects, elopes with Lydia Bennet and then marries her, transferring from the militia to a commission in the regular army. *His appearance was greatly in his favour, he had all the best part of beauty, a fine countenance, a good figure, and very pleasing address.*

Mr. Wickham was the happy man towards whom almost every female eye was turned, and Elizabeth was the happy woman by whom he finally seated himself; and the agreeable manner in which he immediately fell into conversation, though it was only on its being a wet night, and on the probability of a rainy season, made her feel that the commonest, dullest, most threadbare topic might be rendered interesting by the skill of the speaker. (*Pride & Prejudice*)

WILLIAMS, ELIZA: Colonel Brandon's loved one from childhood, married instead to his brother, who later divorced her. Colonel Brandon found her in a debtors'-house in the last stages of consumption and became guardian to her infant Eliza, 'the offspring of her first guilty connection'. During the story, the child, aged fourteen, leaves the home of the woman in whose care he has placed her to elope with John Willoughby, who subsequently abandons her, pregnant. *'Such,' said Colonel Brandon, after a pause, 'has been the unhappy resemblance between the fate of mother and daughter! And so imperfectly have I discharged my trust!'* (*Sense & Sensibility*)

WILLOUGHBY, JOHN: Heir to his cousin, Mrs Smith of Allenham Court. Marianne Dashwood is passionately in love with him and understands it to be reciprocated; but he elopes with the 14-year-old Eliza, daughter of Colonel Brandon's brother's former wife, abandons her pregnant, fights an ineffectual duel over her with Colonel Brandon, and eventually marries a Miss Grey for her money. *Willoughby was a young man of good abilities, quick imagination, lively spirits, and open affectionate manners. He was exactly formed to engage Marianne's heart; for, with all this, he joined not only a captivating person, but a natural ardour of mind, which was now roused and increased by the example of her own, and which recommended him to her affection beyond everything else ... Marianne began now to perceive that the desperation which had seized her at sixteen and a half, of ever seeing a man who could satisfy her ideas of perfection, had been rash and unjustifiable.* (*Sense & Sensibility*)

WOODHOUSE, EMMA: Younger sister of Mrs John Knightley. She lives with her widowed father and finally marries John Knightley's elder brother, Mr Knightley. *Emma Woodhouse, handsome, clever, and rich, with a comfortable home and happy disposition seemed to unite some of the best blessings of existence; and had lived nearly twenty-one years in the world with very little to distress or vex her.*

'*Such an eye! – the true hazel eye, – and so brilliant! regular features, open countenance, with a true complexion – oh, what a bloom of full health, and such a pretty height and size! such a firm and upright figure! There is health not merely in her bloom, but in her air, her head, her glance. One hears sometimes of a child being "the picture of health"; now, Emma always gives me the idea of being the complete picture of grown-up health. She is loveliness itself.*' – Mrs Weston (*Emma*)

WOODHOUSE, ISABELLA: See KNIGHTLEY, MRS JOHN. (*Emma*)

WOODHOUSE, MR: Of Hartfield, near Highbury, Surrey. Widowed and hypochondriacal father of Isabella Knightley and Emma. *He was a much older man in ways than in years; and though everywhere beloved for the friendliness of his heart and his amiable temper, his talents could not have recommended him at any time ... His spirits required support. He was a nervous man, easily depressed; fond of everybody that he was used to, and hating to part with them; hating change of every kind. Matrimony, as the origin of change, was always disagreeable; and he was by no means yet reconciled to his own daughter's marrying, nor could ever speak of her but with compassion, though it had been entirely a match of affection.* (*Emma*)

YATES, THE HON JOHN: Stage-struck friend of Tom Bertram who elopes with, and marries, Julia Bertram. *Had not much to recommend him beyond habits of fashion and expense, and being the younger son of a lord with a tolerable independence . . . He did come rather earlier than had been expected, in consequence of the sudden breaking-up of a large party assembled for gaiety at the house of another friend, which he had left Weymouth to join. He came on the wings of disappointment, and with his head full of acting, for it had been a theatrical party; and the play in which he had borne a part was within two days of representation, when the sudden death of one of the nearest connections of the family had destroyed the scheme and dispersed the performers. To be so near happiness, so near fame, so near the long photograph in favour of the private theatricals at Ecclesford, the seat of the Right Hon. Lord Ravenshaw, in Cornwall, which would of course have immortalised the whole party for at least a twelvemonth!* (*Mansfield Park*)

The Works

LOVE AND FREINDSHIP*

Love and Freindship stands apart from Jane Austen's other juvenile works on the strength of its completeness, its wit, its demonstration of the literary ability and satirical perceptions of the fourteen-year-old author. It is an immensely entertaining revelation of the way she was at that age, and of what she had gained from her wide reading, her father's guidance and her mother's sense of humour.

It was written in 1790 and is dedicated 'To Madame la Comtesse de Feuillide'. This was the former Eliza Hancock, the child of Jane's Aunt Philadelphia, her father's sister. Eliza married a rich Frenchman, Jean Capotte, Comte de Feuillide, but was widowed within a few years when he injudiciously returned from England to his native country at the height of the Terror in order to avert the confiscation of his estates, and was guillotined in 1794. Three years later his lively, flirtatious widow allowed herself to be taken to the altar once more by Jane's brother Henry, then a Militia officer but later the banker who was to prove so helpful in Jane's dealings with her publishers.

Love and Freindship was not published until 1922, by Chatto & Windus, London.

· · · ·

*Jane Austen's own spelling, retained when the work was first published this century. Some commentators and biographers correct it, with or without comment. I prefer to leave it alone, for its reflection of the jolly artlessness of the content and spelling of the work. After all, who would be so pedantic as to amend Daisy Ashford's *The Young Visiters?*

ISABEL writes to her 55-year-old friend, Laura, asking her to keep her promise to relate the misfortunes of her (Laura's) life to Marianne, Isabel's daughter. Supposing herself now out of danger from 'the determined Perseverance of disagreeable Lovers and the cruel Persecutions of obstinate Fathers', Laura consents, and proceeds to tell her strange story in a series of letters.

One December evening, years before, when Laura was an unmarried girl, she had been sitting with her parents in their cottage in the Vale of Usk, in Wales, when they had been astonished by a violent knocking at the door:

My Father started – 'What noise is that,' (said he.) 'It sounds like a loud rapping at the door' – (replied my Mother.) 'it does indeed.' (cried I.) 'I am of your opinion; (said my Father) it certainly does appear to proceed from some uncommon violence exerted against our unoffending door.' 'Yes (exclaimed I) I cannot help thinking it must be somebody who knocks for admittance.'

'That is another point (replied he;) We must not pretend to determine on what motive the person may knock – tho' that someone *does* rap at the door, I am partly convinced.'

Here a second tremendous rap interrupted my Father in his speech, and somewhat alarmed by Mother and me.

'Had we not better go and see who it is? (said she) the servants are out.' 'I think we had.' (replied I.) 'Certainly, (added my Father) by all means.' 'Shall we go now?' (said my Mother.) 'The sooner the better.' (answered he.) 'Oh! let no time be lost' (cried I.)

A third more violent Rap than ever again assaulted our ears. 'I am certain there is somebody knocking at the Door.' (said my Mother). 'I think there must,' (replied my Father) 'I fancy the servants are returned; (said I) I think I hear Mary going to the Door.' 'I'm glad of it (cried my Father) for I long to know who it is.'

I was right in my conjecture; for Mary instantly entering the Room, informed us that a young Gentleman and his Servant were at the door, who had lossed their way, were very cold and begged leave to warm themselves by our fire.

A young man and his servant are admitted. The gentleman

introduces himself as Edward Lindsay, the son of an English baronet whose house in Bedfordshire he had left in order to visit an aunt in Middlesex; but, his geography being faulty, he has found himself benighted, cold and hungry in Wales, and has ventured to apply at the cottage for shelter. He adds that he has a sister 'of the middle size', but no mother. His father is insisting upon his marrying a Lady Dorothea, whom he finds attractive and engaging enough but is determined not to marry, if only to spite his disagreeable parent. This situation is speedily resolved by Edward marrying Laura that same night, the ceremony being conducted by her father, 'who tho' he had never taken orders had been bred to the Church'.

After a few days the couple go to Edward's Aunt Philippa in Middlesex, where they find his sister Augusta. She greets Laura coldly, and upbraids her brother for his impracticality in defying their father's wish:

'My Dear Brother since you were five years old, I entirely acquit you of ever having willingly contributed to the Satisfaction of your Father. But still I am not without apprehensions of your being shortly obliged to degrade yourself in your own eyes by seeking a Support for your Wife in the Generosity of Sir Edward.'

'Never, never Augusta will I so demean myself. (said Edward). Support! What Support will Laura want which she can receive from him?'

'Only those very insignificant ones of Victuals and Drink.' (answered she.)

'Victuals and Drink! (replied my Husband in a most nobly contemptuous Manner) and dost thou then imagine that there is no other support for an exalted Mind (such as is my Laura's) than the mean and indelicate employment of Eating and Drinking?'

'None that I know of, so efficacious.' (returned Augusta).

'And did you then never feel the pleasing Pangs of Love, Augusta? (replied my Edward). Does it appear impossible to your vile and corrupted Palate, to exist on Love? Can you not conceive the Luxury of living in every Distress that Poverty can inflict, with the object of your tenderest Affection?'

'You are too ridiculous (said Augusta) to argue with.'

The argument is interrupted by the entrance of a 'very Handsome Young Woman'. She is Lady Dorothea, Edward's erstwhile betrothed, evidently come to view the woman who has supplanted her. She stays only half an hour, and the meeting is not notable for its warmth.

Lady Dorothea is followed by Edward's father, the 'cruel and unrelenting baronet', Sir Edward Lindsay. Before he can open his mouth to express his rage at the match, his son forestalls him:

'Sir Edward, I know the motive of your Journey here – You come with the base Design of reproaching me for having entered into an indissoluble engagement with my Laura without your Consent. But Sir, I glory in the Act – . It is my greatest boast that I have incurred the displeasure of my Father!'

So saying, he took my hand and whilst Sir Edward, Philippa, and Augusta were doubtless reflecting with Admiration on his undaunted Bravery, led me from the Parlour to his Father's Carriage which yet remained at the Door and in which we were instantly conveyed from the pursuit of Sir Edward.

The couple drive to the home of Edward's close friend, Augustus, who has recently taken a young bride, Sophia, also against parental wishes. The girls take to one another immediately. As for their husbands:

Never did I see such an affecting Scene as was the meeting of Edward and Augustus.

'My Life! my Soul!' (exclaimed the former) 'My Adorable Angel!' (replied the latter) as they flew into each other's arms. It was too pathetic for the feelings of Sophia and myself – We fainted alternately on a sofa.

A letter arrives from Edward's Aunt Philippa, reporting that Sir Edward and Augusta have returned home to Bedfordshire, and inviting them to resume their visit to her in Middlesex when the time comes to leave their friends. They thank her politely, but prefer to remain with Augustus and Sophia for as long as possible. A few weeks later they learn that, 'either to revenge our

Conduct, or releive her own solitude', Aunt Philippa has married a young and illiterate fortune-hunter.

Laura and Edward stay on, content with the society of their young friends and their neighbours. But trouble is approaching. Augustus and Sophia have been living on money he had stolen from his father a few days before the marriage. Now it has all gone, and they are deeply in debt. Augustus's creditors have him arrested, about which there is only one thing the girls can do: 'We sighed and fainted on the sofa.'

Augustus has been carried off to prison in London, and Edward follows him there to see what he can do to help. No word reaches their wives, who at length drive to London to look for Edward, but without success; they leave London without dismounting from their coach. They cannot turn to Laura's parents for comfort, for they had died and have left her virtually nothing. Sophia recollects that she has a relation in Scotland and they contemplate driving straight there, but reflect that it might be too far for the horses to manage. However, by the simple expedient of changing horses, and then travelling Post, they reach a Scottish inn only a few miles from Sophia's relation's home. They write him a pathetic note about their circumstances, proposing that they spend some months with him, and are just about to follow it up in person when a coroneted coach enters the inn-yard and disgorges an old gentleman whom Laura instinctively recognizes to be her grandfather. He acknowledges her as such, and moreover, sees in Sophia another of the granddaughters of his union with Laurina, an Italian opera girl. But this is not all:

Whilst they were tenderly embracing, the Door of the Apartment opened and a most beautifull Young Man appeared. On perceiving him Lord St. Clair started and retreating back a few paces, with uplifted Hands, said, 'Another Grand-child! What an unexpected Happiness is this! to discover in the space of 3 minutes, as many of my Descendants! This, I am certain is Philander the son of my Laurina's third Girl the amiable Bertha; there wants now but the presence of Gustavus to compleat the Union of my Laurina's Grand-children.'

'And here he is; (said a Gracefull Youth who that instant entered the room) here is the Gustavus you desire to see. I am the son of Agatha your Laurina's fourth and Youngest Daughter.' 'I see you are indeed; replied Lord St. Clair – But tell me (continued he looking fearfully towards the Door) tell me, have I any other Grand-children in the House.' 'None my Lord.' 'Then I will provide for you all without farther delay – Here are 4 Banknotes of 50£ each – Take them and remember I have done the Duty of a Grandfather.' He instantly left the Room and immediately afterwards the House.

Far from gratifying the recipients, this gesture is regarded as unworthy of a grandfather, and precipitates further fainting. When the girls recover they find that Gustavus and Philander have gone, and the banknotes with them. Their new distress is relieved by the arrival of Sophia's cousin, Macdonald, who has come to escort them to his mansion. There they meet his fifteen-year-old daughter Janetta and her betrothed, Graham. They do not like the look of the latter, and Janetta confides that she has become engaged only because it is her father's wish. She claims no other particular preference; only a slight inclination towards a Captain M'Kenzie. This is enough for Sophia and Laura to work upon, which they do by persuading Janetta that she is violently in love with M'Kenzie and arranging for him to carry her off to Gretna Green and marriage, which promptly ensues.

Sophia 'happens' to open a private drawer in her relative's library with one of her own keys and finds that it contains a large number of banknotes. She and Laura agree that whenever either of them chances to pass that way again they will remove one or more of the notes, just to teach Macdonald a lesson for trying to marry his daughter off so unsuitably. The series of thefts does not last long, though:

Alas! on the very day of Janetta's Escape, as Sophia was majestically removing the 5th Bank-note from the Drawer to her own purse, she was suddenly most impertinently interrupted in her employment by the entrance of Macdonald himself, in a most abrupt and precipitate Manner. Sophia (who though naturally all winning sweetness could when occasions demanded it call forth the Dignity of her sex) instantly put on a most forbidding look, and darting an angry frown on the undaunted Culprit, demanded in a haughty tone of voice, 'Wherefore her retirement was thus insolently broken in on?' The unblushing Macdonald, without even endeavouring to exculpate himself from the crime he was charged with, meanly endeavoured to reproach Sophia with ignobly defrauding him of his Money. . . . The dignity of Sophia was wounded; 'Wretch (exclaimed she, hastily replacing the Bank-note in the Drawer) how darest thou to accuse me of an Act, of which the bare idea makes me blush?' The base wretch was still unconvinced and continued to upbraid the justly-offended Sophia in such opprobious Language, that at length he so greatly provoked the gentle sweetness of her Nature, as to induce her to revenge herself on him by informing him of Janetta's Elopement, and of the active Part we had both taken in the Affair. At this period of their Quarrel I entered the Library and was as you may imagine equally offended as Sophia at the ill-grounded Accusations of the malevolent and contemptible Macdonald. 'Base Miscreant! (cried I) how canst thou thus undauntedly endeavour to sully the spotless reputation of such bright Excellence? Why dost thou not suspect *my* innocence as soon? Be satisfied Madam (replied he) I *do* suspect it, and therefore must desire that you will both leave this House in less than half an hour.'

'We shall go willingly; (answered Sophia) our hearts have long detested thee, and nothing but our freidnship for thy Daughter could have induced us to remain so long beneath thy roof.'

The aggrieved ladies pack their bags and depart from Macdonald Hall on foot. Having travelled a mile and a half they are sitting beneath some elms, resting their exhausted limbs, when a phaeton overturns on the road nearby. Sophia and Laura run to it, to find two gentlemen lying bleeding. They are their respective husbands, August and Edward:

Sophia shreiked and fainted on the Ground – I screamed and instantly ran mad –. We remained thus mutually deprived of our Senses, some minutes, and on regaining them were deprived of them again. For an Hour and a Quarter did we continue in this unfortunate Situation – Sophia fainting every moment and I running Mad as often. At length a groan from the hapless Edward (who alone retained any share of Life) restored us to ourselves. Had we indeed before imagined that either of them lived, we should have been more sparing of our Greif – but as we had supposed when we first beheld them that they were no more, we knew that nothing could remain to be done but what we were about.

But Edward had groaned too late: both men die. Their grief-stricken widows, realistically recognizing that they had better find lodgings for the night, are admitted to an old woman's cottage. The following day Sophia is found to be ill, presumably chilled through having spent so long on the ground in her faints, a fate from which Laura presumes herself to have been saved by her frenzy stimulating her circulation. It is soon apparent that Sophia's disorder is serious. It turns into galloping consumption, and within a few days she, too, is dead.

Laura travels to Edinburgh in a stage coach. She boards the coach in darkness and so is unable to see the faces of her fellow passengers, one of whom snores disgustingly. When daylight reveals his and the others' identity, Laura is unpleasantly surprised:

It was Sir Edward the father of my Deceased Husband. By his side, sate Augusta, and on the same seat with me were your Mother and Lady Dorothea. Imagine my Surprise at finding myself thus seated amongst my old Acquaintance. Great as was my astonishment, it was yet increased, when on looking out of Windows, I beheld the Husband of Philippa, with Philippa by his side, on the Coachbox, and when on looking behind I beheld, Philander and Gustavus in the Basket. 'Oh! Heavens, (exclaimed I) is it possible that I should so unexpectedly be surrounded by my nearest Relations and Connections'? These words rouzed the rest of the Party, and every eye was directed to the corner in which I sat. 'Oh! my Isabel (continued I throwing myself across Lady Dorothea into her arms) receive once more to your Bosom the unfortunate Laura.

She relates her tragic story. When they reach Edinburgh Sir Edward asks her, as the widow of his son, to accept £400 a year. She accepts graciously and goes off to live in a romantic High-land village, where she can, 'uninterrupted by unmeaning Visits, indulge in a melancholy solitude, my unceasing Lamentations for the Death of my Father, my Mother, my Husband and my Freind.'

Augusta marries Graham; Sir Edward marries Lady Dorothea; Philander and Gustavus succeed in the theatre under the stage names of Lewis and Quick; and Philippa's husband, eventually widowed, 'still continues to drive the Stage-Coach from Edinburgh to Sterling.'

THE WATSONS

NOT only did the Austen family's removal from Steventon to Bath in 1801 upset Jane by its suddenness; it affected her in the longer term as well. She never came to care for Bath itself, and in the five years spent there wrote little. *Susan* (later *Northanger Abbey*) was revised and sold, but not published; the brief sketch *Lady Susan* was worked on and laid aside; and in 1803 or 1804 a novel was started, never to be finished.

Why she never went on with what we know as *The Watsons* is not certain. Her nephew, James Edward Austen-Leigh, in his *Memoir* of her, says it was because she recognized 'the evil of having placed her heroine too low, in a position of poverty and obscurity, which, though not necessarily connected with vulgarity, has a sad tendency to degenerate into it.' This is less than convincing: Emma Watson's situation is not so 'low' as all that, and by the time the fragment ends is showing considerable potential for improvement. More likely, Jane simply found the theme unrewarding: one of those false starts familiar to most writers. Furthermore, as we have seen, any untoward occurrence could burden her mind and disrupt her work. The death of her dearly beloved father in 1804, preceded only a few weeks by that of a close friend, Mrs Lefroy, in a riding accident, probably caused her finally to give up work on a book which was already troubling her. The effort that had gone into it cannot have been wasted, however; especially if, as has been suggested, she later drew upon *The Watsons* when writing *Emma*.

The fragment was first published in her nephew's *Memoir* in 1871.

. . . .

The first winter assembly in 'the Town of D. in Surry' (presumed to be Dorking, Surrey) is about to take place. Many of the leading families of the surrounding country are certain to attend, including, it is hoped, the grand Osbornes of Osborne Castle.

On a lower scale are the Edwards,* who have money and a coach; and, lower still – a good deal lower – the Watsons, who have neither coach nor money. Mr Watson, a widower, is a sickly man, who prefers to stay at home, patiently tended by his eldest daughter, Elizabeth, who is twenty-eight and a spinster, though she might once have married a Mr Purvis if her sister Penelope had not prevented it.

The Watsons live in Stanton, a village some three miles from D., and it is the Edwards's generous custom to invite those of them who are able to attend the assemblies to dress, dine and stay overnight at their house. On this occasion there is only one to be accommodated: the nineteen-year-old Emma, who has just returned to her family after having been brought up by an aunt. The aunt has suddenly married again and has gone to live in Ireland with her Captain O'Brien, and Emma consequently finds herself back on her native heath after fourteen years, a stranger to everyone. The ball will serve to introduce her, and Elizabeth, who will be staying behind to look after their father, is escorting her to D., and taking the opportunity to give her some background information on many of the people she is likely to meet. Most of this concerns the various females' quests for husbands, a preoccupation with which Emma does not sympathize:

'To be so bent on Marriage – to pursue a Man merely for the sake of situation – is a sort of thing that shocks me; I cannot understand it. Poverty is a great Evil, but to a woman of Education & feeling it ought not, it cannot be the greatest. – I would rather be Teacher at a school (and I can think of nothing worse) than marry a Man I did not like.' – 'I would rather do any thing that be Teacher at a school – said her sister. *I* have been at school, Emma, & know what a Life they lead; *you* never have. – I should not like marrying a disagreable Man any more than yourself, – but I do not think there *are* many very disagreable Men; – I think I could like any good humoured Man with a comfortable Income.'

Elizabeth fears that her sister's aunt has brought her up to be

*Often given as 'Edwardes' in the original text, but 'Edwards' is used consistently here for the sake of clarity.

too refined for her good, and is evidently relishing the almost inevitable encounter at the ball between Emma and Tom Musgrave, a notorious ladies' man, irresistible to most women and always eager to bestow his attention upon a new one. She is also anxious to have Emma's report as to who dances with the eligible Miss Mary Edwards, so that she may write and tell their brother, Sam Watson, who is much attached to that lady, but cannot get away from his duties as a surgeon in 'Guilford' (Guildford) to partner her himself. In any case, Elizabeth confides, Sam is wasting his time pursuing Miss Edwards, who is an only child with an expectation of at least ten thousand pounds a year. Her parents and she will want to do much better for her than an impecunious medical man. In fact, sighs Elizabeth, her mind on her own disappointment, the only lucky Watson has been their eldest brother Robert, who is a successful attorney at Croydon, having married his former partner's daughter, who had brought him £6,000.

This summing-up of her family's inferior status somewhat depresses Emma's spirit, and she discerns in the Edwards ladies' reception of her a certain reserve behind the civility. Mr Edwards proves breezier and garrulous, coming home full of the news that the Osborne Castle party will definitely be at the ball. The ladies are fussed into getting dressed in good time, and this enforced intimacy does something to ease their relationship. Emma hears little of value about Mary Edwards's feelings towards her brother. At dinner, Mr Edwards, an indefatigable collector of material for his gossiping, wants to know the details of Emma's aunt's marriage. It is her second, and if she is indeed the lady he had once danced with at Bath some thirty years earlier she cannot exactly be termed young. This provokes some slight discussion:

'Elderly Ladies should be careful how they make a second choice,' observed Mr. Edwards. – 'Carefulness – Discretion – should not be confined to Elderly Ladies, or to a second choice added his wife. It is quite as necessary to young Ladies in their first.' – 'Rather more so, my dear – replied he, because young Ladies are likely to feel the effects of it longer.

When an old Lady plays the fool, it is not in the course of nature that she should suffer from it many years.'

Dinner over, there is an impatient period of waiting for the time of the ball, partially whiled away with tea and muffins. A little before eight o'clock a neighbour's carriage is heard to pass, which is accepted by Mrs Edwards as the cue to order theirs. They are amongst the first to arrive at the inn where the ball is being held, and as they pass along a corridor they encounter a young man lounging in a bedroom doorway:

'Ah! Mrs. E – how do you do? – How do you do Miss E.? – he cried, with an easy air; – You are determined to be in good time I see, as usual. – The Candles are but this moment lit' – 'I like to get a good seat by the fire you know, Mr. Musgrave.' replied Mrs. E. 'I am this moment going to dress,' said he – 'I am waiting for my stupid fellow. –We shall have a famous Ball, The Osbornes are certainly coming; you may depend upon *that* for I was with Ld. Osborne this morning.'

Mary whispers to Emma as they pass that he is the celebrated Tom Musgrave. The assembly room is cold and underpopulated at this early time, but it soon begins to fill and an atmosphere of enjoyment develops. Emma, the stranger in the midst, is examined by all eyes, identified, and admired, and she soon finds herself dancing with an officer. He is introduced to her by Captain Hunter who, she notes, is the man whom her brother Sam will have to be told partnered Mary Edwards in not only the first, but also the second dance.

More carriages are heard and excited word runs round the room that 'the Osbornes are coming'. This important group proves to consist in the main of the young and aloof Lord Osborne; his mother, Lady Osborne; his unmarried sister; his former tutor, Mr Howard, now a local clergyman; Mr Howard's widowed sister, Mrs Blake, with her ten-year-old son Charles – and Tom Musgrave.

Little Charles Blake has a passion for dancing and cannot wait to get out on to the floor; but Miss Osborne, who has promised him the first two dances, decides instead to partner a Colonel

Beresford. Emma sees that the little boy is near to tears as a result,
and without a second thought offers herself. He accepts with
touching gratitude, and they join the set. This partnership of
nineteen-year-old girl and ten-year-old boy attracts more notice
for Emma, even from Lord Osborne, who relaxes his forbidding
dignity to stare openly at her. Her kind action has won her the
gratitude of Charles Blake's mother, and she introduces Emma to
her brother, Mr Howard. He partners her in further dancing,
proving an intelligent, friendly man; but she has little time to
enjoy his company, for the Osborne party is leaving and he must
accompany them. Emma has clearly made her impression,
though. Miss Osborne gives her the hint of a curtsey as she
passes, and Lord Osborne 'actually came back after the others
were out of the room, to "beg her pardon", & look in the
window seat behind her for the gloves which were visibly compressed in his hand.'

Emma's enjoyment of the evening has been complete, and next
day brings a host of callers to the Edwards's house, all of whom
are curious 'to look again at the girl who had been admired the
night before by Lord Osborne', either to admire her for themselves or to seek for real or imaginary flaws in her beauty.

One caller is Tom Musgrave. He brings a note from Emma's
sister, whom he had chanced to encounter while riding through
Stanton, to the effect that Mr Watson is enjoying one of his days
of better health and has decided to attend a religious Visitation in
R. (presumed to be Reigate). This means that his Chair is not
available to fetch Emma home as arranged, and she must stay
another night with the Edwards family. Mr Musgrave has a
verbal postscript of his own to add, however: his curricle is
at the door, and it will be his pleasure to drive Emma home
himself:

Emma felt distressed; she did not like the proposal – she did not wish to
be on terms of intimacy with the Proposer – & yet fearful of encroaching
on the Edwards', as well as wishing to go home herself, she was at a loss
how entirely to decline what he offered – Mrs. E. continued silent, either
not understanding the case, or waiting to see how the young Lady's

inclination lay. Emma thanked him – but professed herself very unwilling to give him so much trouble. 'The Trouble was of course, Honour, Pleasure, Delight. What had he or his Horses to do?' – Still she hesitated. 'She believed she must beg leave to decline his assistance – she was rather afraid of the sort of carriage –. The distance was not beyond a walk. –' Mrs. E. was silent no longer. She enquired into the particulars – & then said 'We shall be extremely happy Miss Emma, if you can give us the pleasure of your company till tomorrow – but if you can not conveniently do so, our Carriage is quite at your Service, & Mary will be pleased with the opportunity of seeing your Sister.' This was precisely what Emma had longed for; & she accepted the offer most thankfully; acknowledging that as Eliz: was entirely alone, it was her wish to return home to dinner. – The plan was warmly opposed by their Visitor. 'I cannot suffer it indeed. I must not be deprived of the happiness of escorting you. I assure you there is not a possibility of fear with my Horses. You might guide them yourself. *Your Sisters* all know how quiet they are; They have none of them the smallest scruple in trusting themselves with me, even on a Race Course. Believe me – added he lowering his voice – *You* are quite safe, the danger is only *mine*.' – Emma was not more disposed to oblige him for all this. – 'And as to Mrs. Edwards' carriage being used the day after a Ball, it is a thing quite out of rule I assure you – never heard of before – the old Coachman will look as black as his Horses –Won't he Miss Edwards?' – No notice was taken. The Ladies were silently firm, & the gentleman found himself obliged to submit.

Emma duly escapes and reaches home in safety to regale Elizabeth with every detail of the ball, impress her with the friendship she has gained so quickly with the people from Osborne Castle, and amaze her by her failure to be captivated by Tom Musgrave. That she has danced with Mr Howard particularly astonishes Elizabeth, for he is 'quite one of the great & Grand ones.' When Mr Watson returns home at last it transpires that none other than Mr Howard had delivered the sermon at the Visitation. Mr Weston cannot recall having heard better preaching; but, what had impressed him as much was that afterwards Mr Howard had paid him personal attention, assisting him to walk on his gouty foot into the room where dinner was to be served:

'It struck me as very becoming in so young a Man, but I am sure I had no claim to expect it; for I never saw him before in my Life. – By the bye, he enquired after one of my Daughters, but I do not know which. I suppose you know among yourselves.'

Three days after the ball Mr Weston is not well again, and Elizabeth and Emma are just about to sit down alone to an informal afternoon meal in the parlour when visitors are shown in. They are Lord Osborne and Tom Musgrave. Flattered that the call must be on account of herself, Emma is, nevertheless, embarrassed to be caught out in what must appear to such people a very inelegant habit. The awkwardness of the moment is not relieved by Lord Osborne, who, beyond hoping that Emma had not caught cold at the ball, can find little to say, though his eyes are glancing over her busily:

Emma was not inclined to give herself much trouble for his Entertainment – & after hard labour of mind, he produced the remark of it's being a very fine day, & followed it up with the question of, 'Have you been walking this morning?' 'No, my Lord. We thought it too dirty.' 'You should wear half-boots.' – After another pause, 'Nothing sets off a neat ankle more than a half-boot; nankin galoshed with black looks very well. – Do not you like Half boots? 'Yes – but unless they are so stout as to injure their beauty, they are not fit for Country walking.' – 'Ladies should ride in dirty weather. – Do you ride?' 'No my Lord.' 'I wonder every Lady does not. – A woman never looks better than on horseback. –' 'But every woman may not have the inclination, or the means.' 'If they knew how much it became them, they would all have the inclination, & I fancy Miss Watson – when once they had the inclination, the means would soon follow.' – 'Your Lordship thinks we always have our own way. – *That* is a point on which Ladies & Gentlemen have long disagreed – But without pretending to decide it, I may say that there are some circumstances which even *Women* cannot controul. – Female Economy will do a great deal my Lord, but it cannot turn a small income into a large one.' – Lord Osborne was silenced. Her manner had been neither sententious nor sarcastic, but there was a something in it's mild seriousness, as well as in the words themselves which made his Lordship think; – and when he addressed her again, it was with a degree of considerate propriety, totally unlike the half-awkward, half-fearless stile of his former remarks. – It was a new thing with him to wish to please a woman; it was the first time that he had ever felt what was due to a woman, in Emma's situation.

The interview is cut short by the housekeeper's entry with the inquiry, 'Please Ma'am, Master wants to know why he be'nt to have his dinner.' The gentlemen take their leave, Lord Osborne casually mentioning that his hounds will be hunting next week, should Emma be tempted to see them start off. Elizabeth is amazed that two such splendid men should have visited their humble home; but it does not escape Emma's thoughts that it would have been nicer if Mr Howard had come, too.

A fortnight or so later the Watsons are visited by brother Robert from Croydon, with his wife Jane, whom Emma has never met. She is not much attracted by this pert woman, and even less by her own sister Margaret, who has been staying at Croydon and has returned with them: she is too falsely affectionate, and full of the superior amenities and society of Croydon. Mr Watson is not well enough to dine with them, but comes down afterwards for tea and a game of cards. This is interrupted by the entrance of Tom Musgrave, who is on his way home from London and has decided to call on the Westons for a few minutes before going on to his dinner, which is served at a more fashionable hour than theirs. He is warmly welcomed and urged to join in the game, which he does for an hour, enlivening the gathering with his customary raillery, anecdotes and mimicry of the company at Osborne.

When he leaves at last it is with an invitation from Elizabeth, prompted by Margaret, to dine the following day. He will not commit himself, but promises to come if he can. A whole day is spent preparing for the guest, who Margaret admits to Emma is 'more interesting to me than perhaps you may be aware'; but after hours of suspense he does not arrive. This provokes general peevishness, and Emma is thankful to escape to sit with her father in the quiet of his room.

Robert and Jane invite Emma to return to Croydon with them, and Elizabeth urges her to accept, since she herself is more used to the disagreeable Margaret's manner than Emma is and can tolerate her more easily. Emma declines, however, and the visitors depart without her.

(The manuscript ends at this point. In later years, Cassandra Austen is said to have shown it to some nieces and told them what she alone knew of the author's intentions: that Mr Watson would soon die, compelling Emma to depend for a home on Robert and Jane; and that she would refuse an offer of marriage from Lord Osborne, eventually accepting one from Mr Howard.)

LADY SUSAN

Lady Susan was Jane Austen's last work in epistolary form. It is not know for certain when she wrote it, since the only evidence rests on the watermark of the paper on which the surviving fair copy was written out by her in 1805. The original may have been wholly composed before the move from Steventon; or, like *The Watsons*, it may belong to the unsettled years at Bath. In *Jane Austen and her Art* Mary Lascelles suggests the possibility that it was written at Steventon, where *Elinor and Marianne* (later *Sense and Sensibility*) was similarly drafted in the form of a series of letters, and that when Jane took up the work again at Bath, with the thought of finishing it, she found she could not return to the old device, so simply added the postscript to round off the story. At any rate, at the point where the series of letters ceases and the brief summary of subsequent events is tacked on, the story has virtually reached its conclusion and all the points have been made.

In *The Double Life of Jane Austen*, Jane Aiken Hodge makes an assessment of *Lady Susan* which I find astonishing: 'This curiously cold-blooded study of a wicked woman is almost entirely without humour. Until the very end, the laughter is silent.' I would submit that *Lady Susan* is a brilliantly humorous work, full of ironic innuendo, and its central character a most witty portrayal of the kind of enchantress who can be admired as much for her brazen machinations as deplored for the unscrupulous way in which she pursues her self-interests.

Lady Susan was first published with other short pieces in a second edition of James Edward Austen-Leigh's *A Memoir of Jane Austen* in 1871.

. . . .

The recently-widowed Lady Susan Vernon writes to her brother-in-law, Charles Vernon, accepting his invitation to stay with him and his wife Catherine at their home, Churchill, in Sussex. She has not yet met his wife and children and impatiently looks forward to 'the hour when I shall be admitted into your delightful retirement'. The people with whom she is staying at present, the Manwarings of Langford, are, she explains, too 'chearful' and fond of society for a bereaved woman's comfort. And, an additional burden is about to oppress her: she is to be parted from her dear daughter, who is to enter a private school in London.

Having finished her letter, Lady Susan draws forward more writing paper and begins another, franker, one. This is to her intimate friend, Mrs Alicia Johnson, of Edward Street, London, and it reveals both the real reason for her decision to quit Langford and her true feelings towards her daughter. The women of Langford are united against Lady Susan:

'My dear Creature, I have admitted no one's attentions but Manwaring's, I have avoided all general flirtation whatever, I have distinguished no Creature besides of all the Numbers resorting hither, except Sir James Martin, on whom I bestowed a little notice in order to detach him from Miss Manwaring. But if the World could know my motive *there*, they would honour me. I have been called an unkind Mother, but it was the sacred impulse of maternal affection, it was the advantage of my Daughter that led me on; and if that Daughter were not the greatest simpleton on Earth, I might have been rewarded for my Exertions as I ought. – Sir James did make proposals to me for Frederica – but Frederica, who was born to be the torment of my life, chose to set herself so violently against the match, that I thought it better to lay aside the scheme for the present, I have more than once repented that I did not marry him myself, & were he but one degree less contemptibly weak I certainly should, but I must own myself rather romantic in that respect, & that Riches only will not satisfy me. The event of all this is very provoking. Sir James is gone, Maria highly incensed, and Mrs. Manwaring insupportably jealous ... No house was ever more altered; the whole family are at war, & Manwaring scarcely dares speak to me. It is time for me to be gone.'

Hence her transfer to Churchill, a resolution taken despite the fact that she detests Charles Vernon and is afraid of his wife, whom she had tried to prevent his marrying at all. Lack of enthusiasm for the visit is voiced by Mrs Vernon in a letter to her mother, Lady

De Courcy, regretting that it will prevent her family being able to pay their planned Christmas visit, all as a result of Charles Vernon's excessive kindness to the widow. It is Catherine Vernon's brother, Reginald De Courcy, who immediately answers this letter, amusedly telling her the truth about Lady Susan's behaviour at Langford, as passed on to him by a Mr Smith, one of the Manwarings' neighbours:

What a Woman she must be! I long to see her, & shall certainly accept your kind invitation, that I may form some idea of those be-witching powers which can do so much – engaging at the same time & in the same house the affections of two Men who were neither of them at liberty to bestow them – & all this, without the charm of Youth. I am glad to find that Miss Vernon does not come with her Mother to Churchill, as she has not even Manners to recommend her, & according to Mr. Smith's account, is equally dull & proud. Where Pride & Stupidity unite, there can be no dissimulation worthy notice, & Miss Vernon shall be consigned to unrelenting contempt; but by all that I can gather, Lady Susan possesses a degree of captivating Deceit which must be pleasing to witness & detect. I shall be with you very soon, & am

your affec. Brother R. DE COURCY.'

Lady Susan is soon installed at Churchill and reporting to Mrs Johnson about the elegance of the house, Charles Vernon's wealth, Catherine's polite but undelighted reception of her, and her own determination to force herself to be liked, towards which end she is cultivating the affection of the Vernon children – 'I know all their names already'. The infatuated Manwaring has written, missing her sorely, and she is going to pretend to the Vernons that her correspondence with him is really between her and Mrs Manwaring.

In another room Catherine Vernon is writing simultaneously to her brother:

'Well my dear Reginald, I have seen this dangerous creature, & must give you some description of her, tho' I hope you will soon be able to form your own judgement. She is really excessively pretty. However you may chuse to question the allurements of a Lady no longer young, I must for my own part declare that I have seldom seen so lovely a Woman as Lady Susan. She is delicately fair, with fine grey eyes & dark eyelashes; & from her appearance one would not suppose her more than five & twenty, tho' she must in fact be ten years older. I was certainly not disposed to admire her, tho' always hearing she was beautiful; but I cannot help feeling that she possesses an uncommon union of Symmetry, Brilliancy and Grace. Her address to me was so gentle, frank & even affectionate, that if I had not known how much she has always disliked me for marrying Mr. Vernon, & that we have never met before, I should have imagined her an attached friend. One is apt I believe to connect assurance of manner with coquetry, & to expect that an impudent adddress will necessarily attend an impudent mind; at least I was myself prepared for an improper degree of confidence in Lady Susan; but her Countenance is absolutely sweet, & her voice & manner winningly mild. I am sorry it is so, for what is this but Deceit? Unfortunately one knows her too well. She is clever & agreable, has all that knowledge of the world which makes conversation easy, & talks very well, with a happy command of Language, which is too often used I believe to make Black appear White. She has already almost persuaded me of her being warmly attached to her daughter, tho' I have so long been convinced of the contrary. She speaks of her with so much tenderness & anxiety, lamenting so bitterly the neglect of her education, which she represents however as wholly unavoidable, that I am forced to recollect how many successive Springs her Ladyship spent in Town, while her daughter was left in Staffordshire to the care of servants or a Governess very little better.'

The story Reginald has heard from his friend Smith cannot be quite true, she objects, or Lady Susan would surely not be corresponding amiably with Mrs Manwaring: besides which, it is scarcely possible that two men could be taken in by her at the same time.

Lady Susan writes to thank Mrs Johnson for allowing Frederica to visit her in London, but asking her not to do so again: she wishes the girl to be so uncomfortable there that she will be only too glad to accept Sir James Martin and escape from school. Life at Churchill, insufferably dull for the first week, has been improved by the arrival of Reginald De Courcy. Lady Susan proposes to amuse herself by bewitching him, thereby demonstrating the superiority of her charms over the pride of the De Courcy clan.

She is evidently succeeding rapidly, to judge from Catherine Vernon's next letter to her mother, which contains the news that Reginald has decided to prolong his stay at Churchill and has sent home for his horses, with the intention of getting in some hunting while the weather holds. Mrs Vernon is certain that the hunting so far has been done by Lady Susan, and that Reginald is the quarry upon whom she is gaining fast. Yet there is nothing about Lady Susan's conduct that can be criticized at all: her manner towards them all has been impeccable.

Mrs Johnson advises Lady Susan to marry Reginald, whose inheritance, from a father already infirm, will be considerable. Sir James Martin has called on Mrs Johnson several times, and she is sure he would marry either Frederica or Lady Susan herself at the least prompting. Lady Susan replies that, although she is quite aware that she could bring Reginald De Courcy to the point of marriage with ease, she has no intention of doing so: she is rich already, and prefers her freedom. Her sole object is to humiliate him and his family.

Mrs Vernon reports to her mother her unease about Reginald's growing interest in Lady Susan and his refusal any longer to believe that the stories about her character are true. Unfortunately, when Lady De Courcy receives this letter she is suffering from so severe a cold that her streaming eyes cannot read it. Her husband, Sir Reginald, reads it out to her and is appalled to learn for the first time that his son is becoming embroiled with a notorious widow twelve years his senior. He writes Reginald a fatherly note, containing just a hint of what might eventuate if he is not heeded:

'You know your own rights, & that it is out of my power to prevent your inheriting the family Estate. My Ability of distressing you during my Life, would be a species of revenge to which I should hardly stoop under any circumstances. I honestly tell you my Sentiments & Intentions. I do not wish to work on your Fears, but on your Sense & Affection. It would destroy every comfort of my Life, to know that you were married to Lady Susan Vernon. It would be the death of that honest Pride with which I have hitherto considered my son, I should blush to see him, to hear of him, to think of him.'

Reginald replies by return of post. He has no matrimonial intentions towards Lady Susan – 'Our difference of age must be an insuperable objection' – but he resents strongly the imputations against that lady; the result, in his opinion, of Catherine Vernon's prejudice against her, and the scandalous tales invented by Mr Smith about the activities at Langford. Lady Susan has been misrepresented, misunderstood and mistreated, not least by her unworthy daughter, Frederica, who is evidently blind to her mother's affectionate concern for her.

Sir Reginald, relieved to hear this, passes his son's letter to Lady De Courcy, who in turn sends it to their daughter, Catherine sends it back again, rejoicing that her father's mind has been made easier, but adding her misgiving that even if Reginald has no *present* intention of marrying Lady Susan, what he may do in three months' time is a different question. However, even Catherine is feeling sorry for Lady Susan at this moment, for the poor woman has just received word that her daughter has tried to run away from school. Charles Vernon has hurried to London to try to persuade her schoolmistress to keep her on. If she refuses, Frederica will have to join them at Churchill, much against the wishes of Lady Susan, who is blaming herself for having promoted the girl's defects by over-indulging her in the past.

The truth of Frederica's attempted escape is contained in a letter Lady Susan writes to her friend Mrs Johnson. It is plainly the girl's ungrateful reaction to a letter her mother had sent her insisting that she marry Sir James Martin. 'But,' Lady Susan adds, 'she *shall* be punished, she *shall* have him.' As for her own progress, Reginald is proving thoroughly attentive, though a little tedious with his habit of demanding every detail of everything he has heard about her past life:

'This is *one* sort of Love – but I confess it does not particularly recommend itself to me. I infinitely prefer the tender & liberal spirit of Manwaring, which impressed with the deepest conviction of my merit, is satisfied that whatever I do must be right; & look, with a degree of contempt on the inquisitive & doubting Fancies of that Heart which seems always debating on the reasonableness of it's Emotions. Manwaring is indeed beyond compare superior to Reginald – superior in everything but the power of being with me. Poor fellow! he is quite distracted by Jealousy, which I am not sorry for, as I know no better support of Love. He has been teizing me to allow of his coming into this country, & lodging somewhere near me *incog*. – but I forbid anything of the kind. Those women are inexcusable who forget what is due to themselves & the opinion of the World.'

Mrs Vernon writes again to her mother, Lady De Courcy. Frederica's schoolmistress has proved adamant, and Charles has brought the girl back to Churchill. She is a pretty, pathetic thing, and Catherine is vexed by her brother's echoing Lady Susan's contempt for her. A certain excitement colours Mrs Vernon's next letter to her mother, however: Frederica is growing discernibly partial to Reginald, for 'Thoughtful & pensive in general, her countenance always brightens with a smile when Reginald says anything amusing; & let the subject be ever so serious that he may be conversing on, I am much mistaken if a syllable of his uttering escape her.' If only he could be made to see this, Catherine feels, it might prove Reginald's salvation.

Lady Susan has, of course, perceived the same symptoms, as she informs Mrs Johnson; but such is her contempt for her daughter's artlessness and ignorance that she has no fear of Reginald being anything more than indifferent towards her.

An unexpected visitor arrives at Churchill: Sir James Martin. Frederica is clearly dismayed, and Lady Susan rather put out. The latter has taken the unusual step of visiting Mrs Vernon in her dressing room, to confide in her, in sisterly fashion, that Sir James is passionately in love with the girl, and to solicit the Vernons' support in furthering the match. Her concluding words are:

'I am not apt to deal in professions, my dear Mrs. Vernon, & I never had the convenient talent of affecting sensations foreign to my heart; &

therefore I trust you will believe me when I declare that much as I had heard in your praise before I knew you, I had no idea that I should ever love you as I now do; & I must farther say that your friendship towards me is more particularly gratifying, because I have reason to believe that some attempts were made to prejudice you against me. I only wish that They – whoever they are – to whom I am endebted for such kind intentions, could see the terms on which we now are together, & understand the real affection we feel for each other! But I will not detain you any longer. God bless you, for your goodness to me & my girl, & continue to you all your present happiness.'

This leaves Catherine Vernon perplexed but still wary. She determines to get Frederica on her own to discover her feelings for Sir James. In fact, Frederica, at this moment, is describing these feelings in a note to Reginald, begging him, as her mother's close friend, to persuade her to send Sir James away. For her part, Lady Susan is soon writing to Mrs Johnson, giving vent to her fury at Sir James's visit, which has brought to the Vernons' knowledge her intentions concerning Frederica's fate (Lady Susan had preferred that such matters should be accomplished through her own subtle stealth and kept quiet meanwhile). Reginald has had the impudence to intercede with her on Frederica's behalf. Lady Susan had lost her temper, he had lost his, and the interview was ended on a high note of mutual indignation.

This clash has brought relief and delight to Catherine Vernon, who is able to write to his mother that Reginald is leaving for home that very day, having told her of Frederica's distaste for Sir James Martin and of Lady Susan's injustice in seeking to force the match. Catherine concludes her letter, 'When I next write, I shall be able I hope to tell you that Sir James is gone, Lady Susan vanquished, & Frederica at pease.' Instead:

'Little did I imagine my dear Mother, when I sent off my last letter, that the delightful perturbation of spirits I was then in, would undergo so speedy, so melancholy a reverse! I never can sufficiently regret that I wrote to you at all. Yet who could have foreseen what has happened? My dear Mother, every hope which but two hours ago made me so happy, is vanished. The quarrel between Lady Susan & Reginald is made up, & we are all as we were before. One point only is gained; Sir James Martin is dismissed. What are we now to look forward to? I am indeed disappointed. Reginald was all but gone; his horse was ordered, & almost brought to the door! Who would not have felt safe?'

It appears that on hearing of Reginald's imminent departure Lady Susan had hastened to beg him not to sacrifice the comfort of staying with his relatives because of a quarrel with her:

'My remaining here cannot give that pleasure to Mr. & Mrs. Vernon which your society must; & my visit has already perhaps been too long. My removal therefore, which must at any rate take place soon, may with perfect convenience be hastened; & I make it my particular request that I may not in any way be instrumental in separating a family so affectionately attached to each other. Where *I* go is of no consequence to anyone; of very little to myself; but *you* are of importance to all your connections.'

Sir James has left. Lady Susan has explained to the Vernons that she had never dreamed that her daughter was so passionately opposed to him, Now. Catherine fears, it seems more likely than ever that Reginald and Lady Susan will marry and will leave them to care for the unwanted Frederica.

Lady Susan tells Mrs Johnson how she has successfully overcome this latest crisis. She intends visiting London with Frederica, both to further her plans regarding Sir James Martin and to enjoy Mrs Johnson's society ' & a little Dissipation for a ten weeks' penance at Churchill'. Mrs Johnson answers swiftly, urging her not to bother further about Frederica, who has plagued her enough, but to get herself well established with the Vernons by marrying Reginald. Manwaring has called on Mrs Johnson several times, filled with anxiety to see Lady Susan and jealous of what he has heard of her relationship with Reginald. He is threatening to turn up at Churchill: Lady Susan could best avert an ugly situation by marrying Reginald and sending Manwaring back to his wife. The most welcome news in Mrs Johnson's letter is that her husband, who has always disapproved of Lady Susan and forbids his wife to have her to stay in his house, is going to

Bath, to take a cure for his gout. Mrs Johnson can get her friend a nice apartment in Upper Seymour Street, and they shall enjoy whatever company they please and some high times together. In fact, it would be better if Lady Susan were to leave Frederica at Churchill, and visit London alone.

This arrangement is no sooner accepted than it is upset by the tiresome Mr Johnson. Having heard that Lady Susan is to visit town, he has had an attack of gout so severe that he is unable to leave for Bath. However, the lodgings are taken, and Lady Susan duly installs herself in them. Manwaring promptly visits her. His virile appearance contrasts markedly with Reginald De Courcy's softness, and Lady Susan hesitates over taking Mrs Johnson's advice and settling for Reginald and respectability. Reginald has arranged to visit her in town: he must be put off until Manwaring has gone. Accordingly, she writes to Reginald, postponing his visit and suggesting that their marriage, for which he is by now eager, ought to be delayed, for reasons of delicacy due to her recent widowhood, and in order not to lose him the favour of his father and family.

The only effect of this is to bring Reginald hastening to see her, full of passionate entreaty. Flattered but alarmed – Manwaring is due to call – Lady Susan sends Reginald to spend the evening with Mrs Johnson, bearing a note permitting her friend to flirt with him as much as she wishes. Catastrophe ensues. Reginald's visit to Mrs Johnson's coincides with the stormy arrival there of Mrs Manwaring – Mr Johnson's ward – demanding help in reclaiming her husband from his embroilment with Lady Susan.

'The spell is removed,' writes Reginald to Lady Susan, after hearing that the stories he had come to disbelieve about her and Manwaring are true after all. But she is imperturbably confident that she can win him over yet again, and answers his farewell note with expressions of surprise that he should be taken in by the slanders of the jealous and ill-natured Mrs Manwaring. If he will only visit her at once, and tell her what has been alleged, she will refute everything to his face. This time, though, her spell fails. His reply challenges her to deny truthfully that she has been corresponding constantly with Manwaring, or that Manwaring has visited her London lodgings daily.

Knowing that an honest denial is not possible, and that Reginald's mind is made up finally, Lady Susan indulges in the dignity of womanly scorn:

'I am satisfied – & will trouble you no more when these few lines are dismissed. The Engagement which you were eager to form a fortnight ago, is no longer compatible with your views, & I rejoice to find that the prudent advice of your Parents has not been given in vain. Your restoration to Peace will, I doubt not, speedily follow this act of filial Obedience, & I flatter myself with the hope of surviving *my* share in this disappointment.'

Reginald's is not the only departure from Lady Susan's life at this time: Mrs Johnson has been threatened by her husband that if she persists in her connection with her he will take her away to settle in the country for the rest of his life – ' & you know it is impossible to submit to such an extremity while any other alternative remains'. Regrettably, the two women's long friendship must cease. Two final items of news, however, are that Mr and Mrs Manwaring are separating, and that Miss Manwaring has arrived in town, determined to secure Sir James Martin before she leaves again.

Lady Susan writes Alicia Johnson an understanding reply of farewell, summarizing her situation. She is finished with Reginald, but determined that Frederica shall not have him: she is fetching the girl from Churchill at once, ' & let Maria Manwaring tremble for the consequence. Frederica shall be Sir James's wife before she quits my house.' She herself could even make the sacrifice of matrimony, should Manwaring become free to offer himself: perhaps Mrs Johnson can speed this by keeping his wife in a state of irritation with him. As to Mrs Johnson's own future: 'Adeiu, dearest of Friends. May the next Gouty Attack be more favourable.'

The events which have been reported in this series of letters are briefly rounded off in a 'Conclusion', which begins:

This Correspondence, by a meeting between some of the Parties & a separation between the others, could not, to the great detriment of the Post office Revenue, be continued longer.

Frederica is living in London with her mother. Having heard enough from Reginald to convince them even more of Lady Susan's unsuitability to care for the girl, the Vernons visit London and Catherine calls on Lady Susan, whom she is surprised to find irrepressibly affectionate and unrepentant. Frederica still appears timid and apprehensive, but there is no mention of Sir James Martin, beyond the fact that he is not in London. Lady Susan seems to have acquired a deep devotion to her daughter; only she expresses little concern that London may not be agreeing with the girl, who she feels is not looking so well as she had done at Churchill. This seemingly fortuitous observation enables Catherine Vernon to propose that Frederica return to Sussex with her and her husband. Lady Susan is moved by the gesture, but cannot bring herself to part with her daughter, even for a few weeks. Mrs Vernon returns to the subject several times over the next few days, but Lady Susan remains adamant, until an influenza epidemic is heard to be spreading. Solicitous only for Frederica's health, she allows the Vernons to take her with them.

Three weeks later it is announced that Lady Susan and Sir James Martin are married. One or two affectionate letters reach Frederica at Churchill, inviting her to return to her mother. Her intended six weeks' stay extends to two months, and then two more, by which time the letters from Lady Susan have ceased:

Frederica was therefore fixed in the family of her Uncle & Aunt, till such time as Reginald De Courcy could be talked, flattered & finessed into an affection for her – which, allowing leisure for the conquest of his attachment to her Mother, for his abjuring all future attachments & detesting the Sex, might be reasonably looked for in the course of a Twelvemonth. Three Months might have done it in general, but Reginald's feelings were no less lasting than lively.

Whether Lady Susan was, or was not happy in her second Choice – I do not see how it can ever be ascertained – for who would take her assurance of it, on either side of the question? The World must judge from Probability. She had nothing against her, but her Husband, & her Conscience.

SENSE AND SENSIBILITY

SOMETIME before 1796 Jane Austen drafted a novel in the form of a series of letters to which she gave the title *Elinor and Marianne*. In November 1797, the month in which her *First Impressions* (later *Pride and Prejudice*) was so abruptly declined, she began to re-work the draft into a novel in narrative form, which at some stage received the title *Sense and Sensibility*. It was not offered for publication in that century, and no one can say when, in the years preceding publication, or to what extent, revision was carried out.

Elinor and Marianne has not survived, and there are no clues in those of Jane Austen's letters which escaped destruction to lead to the details of its reconstruction into the form we know. One imagines the final rewriting took place in 1810, for it was in the hands of the printer early the following year, in the April of which she was answering an inquiry of Cassandra's about it: 'No indeed, I am never too busy to think of S & S. I can no more forget it, than a mother can forget her sucking child. . . . I have had two sheets to correct, but the last only brings us to W.s [Willoughby's] first appearance.'

Sense and Sensibility, by 'A Lady', was published by Thomas Egerton, of London, in November 1811, the first of her works to appear. In July 1813 she was pleased to be able to report to her brother Francis that the first edition was exhausted and had brought her altogether £140. The copyright also reverted to her at this point, and a second edition, with corrections, was published in 1813. First American publication was in Bentley's Standard Novels series, Philadelphia, in 1833, sixteen years after her death.

. . . .

Henry Dashwood inherits the estate of Norland Park, Sussex, from his uncle, with whom he and his second family have been living for several years. By his first wife Dashwood has a married son, John, and by his second, three daughters, Elinor, Marianne and Margaret. It is expected that the girls will be well provided for in the deceased relation's will; but surprisingly, the old gentleman has left the estate to be held in trust for the engaging four-year-old Harry Dashwood, John's only child, and the girls receive a meagre legacy of £300 each.

A year later Henry Dashwood himself dies and the estate passes to John. His widow and three daughters are left with only £10,000 to support them. John's wife, Fanny, arrives immediately after the funeral and installs herself as mistress of the house. Henry's widow is tempted to leave Norland Park rather than suffer this insult, but is persuaded by her sensible eldest daughter, Elinor, not to cause a breach between them and John. On his death-bed, Henry had urged John to make some extra provision for his step-mother and sisters, and in the first flush of his inheritance he plans to make over to each of the girls £1,000, which he can well spare. His wife thinks otherwise:

'It was my father's last request to me,' replied her husband, 'that I should assist his widow and daughters.'

'He did not know what he was talking of, I dare say; ten to one but he was light-headed at the time. Had he been in his right senses, he could not have thought of such a thing as begging you to give away half your fortune from your own child.'

'He did not stipulate for any particular sum, my dear Fanny; he only requested me, in general terms, to assist them, and make their situation more comfortable than it was in his power to do. Perhaps it would have been as well if he had left it wholly to myself. He could hardly suppose I should neglect them. But as he required the promise, I could not do less than give it: at least I thought so at the time. The promise, therefore, was given, and must be performed. Something must be done for them whenever they leave Norland and settle in a new home.'

'Well, then, *let* something be done for them; but *that* something need not be three thousand pounds. Consider,' she added, 'that when the money is once parted with, it never can return. Your sisters will marry, and it will be gone for ever. If, indeed, it could ever be restored to our poor little boy –'

'Why, to be sure,' said her husband, very gravely, 'that would make a great difference. The time may come when Harry will regret that so large a sum was parted with. If he should have a numerous family, for instance, it would be a very convenient addition.'

'To be sure it would.'

'Perhaps, then, it would be better for all parties if the sum were diminished one half. – Five hundred pounds would be a prodigious increase to their fortunes!'

'Oh! beyond any thing great! What brother on earth would do half as much for his sisters, even if *really* his sisters! And as it is – only half blood! – But you have such a generous spirit!'

'I would not wish to do any thing mean,' he replied. 'One had rather, on such occasions, do too much than too little. No one, at least, can think I have not done enough for them: even themselves, they can hardly expect more.'

'There is no knowing what *they* may expect,' said the lady, 'but we are not to think of their expectations: the question is, what you can afford to do.'

'Certainly – and I think I may afford to give them five hundred pounds a-piece. As it is, without any addition of mine, they will each have above three thousand pounds on their mother's death – a very comfortable fortune for any young woman.'

'To be sure it is: and, indeed, it strikes me that they can want no addition at all. They will have ten thousand pounds divided amonst them. If they marry, they will be sure of doing well, and if they do not, they may all live very comfortably together on the interest of ten thousand pounds.'

'That is very true, and, therefore, I do not know whether, upon the whole, it would not be more advisable to do something for their mother while she lives rather than for them – something of the annuity kind, I mean. – My sisters would feel the good effects of it as well as herself. A hundred a year would make them all perfectly comfortable.'

His wife hesitated a little, however, in giving her consent to this plan.

'To be sure,' said she, 'it is better than parting with fifteen hundred pounds at once. But then if Mrs. Dashwood should live fifteen years, we shall be completely taken in.'

'Fifteen years! my dear Fanny; her life cannot be worth half that purchase.'

'Certainly not; but if you observe, people always live for ever when there is any annuity to be paid them; and she is very stout and healthy, and hardly forty. An annuity is a very serious business; it comes over and over every year, and there is no getting rid of it. You are not aware of what you are doing. I have known a great deal of the trouble of annuities; for my mother was clogged with the payment of three to old super-annuated servants by my father's will, and it is amazing how disagree-able she found it. Twice every year, these annuities were to be paid; and then there was the trouble of getting it to them; and then one of them was said to have died, and afterwards it turned out to be no such thing. My mother was quite sick of it. Her income was not her own, she said, with such perpetual claims on it; and it was the more unkind in my father, because, otherwise, the money would have been entirely at my mother's disposal, without any restriction whatever. It has given me such an abhorrence of annuities, that I am sure I would not pin myself down to the payment of one for all the world.'

'It is certainly an unpleasant thing,' replied Mr. Dashwood, 'to have those kind of yearly drains on one's income. One's fortune, as your mother justly says, is *not* one's own. To be tied down to the regular pay-ment of such a sum, on every rent day, is by no means desirable: it takes away one's independence.'

'Undoubtedly; and after all you have no thanks for it. They think themselves secure, you do no more than what is expected, and it raises no gratitude at all. If I were you, whatever I did should be done at my own discretion entirely. I would not bind myself to allow them any thing yearly. It may be very inconvenient some years to spare a hundred, or even fifty pounds from our own expenses.'

'I believe you are right, my love; it will be better that there should be no annuity in the case; whatever I may give them occasionally will be of far greater assistance than a yearly allowance, because they would only enlarge their style of living if they felt sure of a larger income, and would not be sixpence the richer for it at the end of the year. It will certainly be much the best way. A present of fifty pounds, now and then, will prevent their ever being distressed for money, and will, I think, be amply discharging my promise to my father.'

'To be sure it will. Indeed, to say the truth, I am convinced within myself that your father had no idea of your giving them any money at all. The assistance he thought of, I dare say, was only such as might be reasonably expected of you; for instance, such as looking out for a comfortable small house for them, helping them to move their things, and sending them presents of fish and game, and so forth, whenever they are in season. I'll lay my life that he meant nothing farther; indeed, it would be very strange and unreasonable if he did. Do but consider, my dear Mr. Dashwood, how excessively comfortable your mother-in-law and her daughters may live on the interest of seven thousand pounds, besides the thousand pounds belonging to each of the girls, which brings them in fifty pounds a-year a-piece, and, of course, they will pay their mother for their board out of it. Altogether, they will have five hundred a-year amongst them, and what on earth can four women want for more than that? – They will live so cheap! Their housekeeping will be nothing at all. They will have no carriage, no horses, and hardly any servants; they will keep no company, and can have no expenses of any kind! Only conceive how comfortable they will be! Five hundred a-year! I am sure I cannot imagine how they will spend half of it; and as to your giving them more, it is quite absurd to think of it. They will be much more able to give *you* something.'

'Upon my word,' said Mr. Dashwood, 'I believe you are perfectly right. My father certainly could mean nothing more by his request to me than what you say. I clearly understand it now, and I will strictly fulfil my engagement by such acts of assistance and kindness to them as you have described. When my mother removes into another house, my services shall be readily given to accommodate her as far as I can. Some little present of furniture, too, may be acceptable then.'

'Certainly,' returned Mrs. John Dashwood. 'But, however, *one* thing must be considered. When your father and mother moved to Norland, though the furniture of Stanhill was sold, all the china, plate, and linen was saved, and is now left to your mother. Her house will therefore be almost completely fitted up as soon as she takes it.'

'That is a material consideration undoubtedly. A valuable legacy indeed! And yet some of the plate would have been a very pleasant addition to our own stock here.'

'Yes; and the set of breakfast china is twice as handsome as what belongs to this house. A great deal too handsome, in my opinion, for any place *they* can ever afford to live in. But, however, so it is. Your father thought only of *them*. And I must say this: that you owe no particular gratitude to him, nor attention to his wishes, for we very well know that if he could, he would have left almost every thing in the world to them.'

This argument was irresistible. It gave to his intentions whatever of decision was wanting before; and he finally resolved, that it would be absolutely unnecessary, if not highly indecorous, to do more for the widow and children of his father, than such kind of neighbourly acts as his own wife pointed out.

Edward Ferrars, Fanny Dashwood's brother, comes to stay at the house and a warm attachment soon develops between him and Elinor. Mrs Dashwood encourages the friendship, but her second daughter, Marianne, considers the young man spiritless and tame and tries to persuade Elinor likewise. Fanny spitefully tells Mrs Dashwood that her daughter is no match for Edward, after this crowning insult the widow is only too grateful to accept an invitation from a relative, Sir John Middleton, to take up residence with her daughters at Barton Cottage on his estate in Devonshire.

After their arrival and installation in the cottage, half a mile from Barton Park itself, Sir John introduces the Dashwood ladies to his young wife. They find her handsome, but very reserved, and her children undisciplined and spoiled. The day following this meeting Mrs Dashwood and her daughters dine with the Middletons. They discover Sir John 'delighted in collecting about him more young people than his house would hold', while his wife 'piqued herself upon the elegance of her table, and all her domestic arrangements'. Lady Middleton's mother, Mrs Jennings, and Colonel Brandon, a bachelor 'on the wrong side of five and thirty', complete the company. The evening passes uncomfortably: Mrs Jennings is a boisterous and vulgar woman, Brandon silent and grave, and the Middleton children little pests. Finally, Marianne is invited to play for them:

Marianne's performance was highly applauded. Sir John was loud in his admiration at the end of every song, and as loud in his conversation with the others while every song lasted. Lady Middleton frequently called him to order, wondered how any one's attention could be diverted from music for a moment, and asked Marianne to sing a particular song which Marianne had just finished. Colonel Brandon alone, of all the party, heard her without being in raptures. He paid her only the compliment of attention; and she felt a respect for him on the occasion, which the others had reasonably forfeited by their shameless want of taste. His pleasure in music, though it amounted not to that extatic delight which alone could sympathize with her own, was estimable when contrasted against the horrible insensibility of the others; and she was reasonable enough to allow that a man of five and thirty might well have outlived all acuteness of feeling and every exquisite power of enjoyment. She was perfectly disposed to make every allowance for the colonel's advanced state of life which humanity required.

Mrs Jennings, having married off her two daughters, is pre-occupied with making matches for others, and is convinced that Brandon has fallen deeply in love with Marianne. The girl is aghast at the idea:

'A woman of seven and twenty,' said Marianne, after pausing a moment, 'can never hope to feel or inspire affection again, and if her home be uncomfortable, or her fortune small, I can suppose that she might bring herself to submit to the offices of a nurse, for the sake of the provision and security of a wife. In his marrying such a woman therefore there would be nothing unsuitable. It would be a compact of convenience, and the world would be satisfied. In my eyes it would be no marriage at all, but that would be nothing. To me it would seem only a commercial exchange, in which each wished to be benefited at the expense of the other.'

'It would be impossible, I know,' replied Elinor, 'to convince you that a woman of seven and twenty could feel for a man of thirty-five any thing near enough to love to make him a desirable companion to her. But I must object to your dooming Colonel Brandon and his wife to the constant confinement of a sick chamber, merely because he chanced to complain yesterday (a very cold damp day) of a slight rheumatic feel in one of his shoulders.'

'But he talked of flannel waistcoats,' said Marianne; 'and with me a flannel waistcoat is invariably connected with aches, cramps, rheuma-tisms, and every species of ailment than can afflict the old and the feeble.'

'Had he been only in a violent fever, you would not have despised him half so much. Confess, Marianne, is not there something interesting to you in the flushed cheek, hollow eye, and quick pulse of a fever?'

Marianne confides to her mother that she fears Edward

Ferrars is unwell, since he has not kept his promise to visit them at Barton Cottage.

One morning Marianne and Margaret go out for a walk along the nearby valley of Allenham. They are caught in a sudden downpour and hurry home, but Marianne trips and falls, twisting her foot. A gentleman happens to be passing and carries her back to the cottage. Mrs Dashwood invites him to stay. He is dirty and wet and refuses the invitation, but begs to be allowed to call the next day. He tells them his name is Willoughby and that he lives nearby at Allenham. Shortly afterwards, Sir John calls, and on hearing what has occurred, declares he will invite Willoughby to dinner the following Thursday. He tells the Dashwoods that the young man is staying with his elderly relative at Allenham Court, which he will inherit on her death, and that he owns a small estate in Somerset:

'He is as good a sort of fellow, I believe, as ever lived,' repeated Sir John. 'I remember last Christmas, at a little hop at the park, he danced from eight o'clock till four, without once sitting down.'

'Did he indeed?' cried Marianne, with sparkling eyes, 'and with elegance, with spirit?'

'Yes; and he was up again at eight to ride to covert.'

'That is what I like; that is what a young man ought to be. Whatever be his pursuits, his eagerness in them should know no moderation, and leave him no sense of fatigue.'

'Aye, aye, I see how it will be,' said Sir John, 'I see how it will be. You will be setting your cap at him now, and never think of poor Brandon.'

'That is an expression, Sir John,' said Marianne, warmly, 'which I particularly dislike. I abhor every common-place phrase by which wit is intended; and "setting one's cap at a man," or "making a conquest," are the most odious of all. Their tendency is gross and illiberal; and if their construction could ever be deemed clever, time has long ago destroyed all its ingenuity.'

Sir John did not much understand this reproof; but he laughed as heartily as if he did, and then replied,

'Aye, you will make conquests enough, I dare say, one way or other. Poor Brandon! he is quite smitten already, and he is very well worth setting your cap at, I can tell you, in spite of all this tumbling about and spraining of ancles.'

Willoughby calls next morning and the attraction Marianne already feels for him becomes mutual as they discover how many tastes they have in common. He begins to call at Barton Cottage every day, encouraged by Mrs Dashwood; but Elinor is concerned about the effect this deepening friendship might have on Colonel Brandon, whom she now believes to be very much in love with Marianne. She defends the colonel warmly when Willoughby and her sister make fun of him.

As the autumn advances Sir John Middleton commences a series of balls at Barton Park, and Willoughby is constantly at Marianne's side. Elinor finds hereslf frequently in the company of Brandon, for whom her compassion increases. Willoughby promises Marianne a horse, but Elinor persuades her to decline the gift. She is now convinced that Willoughby's intentions towards her sister are serious, and her belief is shared by the sagacious Margaret, who has witnessed several little incidents between the pair. It is arranged that the Dashwoods and Middletons visit Whitwell, the home of a brother-in-law of Brandon, twelve miles from Barton. Just as the party is about to start off, Brandon receives a letter. Its contents clearly distract him, and he tells them that the visit will have to be cancelled since he has to leave immediately for London. Mrs Jennings believes she knows the reason:

'It is about Miss Williams, I am sure.'
'And who is Miss Williams?' asked Marianne.
'What! do not you know who Miss Williams is? I am sure you must have heard of her before. She is a relation of the Colonel's, my dear; a very near relation. We will not say how near, for fear of shocking the young ladies.' Then lowering her voice a little, she said to Elinor, 'She is his natural daughter.'
'Indeed!'
'Oh! yes; and as like him as she can stare. I dare say the Colonel will leave her all his fortune.'

Marianne and Willoughby drive over to Allenham Court and

spend the morning walking in the garden and going over the house. When this is disclosed at dinner that evening, Elinor is vexed with her sister's improper conduct in entering the house in the absence of its owner, Mrs Smith. Marianne replies that such niceties hardly matter, since the house will be hers one day.

A week later Willoughby suddenly announces that he is leaving for London immediately on business for Mrs Smith. The Dashwoods are upset, not only because he cannot say when he will return, but because he goes without having made an offer for Marianne's hand.

The two sisters are walking out one day some time later when they encounter Edward Ferrars. He returns with them to Barton Cottage and discloses that he has already been in Devonshire a fortnight, staying near Plymouth with friends. It hurts Elinor to think he had not called to see her during this time, and she is distressed by his distant manner and polite reserve. But she is flattered when, the following day, she notices that he wears a ring with a plait of what she fancies is her hair at the centre: though he pretends that the hair is his sister's, Fanny Dashwood's.

Edward remains at Barton Cottage a week, then declares that he must regretfully terminate his visit. He departs as coldly as he had arrived. Some days later the Middletons and Mrs Jennings arrive at the cottage with Charlotte Palmer, Lady Middleton's sister, and her husband. Mrs Palmer, whom Elinor finds as noisy and silly as her mother, Mrs Jennings, is expecting a child in February. She discloses to Elinor that she had met Colonel Brandon in London and that he had told her of the attachment between Marianne and Willoughby. Mrs Palmer knows Willoughby well, since his estate at Combe Magna in Somerset is not far from the Palmers' home, Cleveland. She has also known Brandon some time, and might once have married him, had not Mrs Jennings disapproved of the match.

The Palmers depart and their places as guests at Barton Park are taken by the Misses Steele, two young relatives of Mrs Jennings. Anne and Lucy Steele display a tactless curiosity about Edward Ferrars when they visit the Dashwoods, and, while out

walking with Lucy some days later, Elinor is astonished to learn
than she hopes to marry Edward:

'You may well be surprised,' continued Lucy; 'for to be sure you could
have had no idea of it before; for I dare say he never dropped the smallest hint of it to you or any of your family; because it was always meant
to be a great secret, and I am sure has been faithfully kept so by me to this
hour. Not a soul of all my relations know of it but Anne, and I never
should have mentioned it to you, if I had not felt the greatest dependence
in the world upon your secrecy; and I really thought my behaviour in
asking so many questions about Mrs. Ferrars, must seem so odd, that it
ought to be explained. And I do not think Mr. Ferrars can be displeased
when he knows I have trusted you, because I know he has the highest
opinion in the world of all your family, and looks upon yourself and the
other Miss Dashwoods, quite as his own sisters.' – She paused.

Elinor for a few moments remained silent. Her astonishment at what she
heard was at first too great for words; but at length forcing herself to
speak, and to speak cautiously, she said with a calmness of manner, which
tolerably well concealed her surprise and solicitude – 'May I ask if your
engagement is of long standing?'

'We have been engaged these four years.'

'Four years'.

'Yes.'

Elinor though greatly shocked, still felt unable to believe it.

'I did not know,' said she, 'that you were even acquainted till the other
day.'

'Our acquaintance, however, is of many years' date. He was under
my uncle's care, you know, a considerable while.'

'Your uncle!'

'Yes; Mr. Pratt. Did you never hear him talk of Mr. Pratt?'

'I think I have,' replied Elinor, with an exertion of spirits which
increased with her increase of emotion.

'He was four years with my uncle, who lives at Longstaple, near
Plymouth. It was there our acquaintance begun, for my sister and me was
often staying with my uncle, and it was there our engagement was
formed, though not till a year after he had quitted as a pupil; but he
was almost always with us afterwards.'

Lucy tells Elinor that it was with them that Edward had been staying before his visit to Barton Cottage, and that she had given him a ring containing a lock of her hair. After an initial period of deep distress, Elinor decides to put a brave face on the matter and takes every opportunity to show her unwitting rival how unmoved she is. At a dinner, she points out to Lucy the disadvantages implied in her engagement to Edward: his small income, his slender hopes of advancement, the infrequency of their meetings. Lucy begs Elinor to advise her, but the latter recognizes the insincerity of the request and pretends complete indifference:

From this time the subject was never revived by Elinor, and when entered on by Lucy, who seldom missed an opportunity of introducing it, and was particularly careful to inform her confidante, of her happiness whenever she received a letter from Edward, it was treated by the former with calmness and caution, and dismissed as soon as civility would allow; for she felt such conversations to be an indulgence which Lucy did not deserve, and which were dangerous to herself.

Mrs Jennings invites Marianne and Elinor to accompany her on visit to her London house. Marianne is eager to see Willoughby again and agrees readily, but Elinor is more reluctant and has to be persuaded by her mother. The journey takes three days, and as soon as they are settled in the house Marianne writes to Willoughby, expecting him to come immediately. Brandon arrives instead, but does not stay long. He repeats his visit during the following days, while Marianne grows more and more desperate at Willoughby's prolonged silence.

The Middletons arrive in London and invite everyone to a ball. Marianne is delighted to see Willoughby there, though he is earnestly conversing with a fashionable looking young woman; but his reaction when she addresses him shows too plainly that her pleasure is not reciprocated.

He approached, and addressing himself rather to Elinor than Marianne, as if wishing to avoid her eye, and determined not to observe her attitude, inquired in a hurried manner after Mrs. Dashwood, and asked how long they had been in town. Elinor was robbed of all presence of mind by such an address, and was unable to say a word. But the feelings of her sister were instantly expressed. Her face was crimsoned over, and she exclaimed in a voice of the greatest emotion, 'Good God! Willoughby, what is the meaning of this? Have you not received my letters? Will you not shake hands with me?'

He could not then avoid it, but her touch seemed painful to him, and he held her hand only for a moment. During all this time he was evidently struggling for composure. Elinor watched his countenance and saw its expression becoming more tranquil. After a moment's pause, he spoke with calmness.

'I did myself the honour of calling in Berkeley-street last Tuesday, and very much regretted that I was not fortunate enough to find yourselves and Mrs. Jennings at home. My card was not lost, I hope.'

'But have you not received my notes?' cried Marianne in the wildest anxiety. 'Here is some mistake I am sure – some dreadful mistake. What can be the meaning of it? Tell me, Willoughy; for heaven's sake tell me, what is the matter?'

He made no reply; his complexion changed and all his embarrassment returned; but as if, on catching the eye of the young lady with whom he had been previously talking, he felt the necessity of instant exertion, he recovered himself again, and after saying, 'Yes, I had the pleasure of receiving the information of your arrival in town, which you were so good as to send me,' turned hastily away with a slight bow and joined his friend.

Willoughby leaves the party with his lady friend, and Marianne is taken home in a state of shock by her sister. The following morning she sends a letter to Willoughby, and receives his immediate reply: it is a polite note informing her that he is shortly to marry another woman. Marianne is prostrated with grief:

Mrs. Jennings came immediately to their room on her return, and without waiting to have her request of admittance answered, opened the door and walked in with a look of real concern.

'How do you do my dear?' – said she in a voice of great compassion to Marianne, who turned away her face without attempting to answer.

'How is she, Miss Dashwood? – Poor thing! she looks very bad. – No wonder. Aye, it is but too true. He is to be married very soon – a good-for-nothing fellow! I have no patience with him. Mrs. Taylor told me of it half an hour ago, and she was told it by a particular friend of Miss Grey herself, else I am sure I should not have believed it; and I was almost ready to sink as it was. Well, said I, all I can say is, that if it is true, he has used a young lady of my acquaintance abominably ill, and I wish with all my soul his wife may plague his heart out. And so I shall always say, my dear, you may depend on it. I have no notion of men's going on in this way: and if ever I meet him again, I will give him such a dressing as he has not had this many a day. But there is one comfort, my dear Miss Marianne; he is not the only young man in the world worth having; and with your pretty face you will never want admirers. Well, poor thing! I won't disturb her any longer, for she had better have her cry out at once and have done with it. The Parry's and Sandersons luckily are coming to-night you know, and that will amuse her.'

She then went away, walking on tiptoe out of the room, as if she supposed her young friend's affliction could be increased by noise.

Marianne, to the surprise of her sister, determined on dining with them. Elinor even advised her against it. But 'no, she would go down; she could bear it very well, and the bustle about her would be less.' Elinor, pleased to have her governed for a moment by such a motive, though believing it hardly possible that she could sit out the dinner, said no more; and adjusting her dress for her as well as she could, while Marianne still remained on the bed, was ready to assist her into the dining room as soon as they were summoned to it.

When there, though looking most wretchedly, she ate more and was calmer than her sister had expected. Had she tried to speak, or had she been conscious of half Mrs. Jennings's well-meant but ill-judged attentions to her, this calmness could not have been maintained; but not a syllable escaped her lips, and the abstraction of her thoughts preserved her in ignorance of every thing that was passing before her.

Elinor, who did justice to Mrs. Jennings's kindness, though its effusions were often distressing, and sometimes almost ridiculous, made her those acknowledgments, and returned her those civilities, which her sister could not make or return for herself. Their good friend saw that Marianne was unhappy, and felt that every thing was due to her which might make her at all less so. She treated her therefore, with all the indulgent fondness of a parent towards a favourite child on the last day of its holidays. Marianne was to have the best place by the fire, was to be tempted to eat by every delicacy in the house, and to be amused by the relation of all the news of the day. Had not Elinor, in the sad countenance of her sister, seen a check to all mirth, she could have been entertained by Mrs. Jennings's endeavours to cure a disappointment in love, by a variety of sweetmeats and olives, and a good fire. As soon, however, as the consciousness of all this was forced by continual repetition on Marianne, she could stay no longer. With an hasty exclamation of Misery, and a sign to her sister not to follow her, she directly got up and hurried out of the room.

'Poor soul!' cried Mrs. Jennings, as soon as she was gone, 'how it grieves me to see her! And I declare if she is not gone away without finishing her wine! And the dried cherries too! Lord! nothing seems to do her any good. I am sure if I knew of any thing she would like, I would send all over the town for it. Well, it is the oddest thing to me, that a man should use such a pretty girl so ill! But when there is plenty of money on one side, and next to none on the other, Lord, bless you! they care no more about such things! –'

Brandon arrives at the house next day. Not wishing to see him, Marianne retires to her room, leaving Elinor alone with him, and the colonel, knowing all that has happened, relates his own unhappy story. His supposed natural child is the illegitimate daughter of his childhood sweetheart, Eliza Williams, who had been married off to Brandon's brother, subsequently divorcing him and taking a number of lovers. Brandon had found Eliza dying in poverty and had taken charge of her daughter, also named Eliza, placing her under the care of a respectable woman. After two years, at the age of sixteen, she had suddenly vanished. Brandon had sought news of her for eight months, but had heard nothing until the arrival of the letter which had caused the postponement of the outing to Whitwell and his abrupt departure for London. Young Eliza, he had learned, had eloped with Willoughby, been seduced by him and finally abandoned, pregnant. The outcome had been a duel between Brandon and Willoughby, from which both had emerged unscathed, so that news of it had never become public.

Elinor repeats everything to Marianne, who, while remaining

greatly distressed over Willoughby, begins to treat Brandon with 'a kind of compassionate respect'. A fortnight later word is received of Willoughby's marriage to a Miss Grey.

Anne and Lucy Steele arrive in London, and Lucy renews her unwelcome confidences in Elinor. In a shop, Elinor chances to meet her half-brother, John Dashwood, also just come to town with his wife, and learns that Fanny's mother, Mrs Ferrars, is with them. John believes that Brandon is to marry Elinor, and tells his sister that Mrs Ferrars greatly favours the match. Elinor tries to disabuse him of this belief, but John is too enthusiastic to listen to her. She asks after Edward Ferrars, and learns that Mrs Ferrars is hoping that he will marry an heiress, Miss Morton. The formidable old lady and her family know nothing of his secret engagement to Lucy Steele. At a party at her house in Harley Street Mrs Ferrars openly snubs Elinor, while behaving very graciously towards Lucy. The following day, when the jubilant girl is calling on Elinor, they are surprised by the unexpected arrival of Edward Ferrars. His visit causes some embarrassment, since no one is sure what the others know of the triangular situation.

Mrs Palmer gives birth to a son at her London home, and Mrs Jennings goes every day to visit her daughter, leaving Elinor and Marianne in charge of the Middletons. A fortnight after Mrs Palmer's lying-in, Mrs Jennings arrives home in a state of great excitement, and tells Elinor of a sensational discovery:

'Mr. Edward Ferrars, the very young man I used to joke with you about (but, however, as it turns out, I am monstrous glad there never was any thing in it), Mr. Edward Ferrars, it seems, has been engaged above this twelvemonth to my cousin Lucy! – There's for you, my dear! – And not a creature knowing a syllable of the matter except Nancy! – Could you have believed such a thing possible? – There is no great wonder in their liking one another; but that matters should be brought so forward between them, and nobody suspect it! *That* is strange! – I never happened to see them together, or I am sure I should have found it out directly. Well, and so this was kept a great secret, for fear of Mrs. Ferrars, and neither she nor your brother or sister suspected a word of the matter; – till this very morning, poor Nancy, who, you know, is a well-meaning creature, but no conjurer, popt it all out. "Lord!" thinks she to herself, "they are all so fond of Lucy, to be sure they will make no difficulty about it;" and so, away she went to your sister, who was sitting all alone at her carpet-work, little suspecting what was to come – for she had just been saying to your brother, only five minutes before, that she thought to make a match between Edward and some Lord's daughter or other, I forget who. So you may think what a blow it was to all her vanity and pride. She fell into violent hysterics immediately, with such screams as reached your brother's ears, as he was sitting in his own dressing-room down stairs, thinking about writing a letter to his steward in the country. So up he flew directly, and a terrible scene took place, for Lucy was come to them by that time, little dreaming what was going on. Poor soul! I pity *her*. And I must say, I think she was used very hardly; for your sister scolded like any fury, and soon drove her into a fainting fit. Nancy, she fell upon her knees, and cried bitterly; and your brother, he walked about the room, and said he did not know what to do. Mrs. Dashwood declared they should not stay a minute longer in the house, and your brother was forced to go down upon *his* knees too, to persuade her to let them stay till they had packed up their clothes. *Then* she fell into hysterics again, and he was so frightened that he would send for Mr. Donavan, and Mr. Donavan found the house in all this uproar. The carriage was at the door ready to take my poor cousins away, and they were just stepping in as he came off; poor Lucy in such a condition, he says, she could hardly walk; and Nancy, she was almost as bad. I declare, I have no patience with your sister; and I hope, with all my heart, it will be a match in spite of her. Lord! what a taking poor Mr. Edward will be in when he hears of it! To have his love used so scornfully! for they say he is monstrous fond of her, as well he may. I should not wonder, if he was to be in the greatest of a passion! – and Mr. Donavan thinks just the same. He and I had a great deal of talk about it; and the best of all is, that he is gone back again to Harley-s.reet, that he may be within call when Mrs. Ferrars is told of it, for she was sent for as soon as ever my cousins left the house, for your sister was sure *she* would be in hysterics too; and so she may, for what I care. I have no pity for either of them. I have no notion of people's making such a to-do about money and greatness. There is no reason on earth why Mr. Edward and Lucy should not marry; for I am sure Mrs. Ferrars may afford to do very well by her son and though Lucy has next to nothing herself, she knows better than any body how to make the most of every thing; and I dare say, if Mrs. Ferrars would only allow him five hundred a-year, she would make as good an appearance with it as anybody else would with eight. Lord! how snug they might live in such another cottage as yours – or a little bigger – with two maids and two men; and I believe I could help them to a housemaid, for my Betty has a sister out of place, that would fit them exactly.'

Now Elinor is free to disclose her own unhappiness to Marianne, who is ashamed of having burdened her sister with her grief over Willoughby while she herself was suffering in secret. John Dashwood arrives to inform them that Edward refuses to break off the engagement to Lucy and has been disinherited by his mother in favour of his brother, Robert. Marianne and Elinor recognize that the engagement is a matter of honour with Edward, and do not condemn him.

Elinor meets Anne Steele one morning in Kensington Gardens. The girl has been eavesdropping on conversations between Lucy and Edward, and relates to Elinor how Edward is planning to go to Oxford to be ordained a curate. Next morning Elinor receives a letter from Lucy, reporting how she has tried to persuade Edward to release her. He has refused, and now they are in need of financial help to start their married life.

After two months in London Marianne is becoming increasingly impatient to return to Barton Cottage. The Palmers, who are shortly going back to their home in Somerset, invite her and Elinor to travel with them as far as Cleveland, stay a few days, then continue on to Barton. Elinor thinks this an excellent plan, but Marianne refuses to go anywhere near Somerset, where once she had dreamed of living as Willoughby's wife. Elinor, however, persuades her to accept the Palmers' offer. Brandon calls and asks Elinor to tell Edward Ferrars that he happens to have a vacant living to offer him:

Elinor's astonishment at this commission could hardly have been greater, had the Colonel been really making her an offer of his hand. The preferment, which only two days before she had considered as hopeless for Edward, was already provided to enable him to marry; – and *she*, of all people in the world, was fixed on to bestow it! – Her emotion was such as Mrs. Jennings had attributed to a very different cause; but whatever minor feelings less pure, less pleasing, might have a share in that emotion, her esteem for the general benevolence, and her gratitude for the particular friendship, which together prompted Colonel Brandon to this act, were strongly felt, and warmly expressed. She thanked him for it with all her heart, spoke of Edward's principles and disposition with that praise which she knew them to deserve; and promised to undertake the commission with pleasure, if it were really his wish to put off so agreeable an office to another. But at the same time, she could not help thinking that no one could so well perform it as himself. It was an office in short, from which, unwilling to give Edward the pain of receiving an obligation from *her*, she would have been very glad to be spared herself; – but Colonel Brandon, on motives of equal delicacy declining it likewise, still seemed so desirous of its being given through her means, that she would not on any account make farther opposition. Edward, she believed, was still in town, and fortunately she had heard his address from Miss Steele. She could undertake therefore to inform him of it in the course of the day. After this had been settled, Colonel Brandon began to talk of his own advantage in securing so respectable and agreeable a neighbour, and *then* it was that he mentioned with regret, that the house was small and indifferent; – an evil which Elinor, as Mrs. Jennings had supposed her to do, made very light of, at least as far as regarded its size.

'The smallness of the house,' said she, 'I cannot imagine any inconvenience to them, for it will be in proportion to their family and income.'

By which the Colonel was surprised to find that *she* was considering Mr. Ferrars's marriage as the certain consequence of the presentation; for he did not suppose it possible that Delaford living could supply such an income, as anybody in his style of life would venture to settle on – and he said so.

'This little rectory *can* do no more than make Mr. Ferrars comfortable as a bachelor; it cannot enable him to marry. I am sorry to say that my patronage ends with this; and my interest is hardly more extensive. If, however, by any unforeseen chance it should be in my power to serve him farther, I must think very differently of him from what I now do, if I am not as ready to be useful to him then, as I sincerely wish I could be at present. What I am doing now indeed, seems nothing at all, since it can advance him so little towards what must be his principal, his only object of happiness. His marriage must still be a distant good: – at least, I am afraid it cannot take place very soon. –'

Such was the sentence which, when misunderstood, so justly offended the delicate feelings of Mrs. Jennings; but after this narration of what really passed between Colonel Brandon and Elinor, while they stood at the window, the gratitude expressed by the latter on their parting may perhaps appear in general, not less reasonably excited, nor less properly worded than if it had arisen from an offer of marriage.

Elinor is just about to write to Edward when he arrives at the house. She tells him of Brandon's offer, and he hurries happily away to thank the colonel personally. Elinor goes to call on Fanny Dashwood, who has been indisposed since the Lucy Steele affair, is closely questioned by John about Brandon, and has to listen to Robert's mockery of Edward:

'We may treat it as a joke,' said he at last, recovering from the affected laugh which had considerably lengthened out the genuine gaiety of the moment – 'but upon my soul it is a most serious business. Poor Edward! he is ruined for ever. I am extremely sorry for it – for I know him to be a very good-hearted creature; as well-meaning a fellow, perhaps, as any in the world. You must not judge of him, Miss Dashwood, from *your* slight acquaintance. – Poor Edward! – His manners are certainly not the happiest in nature. – But we are not all born, you know, with the same powers – the same address. – Poor fellow! – to see him in a circle of strangers! – to be sure it was pitiable enough! – but, upon my soul, I believe he has as good a heart as any in the kingdom; and I declare and protest to you I never was so shocked in my life, as when it all burst forth. I could not believe it. – My mother was the first person who told me of it, and I, feeling myself called on to act with resolution, immediately said to her, "My dear madam, I do not know what you may intend to do on the occasion, but as for myself, I must say, that if Edward does marry this young woman, *I* never will see him again." That was what I said immediately. – I was most uncommonly shocked indeed! – Poor Edward! – he has done for himself completely – shut himself out for ever from all decent society! – but as I directly said to my mother, I am not in the least surprised at it; from his style of education it was always to be expected. My poor mother was half frantic.'

In April, Marianne and Elinor leave London with Mrs Palmer and Mrs Jennings, Mr Palmer and Brandon following them a few days later. Marianne again becomes greatly distressed once Cleveland is reached, and spends her evenings wandering about the wet gardens: the result is a violent cold. Mrs Palmer, fearful lest her small baby becomes infected, leaves to stay with a relative and is soon joined by Mr Palmer, leaving Brandon at Cleveland with the Dashwood sisters and Mrs Jennings. Marianne becomes feverish and delirious and the colonel sets off for Barton Cottage, eighty miles away, to fetch Mrs Dashwood. After twelve hours of crisis Marianne begins to recover. That evening, as the sound of a carriage is heard outside, Elinor hurries down to welcome her mother and finds, instead, Willoughby. He pleads with her to hear him:

'I do not know,' said he, after a pause of expectation on her side, and thoughtfulness on his own, – 'how *you* may have accounted for my behaviour to your sister, or what diabolical motive you may have imputed to me. – Perhaps you will hardly think the better of me, – it is worth the trial however, and you shall hear every thing. When I first became intimate in your family, I had no other intention, no other view in the acquaintance than to pass my time pleasantly while I was obliged to remain in Devonshire, more pleasantly than I had ever done before. Your sister's lovely person and interesting manners could not but please me; and her behaviour to me almost from the first, was of a kind – It is astonishing, when I reflect on what it was, and what *she* was, that my heart should have been so insensible! – But at first I must confess, my vanity only was elevated by it. Careless of her happiness, thinking only of my own amusement, giving way to feelings which I had always been too much in the habit of indulging, I endeavoured, by every means in my power, to make myself pleasing to her, without any design of returning her affection.'

Miss Dashwood at this point, turning her eyes on him with the most angry contempt, stopped him, by saying,

'It is hardly worth while, Mr. Willoughby, for you to relate, or for me to listen any longer. Such a beginning as this cannot be followed by any thing. – Do not let me be pained by hearing any thing more on the subject.'

'I insist on your hearing the whole of it,' he replied. 'My fortune was never large, and I had always been expensive, always in the habit of associating with people of better income than myself. Every year since my coming of age, or even before, I believe, had added to my debts; and though the death of my old cousin, Mrs. Smith, was to set me free, yet that event being uncertain, and possibly far distant, it had been for some time my intention to re-establish my circumstances by marrying a woman of fortune. To attach myself to your sister, therefore, was not a thing to be thought of; – and with a meanness, selfishness, cruelty – which no indignant, no contemptuous look, even of yours, Miss Dashwood, can ever reprobate too much – I was acting in this manner, trying to engage her regard, without a thought of returning it. – But one thing may be said for me, even in that horrid state of selfish vanity, I did not know the extent of the injury I meditated, because I did not *then* know what it was to love. But have I ever known it? – Well may it be doubted; for, had I really loved could I have sacrificed my feelings to vanity, to avarice? – or, what is more, could I have sacrificed hers? – But I have done it. To avoid a comparative poverty, which her affection and her society would have deprived of all its horrors, I have, by raising myself to affluence, lost everything that could make it a blessing.'

'You did then,' said Elinor, a little softened, 'believe yourself at one time attached to her.'

'To have resisted such attractions, to have withstood such tenderness! – Is there a man on earth who could have done it! – Yes, I found myself, by insensible degrees, sincerely fond of her; and the happiest hours of my life were what I spent with her, when I felt my intentions were strictly honourable, and my feelings blameless. Even *then*, however, when fully determined on paying my addresses to her, I allowed myself most improperly to put off, from day to day, the moment of doing it, from an unwillingness to enter into an engagement while my circumstances were so greatly embarrassed. I will not reason here – nor will I stop for *you* to expatiate on the absurdity, and the worse than absurdity, of scrupling to engage my faith where my honour was already bound. The event has proved that I was a cunning fool, providing with great circumspection for a possible opportunity of making myself contemptible and wretched for ever. At last, however, my resolution was taken, and I had determined, as soon as I could engage her alone, to justify the attentions I had so invariably paid her, and openly assure her of an affection which I had already taken such pains to display. But in the interim – in the interim of the very few hours that were to pass, before I could have an opportunity of speaking with her in private – a circumstance occurred – an unlucky circumstance, to ruin all my resolution, and with it all my comfort. A discovery took place,' – here he hesitated and looked down. – 'Mrs. Smith had somehow or other been informed, I imagine by some distant relation, whose interest it was to deprive me of her favour, of an affair, a connection – but I need not explain myself farther,' he added, looking at her with an heightened colour and an inquiring eye, – 'your particular intimacy – you have probably heard the whole story long ago.'

'I have,' returned Elinor, colouring likewise, and hardening her heart anew against any compassion for him, 'I have heard it all. And how you will explain away any part of your guilt in that dreadful business, I confess is beyond my comprehension.'

'Remember,' cried Willoughby, 'from whom you received the account. Could it be an impartial one? I acknowledge that her situation and her character ought to have been respected by me. I do not mean to justify myself, but at the same time cannot leave you to suppose that I have nothing to urge – that because she was injured she was irreproachable, and because *I* was a libertine, *she* must be a saint. If the violence of her passions, the weakness of her understanding – I do not mean, however, to defend myself. Her affection for me deserved better treatment, and I often, with great self-reproach, recall the tenderness which, for a very short time, had the power of creating any return. I wish – I heartily wish it had never been. But I have injured more than herself; and I have injured one, whose affection for me – (may I say it?) was scarcely less warm than her's; and whose mind – Oh! how infinitely superior!' –

'Your indifference, however, towards that unfortunate girl – I must say it, unpleasant to me as the discussion of such a subject may well be – your indifference is no apology for your cruel neglect of her. Do not think yourself excused by any weakness, any natural defect of understanding on her side, in the wanton cruelty so evident on yours. You must have known, that while you were enjoying yourself in Devonshire, pursuing fresh schemes, always gay, always happy, she was reduced to the extremest indigence.'

'But, upon my soul, I did *not* know it,' he warmly replied; 'I did not recollect that I had omitted to give her my direction; and common sense might have told her how to find it out.'

'Well, sir, and what said Mrs. Smith?'

'She taxed me with the offence at once, and my confusion may be guessed. The purity of her life, the formality of her notions, her ignorance of the world – everything was against me. The matter itself I could not deny, and vain was every endeavour to soften it. She was previously disposed, I believe, to doubt the morality of my conduct in general, and was moreover discontented with the very little attention, the very little portion of my time that I had bestowed on her, in my present visit. In short, it ended in a total breach. By one measure I might have saved myself. In the height of her morality, good woman! she offered to forgive the past if I would marry Eliza. That could not be – and I was formally dismissed from her favour and her house. The night following this affair – I was to go the next morning – was spent by me in deliberating on what my future conduct should be. The struggle was great – but it ended too soon. My affection for Marianne, my thorough conviction of her attachment to me – it was all insufficient to outweigh that dread of poverty, or get the better of those false ideas of the necessity of riches, which I was naturally inclined to feel, and expensive society had increased. I had reason to believe myself secure of my present wife, if I choose to address her, and I persuaded myself to think that nothing else in common prudence remained for me to do. An heavy scene however awaited me, before I could leave Devonshire; – I was engaged to dine with you on that very day; some apology was therefore necessary for my breaking the engagement. But whether I should write this apology, or deliver it in person, was a point of long debate. To see Marianne, I felt would be dreadul, and I even doubted whether I could see her again, and keep to my resolution. In that point, however, I undervalued my own magnanimity, as the event declared; for I went, I saw her, and saw her miserable, and left her miserable – and left her hoping never to see her again.'

'Why did you call, Mr. Willoughby?' said Elinor, reproachfully; 'a note would have answered every purpose. – Why was it necessary to call?'

'It was necessary to my own pride. I could not bear to leave the country in a manner that might lead you, or the rest of the neighbourhood, to suspect any part of what had really passed between Mrs. Smith and myself – and I resolved therefore on calling at the cottage, in my way to Honiton. The sight of your dear sister, however, was really dreadful; and to heighten the matter, I found her alone. You were all gone I do not know where. I had left her only the evening before, so fully, so firmly resolved within myself on doing right! A few hours were to have engaged her to

me for ever; and I remember how happy, how gay were my spirits, as I
walked from the cottage to Allenham, satisfied with myself, delighted
with every body! But in this, our last interview of friendship, I approached her with a sense of guilt that almost took from me the power
of dissembling. Her sorrow, her disappointment, her deep regret, when
I told her that I was obliged to leave Devonshire so immediately – I
never shall forget it – united too, with such reliance, such confidence in
me! – Oh, God – what an hard-hearted rascal I was!'

He tells Elinor how he was forced to avoid Marianne in London
because of the jealousy of his fiancée, Sophia Grey, and how
Sophia had dictated the note he sent Marianne. In spite of herself,
Elinor pities him, and is moved when he tells how he has driven
all day without stopping, hoping to reach Marianne before she
dies. Reassured of her recovery, Willoughby leaves shortly before
Mrs Dashwood arrives with Brandon.

As the days pass, Marianne's health gradually returns, and the
colonel discloses to Mrs Dashwood that he loves her daughter.
Mrs Dashwood is delighted and discusses with an unenthusiastic
Elinor the likelihood of her living near Marianne at Delaford,
where Edward Ferrars is to be curate.

The Dashwoods return to Barton. One morning, while taking
a walk, Elinor tells Marianne of Willoughby's visit. The story is
later repeated to Mrs Dashwood, and that evening the three
discuss the matter together. It seems that Marianne now realizes
her folly in loving Willoughby so much, and is prepared to
forgive and forget him. Some days later, the manservant reports
to Elinor that 'Mr. Ferrars is married.' The man has just returned
from Exeter, where he had seen Lucy Steele and her new
husband in a chaise. Lucy had spoken to him, sending the
Dashwoods her compliments and promising to call at Barton on
the way back from the west. Then Edward Ferrars arrives at
Barton Cottage and the misunderstanding is cleared up: Lucy
has – unaccountably – married his brother, Robert. Edward is
now free to ask Elinor to marry him.

Disgusted with Robert's marriage, Mrs Ferrars receives
Edward back into the family. He and Elinor are married at

However little known the feelings or views of such a man may be on his first entering a neighbourhood, this truth is so well fixed in the minds of the surrounding families that he is considered as the rightful property of some one or other of their daughters.

Such is the view of Mrs William Bennet of Longbourn, near Meryton, in Hertfordshire; and, with five unmarried daughters for whom to find suitable husbands, she is more than delighted when nearby Netherfield Park acquires a new tenant, the young, wealthy and single Mr Bingley. It is unfortunate that there are no sons in the family, for, by the custom of male inheritance, it implies that when Mr Bennet dies, the attractive estate must go to his clergyman cousin, William Collins. The girls will thus have no fortune of their own, so well-placed husbands are more than usually to be desired. Lydia, Kitty and Mary are silly empty-headed creatures, taking after their mother; but the two eldest girls, Elizabeth and Jane, are as sensible and intelligent as their father, who patiently puts up with his wife, while gently mocking her.

The Bennets attend a ball at the local assembly rooms, which Mr Bingley also attends, with his two sisters, Caroline and Louisa (Mrs Hurst), Mr Hurst, and a friend, Mr Darcy. Bingley soon makes himself agreeable to all the company and partners Jane Bennet, to whom he is obviously attracted. He urges Darcy to dance, but the latter shows his nature to be anything but convivial:

'I certainly shall not. You know how I detest it, unless I am particularly acquainted with my partner. At such an assembly as this it would be insupportable. Your sisters are engaged, and there is not another woman in the room whom it would not be a punishment to me to stand up with.'

'I would not be so fastidious as you are,' cried Bingley, 'for a kingdom! Upon my honour, I never met with so many pleasant girls in my life as I have this evening; and there are several of them you see uncommonly pretty.'

'*You* are dancing with the only handsome girl in the room,' said Mr. Darcy, looking at the eldest Miss Bennet.

'Oh! she is the most beautiful creature I ever beheld! But there is one of her sisters sitting down just behind you, who is very pretty, and I dare say very agreeable. Do let me ask my partner to introduce you.'

'Which do you mean?' and turning round he looked for a moment at Elizabeth, till catching her eye, he withdrew his own and coldly said, 'She is tolerable, but not handsome enough to tempt *me*; and I am in no humour at present to give consequence to young ladies who are slighted by other men. You had better return to your partner and enjoy her smiles, for you are wasting your time with me.'

Sir William and Lady Lucas are neighbours of the Bennets and Charlotte Lucas is Elizabeth's close friend. When they give a ball, which the Bingleys, the Bennets, and Darcy attend, Elizabeth has the pleasure of repaying Darcy's rudeness by refusing to dance with him. Her spirited rebuff arouses Darcy's interest.

Bingley's sisters invite Jane over to Netherfield. She rides there on horseback in a downpour and arrives drenched to the skin, which results in a bad chill. Mrs Bennet is only too pleased to learn that this will necessitate her remaining at Netherfield to recuperate, and gladly despatches Elizabeth to join her. Elizabeth walks there, making a mud-bespattered arrival, which arouses the scorn of Bingley's sisters, but increases Darcy's admiration of her. She remains hostile to him, and they hold barbed conversations during which Elizabeth makes her feelings quite clear. Romance is burgeoning elsewhere in the house, though. As Mrs Bennet had hoped, Bingley has fallen in love with Jane and she with him, in spite of a natural reserve which does not allow her to show her feelings openly.

An unexpected letter reaches Mr Bennet from Hunsford, near Westerham, Kent. It is from his cousin, William Collins, to say that he has been appointed to the living there by a grand patroness, Lady Catherine de Bourgh. His clerical conscience has been troubling him with the thought that he is to inherit Longbourn, to the detriment of the girls, and he proposes to pay a visit there to propose making some amends. The family speculate upon his intentions:

'At four o'clock, therefore, we may expect this peace-making gentleman,' said Mr. Bennet, as he folded up the letter. 'He seems to be a most conscientious and polite young man, upon my word, and I doubt not will prove a valuable acquaintance, especially if Lady Catherine should be so indulgent as to let him come to us again.'

'There is some sense in what he says about the girls, however, and if he is disposed to make them any amends, I shall not be the person to discourage him.'

'Though it is difficult,' said Jane, 'to guess in what way he can mean to make us the atonement he thinks our due, the wish is certainly to his credit.'

Elizabeth was chiefly struck with his extraordinary deference for Lady Catherine, and his kind intention of christening, marrying, and burying his parishioners whenever it were required.

'He must be an oddity, I think,' said she. 'I cannot make him out. – There is something very pompous in his style. – And what can he mean by apologizing for being next in the entail? – We cannot suppose he would help it if he could. – Can he be a sensible man, sir?'

'No, my dear; I think not. I have great hopes of finding him quite the reverse. There is a mixture of servility and self-importance in his letter, which promises well. I am impatient to see him.'

'In point of composition,' said Mary, 'his letter does not seem defective. The idea of the olive-branch perhaps is not wholly new, yet I think it is well expressed.'

Mr Collins, on arrival, proves to be as pompous as his writing style, and his intentions soon become plain: he has heard much about the beautiful Bennet girls and has come to examine them, with a view to choosing a wife. Mr Bennet treats him with veiled dislike, but Mrs Bennet is pleased that one of her daughters at least shall be settled, and encourages Collins. He first picks Jane, but is told she is virtually engaged already, so transfers his attentions to Elizabeth, to her dismay.

The girls spend an evening with their uncle and aunt, Mr and Mrs Philips, accompanied by Mr Collins. There Elizabeth meets a handsome officer, George Wickham. They discuss Darcy, and hearing her term Darcy as disagreeable, he has some confirmatory comments to add:

'I have no right to give *my* opinion,' said Wickham, 'as to his being agreeable or otherwise. I am not qualified to form one. I have known him too long and too well to be a fair judge. It is impossible for *me* to be impartial. But I believe your opinion of him would in general astonish – and perhaps you would not express it quite so strongly anywhere else. Here you are in your own family.'

'Upon my word, I say no more *here* than I might say in any house in the neighbourhood, except Netherfield. He is not at all liked in Hertfordshire. Everybody is disgusted with his pride. You will not find him more favourably spoken of by anyone.'

'I cannot pretend to be sorry,' said Wickham, after a short interruption, 'that he or that any man should not be estimated beyond their deserts; but with *him* I believe it does not often happen. The world is blinded by his fortune and consequence, or frightened by his high and imposing manners, and sees him only as he chuses to be seen.'

'I should take him, even on *my* slight acquaintance, to be an ill-tempered man.' Wickham only shook his head.

'I wonder,' said he, at the next opportunity of speaking, 'whether he is likely to be in this country much longer.'

'I do not at all know; but I *heard* nothing of his going away when I was at Netherfield. I hope your plans in favour of the-shire will not be affected by his being in the neighbourhood.'

'Oh! no – it is not for *me* to be driven away by Mr. Darcy. If *he* wishes to avoid seeing *me*, he must go. We are not on friendly terms, and it always gives me pain to meet him, but I have no reason for avoiding *him* but what I might proclaim before all the world, – a sense of very great ill-usage, and most painful regrets at his being what he is. His father, Miss Bennet, the late Mr. Darcy, was one of the best men that ever breathed, and the truest friend I ever had; and I can never be in company with this Mr. Darcy without being grieved to the soul by a thousand tender recollections. His behaviour to myself has been scandalous; but I verily believe I could forgive him anything and everything, rather than his disappointing the hopes and disgracing the memory of his father.' . . .

'Indeed!'

'Yes – the late Mr. Darcy bequeathed me the next presentation of the best living in his gift. He was my godfather, and excessively attached to me. I cannot do justice to his kindness. He meant to provide for me amply, and thought he had done it; but when the living fell, it was given elsewhere.'

'Good heavens!' cried Elizabeth; 'but how could *that* be? – How could this will be disregarded? – Why did not you seek legal redress?'

'There was just such an informality in the terms of the bequest as to give me no hope from law. A man of honour could not have doubted the intention, but Mr. Darcy chose to doubt it – or to treat it as a merely conditional recommendation, and to assert that I had forfeited all claim to it by extravagance, imprudence – in short, anything or nothing. Certain it is, that the living became vacant two years ago, exactly as I was of an age to hold it, and that it was given to another man; and no less certain is it, that I cannot accuse myself of having really done any-thing to deserve to lose it. I have a warm, unguarded temper, and I may perhaps have sometimes spoken of my opinion *of* him, and *to* him, too freely. I can recall nothing worse. But the fact is, that we are very different sort of men, and that he hates me.'

'This is quite shocking! – He deserves to be publicly disgraced.'

'Some time or other he *will* be – but it shall not be by *me*. Till I can forget his father I can never defy or expose *him*.'

Elizabeth honoured him for such feelings, and thought him hand-somer than ever as he expressed them.

'But what,' said she, after a pause, 'can have been his motive? – what can have induced him to behave so cruelly?'

'A thorough, determined dislike of me – a dislike which I cannot but attribute in some measure to jealousy. Had the late Mr. Darcy liked me less, his son might have borne with me better: but his father's uncommon attachment to me irritated him, I believe, very early in life. He had not a temper to bear the sort of competition in which we stood – the sort of preference which was often given me.'

'I had not thought Mr. Darcy so bad as this – though I have never liked him, I had not thought so very ill of him. – I had supposed him to be despising his fellow-creatures in general, but did not suspect him of descending to such malicious revenge, such injustice, such inhumanity as this.'

After a few minutes' reflection, however, she continued – 'I *do* remem-ber his boasting one day, at Netherfield, of the implacability of his re-sentments, of his having an unforgiving temper. His disposition must be dreadful.'

'I will not trust myself on the subject,' replied Wickham; 'I can hardly be just to him.'

At a ball at Netherfield, Elizabeth makes it plain to Darcy that she prefers Wickham to him. She is appalled when her mother and younger sisters make foolish exhibitions of themselves before the company, and angered at Darcy's open contempt for them.

The following day Mr Collins proposes to Elizabeth:

'My reasons for marrying are, first, that I think it a right thing for every clergyman in easy circumstances (like myself) to set the example of matrimony in his parish; secondly, that I am convinced it will add very greatly to my happiness; and thirdly – which perhaps I ought to have mentioned earlier, that it is the particular advice and recommendation of the very noble lady whom I have the honour of calling patroness. Twice has she condescended to give me her opinion (unasked too!) on this subject; and it was but the very Saturday night before I left Hunsford – between our pools at quadrille, while Mrs. Jenkinson was arranging Miss de Bourgh's footstool – that she said, "Mr. Collins, you must marry. A clergyman like you must marry. – Chuse properly, chuse a gentlewoman for *my* sake, and for your *own*; let her be an active, useful sort of person, not brought up high, but able to make a small income go a good way. This is my advice. Find such a woman as soon as you can, bring her to Hunsford, and I will visit her." Allow me, by the way, to observe, my fair cousin, that I do not reckon the notice and kindness of Lady Catherine de Bourgh as among the least of the advantages in my power to offer. You will find her manners beyond anything I can describe; and your wit and vivacity, I think, must be acceptable to her, especially when tempered with the silence and respect which her rank will inevitably excite. Thus much for my general intention in favour of matrimony; it remains to be told why my views were directed to Longbourn instead of my own neighbourhood, where, I assure you, there are many amiable young women. But the fact is, that being, as I am, to inherit this estate after the death of your honoured father (who, however, may live many years longer), I could not satisfy myself without resolving to chuse a wife from among his daughters, that the loss to them might be as little as possible, when the melancholy event takes place – which, however, as I have already said, may not be for several years. This has been my motive, my fair cousin, and I flatter myself it will not sink me in your esteem. And now nothing remains for me but to assure you in the most animated language of the violence of my affection. To fortune I am perfectly indifferent, and shall make no demand on that nature on your father, since I am well aware that it could not be complied with; and that one thousand pounds in the four per cents, which will not be yours till after your mother's decease, is all that you may ever be entitled to. On that head, therefore, I shall be uniformly silent; and you may assure yourself that no ungenerous reproach shall ever pass my lips when we are married.'

It was absolutely necessary to interrupt him now.

'You are too hasty, sir,' she cried. 'You forget that I have made no answer. Let me do it without farther loss of time. Accept my thanks for the compliment you are paying me. I am very sensible of the honour of your proposals, but it is impossible for me to do otherwise than decline them.'

'I am not now to learn,' replied Mr. Collins, with a formal wave of the hand, 'that it is usual with young ladies to reject the addresses of the man whom they secretly mean to accept, when he first applies for their favour; and that sometimes the refusal is repeated a second or even a third time. I am therefore by no means discouraged by what you have just said, and shall hope to lead you to the altar ere long.'

'Upon my word, sir,' cried Elizabeth, 'your hope is rather an extra-ordinary one after my declaration. I do assure you that I am not one of those young ladies (if such young ladies there are) who are so daring as to risk their happiness on the chance of being asked a second time. I am perfectly serious in my refusal. You could not make *me* happy, and I am convinced that I am the last woman in the world who would make *you* so. Nay, were your friend Lady Catherine to know me, I am persuaded she would find me in every respect ill qualified for the situation.'

'Were it certain that Lady Catherine would think so,' said Mr. Collins very gravely – 'but I cannot imagine that her ladyship would at all disapprove of you. And you may be certain that when I have the honour of seeing her again, I shall speak in the highest terms of your modesty, economy, and other amiable qualifications.'

'Indeed, Mr. Collins, all praise of me will be unnecessary. You must give me leave to judge for myself, and pay me the compliment of believing what I say. I wish you very happy and very rich, and by refusing your hand, do all in my power to prevent your being otherwise. In making me the offer, you must have satisfied the delicacy of your feelings with regard to my family, and may take possession of Longbourn estate whenever it falls, without any self-reproach. This matter may be considered, therefore, as finally settled.' And rising as she thus spoke, she would have quitted the room, had not Mr. Collins thus addressed her –

'When I do myself the honour of speaking to you next on the subject, I shall hope to receive a more favourable answer than you have now given me; though I am far from accusing you of cruelty at present, because I know it to be the established custom of your sex to reject a man on the first application, and perhaps you have even now said as much to encourage my suit as would be consistent with the true delicacy of the female character.'

'Really, Mr. Collins,' cried Elizabeth with some warmth, 'you puzzle me exceedingly. If what I have hitherto said can appear to you in the form of encouragement, I know not how to express my refusal in such a way as may convince you of its being one.'

'You must give me leave to flatter myself, my dear cousin, that your refusal of my addresses is merely words of course. My reasons for believing it are briefly these: It does not appear to me that my hand is unworthy your acceptance, or that the establishment I can offer would be any other than highly desirable. My situation in life, my connexions with the family of De Bourgh, and my relationship to your own, are circumstances highly in my favour; and you should take it into further consideration, that in spite of your manifold attractions, it is by no means certain that another offer of marriage may ever be made you. Your portion is unhappily so small that it will in all likelihood undo the effects of your loveliness and amiable qualifications. As I must therefore conclude that you are not serious in your rejection of me, I shall chuse to attribute it to your wish of increasing my love by suspense, according to the usual practice of elegant females.'

'I do assure you, sir, that I have no pretensions whatever to that kind of elegance which consists in tormenting a respectable man. I would rather be paid the compliment of being believed sincere. I thank you again and again for the honour you have done me in your proposals, but to accept them is absolutely impossible. My feelings in every respect forbid it. Can I speak plainer? Do not consider me now as an elegant female intending plague you, but as a rational creature, speaking the truth from her heart.'

'You are uniformly charming!' cried he, with an air of awkward gallantry; 'and I am persuaded that, when sanctioned by the express authority of both your excellent parents, my proposals will not fail of being acceptable.'

To such perseverance in wilful self-deception Elizabeth would make no reply, and immediately and in silence withdrew; determined, that if he persisted in considering her repeated refusals as flattering encouragement, to apply to her father, whose negative might be uttered in such a manner as must be decisive, and whose behaviour at least could not be mistaken for the affection and coquetry of an elegant female.

Elizabeth's reply is a firm refusal, but Collins's self-esteem is so considerable that he is hard to convince. Mrs Bennet has hysterics and appeals to her husband, who deals with the matter characteristically:

'Come here, child,' cried her father as she appeared. 'I have sent for you on an affair of importance. I understand that Mr. Collins has made you an offer of marriage. Is it true?' Elizabeth replied that it was. 'Very well – and this offer of marriage you have refused?'

'I have, sir.'

'Very well. We now come to the point. Your mother insists upon your accepting it. Is it not so, Mrs. Bennet?'

'Yes, or I will never see her again.'

'An unhappy alternative is before you, Elizabeth. From this day you must be a stranger to one of your parents. Your mother will never see you again if you do *not* marry Mr. Collins, and I will never see you again if you *do*.'

Mrs Bennet has cause for even more violent hysteria when the resilient Collins soon announces his plan to marry Charlotte Lucas, a move which forbodes the day when the estate will pass to him, and Mrs Bennet, by then a widow, and her daughters, will be cast out. Jane receives a letter from Caroline Bingley, informing her that the Netherfield party have left the district and do not intent to return. Jane and her mother are shocked that Bingley has left without an explanation, or, more importantly, a proposal. Elizabeth suspects that his sisters want him to marry Darcy's sister, Georgiana, whose fortune is so much greater than Jane's. Jane goes to stay in London with her uncle and aunt Gardiner and there receives one formal visit from Caroline which does nothing to ease her pain. Miss Bingley brings no message from her brother, whose engagement to Georgiana Darcy seems beyond doubt.

Elizabeth, too, has had her share of disappointment. Wickham is reported to be courting a Miss King, a plain girl with a large fortune. Elizabeth is glad to receive an invitation from her friend Charlotte, now Mrs Collins, to stay with her at Hunsford Parsonage. Collins's patroness, Lady de Bourgh, is Darcy's aunt, and he and a cousin, Colonel Fitzwilliam, arrive for a stay at her house, Rosings, at the same time as Elizabeth's visit. She and Darcy seem to meet frequently by chance, and the old banter between them continues. Colonel Fitzwilliam, knowing nothing of Elizabeth's background, tells her how Darcy managed to rescue Bingley from an unsuitable match – that is, with Jane Bennet – which, not unnaturally, turns Elizabeth even more against Darcy. She is consequently amazed when he suddenly addresses her agitatedly:

'In vain have I struggled. It will not do. My feelings will not be repressed. You must allow me to tell you how ardently I admire and love you.'

Elizabeth's astonishment was beyond expression. She stared, coloured, doubted, and was silent. This he considered sufficient encouragement; and the avowal of all that he felt, and had long felt for her, immediately followed. He spoke well; but there were feelings besides those of the heart to be detailed, and he was not more eloquent on the subject of tenderness than of pride. His sense of her inferiority – of its being a degradation – of the family obstacles which judgment had always opposed to inclination, were dwelt on with a warmth which seemed due to the consequence he was wounding, but was very unlikely to recommend his suit.

In spite of her deeply rooted dislike she could not be insensible to the compliment of such a man's affection, and though her intentions did not vary for an instant, she was at first sorry for the pain he was to receive; till, roused to resentment by his subsequent language, she lost all compassion in anger. She tried, however, to compose herself to answer him with patience, when he should have done. He concluded with representing to her the strength of that attachment which, in spite of all his endeavours, he had found impossible to conquer; and with expressing his hope that it would now be rewarded by her acceptance of his hand. As he said this, she could easily see that he had no doubt of a favourable answer. He *spoke* of apprehension and anxiety, but his countenance expressed real security. Such a circumstance could only exasperate farther, and, when he ceased, the colour rose into her cheeks, and she said –

'In such cases as this, it is, I believe, the established mode to express a sense of obligation for the sentiments avowed, however unequally they may be returned. It is natural that obligation should be felt, and if I could *feel* gratitude, I would now thank you. But I cannot – I have never desired your good opinion, and you have certainly bestowed it most unwillingly. I am sorry to have occasioned pain to any one. It has been most unconsciously done, however, and I hope will be of short duration. The feelings which, you tell me, have long prevented the acknowledgment of your regard, can have little difficulty in overcoming it after this explanation.'

Mr. Darcy, who was leaning against the mantelpiece with his eyes fixed on her face, seemed to catch her words with no less resentment than surprise. His complexion became pale with anger, and the disturbance of his mind was visible in every feature. He was struggling for the appearance of composure, and would not open his lips till he believed himself to have attained it. The pause was to Elizabeth's feelings dreadful. At length, in a voice of forced calmness, he said –

'And this is all the reply which I am to have the honour of expecting! I might, perhaps, wish to be informed why, with so little *endeavour* at civility, I am thus rejected. But it is of small importance.'

'I might as well inquire,' replied she, 'why, with so evident a design of offending and insulting me, you chose to tell me that you liked me against your will, against your reason, and even against your character? Was not this some excuse for incivility, if I *was* uncivil? But I have other provocations. You know I have. Had not my own feelings decided against you – had they been indifferent, or had they even been favourable, do you think that any consideration would tempt me to accept the man who has been the means of ruining, perhaps for ever, the happiness of a most beloved sister?'

As she pronounced these words, Mr. Darcy changed colour; but the emotion was short, and he listened without attempting to interrupt her, while she continued –

'I have every reason in the world to think ill of you. No motive can excuse the unjust and ungenerous part you acted *there*. You dare not, you cannot deny that you have been the principal, if not the only means of dividing them from each other – of exposing one to the censure of the world for caprice and instability, the other to its derision for disappointed hopes, and involving them both in misery of the acutest kind.'

She paused, and saw with no slight indignation that he was listening with an air which proved him wholly unmoved by any feeling of remorse. He even looked at her with a smile of affected incredulity.

'Can you deny that you have done it?' she repeated.

With assumed tranquillity he then replied, 'I have no wish of denying that I did everything in my power to separate my friend from your sister, or that I rejoice in my success. Towards *him* I have been kinder than towards myself.'

Elizabeth disdained the appearance of noticing this civil reflection, but its meaning did not escape, nor was it likely to conciliate her.

'But it is not merely this affair,' she continued, 'on which my dislike is founded. Long before it had taken place my opinion of you was decided. Your character was unfolded in the recital which I received many months ago from Mr. Wickham. On this subject, what can you have to say? In what imaginary act of friendship can you here defend yourself? Or under what misrepresentation can you here impose upon others?'

'You take an eager interest in that gentleman's concerns,' said Darcy, in a less tranquil tone, and with a heightened colour.

'Who that knows what his misfortunes have been, can help feeling an interest in him?'

'His misfortunes!' repeated Darcy contemptuously; 'yes, his misfortunes have been great indeed.'

'And of your infliction,' cried Elizabeth with energy. 'You have reduced him to his present state of poverty – comparative poverty. You have withheld the advantages which you must know to have been designed for him. You have deprived the best years of his life of that independence which was no less his due than his desert. You have done all this! and yet you can treat the mention of his misfortunes with contempt and ridicule.'

'And this,' cried Darcy, as he walked with quick steps across the room, 'is your opinion of me! This is the estimation in which you hold me! I thank you for explaining it so fully. My faults, according to this calculation, are heavy indeed! But perhaps,' added, he stopping in his walk, and turning towards her, 'these offences might have been overlooked, had not your pride been hurt by my honest confession of the scruples that had long prevented my forming any serious design. These bitter accusations might have been suppressed, had I, with greater policy, concealed my struggles, and flattered you into the belief of my being impelled by unqualified, unalloyed inclination; by reason, by reflection, by everything. But disguise of every sort is my obhorrence. Nor am I ashamed of the feelings I related. They were natural and just. Could you expect me to rejoice in the inferiority of your connections? – to congratulate myself on the hope of relations, whose condition in life is so decidedly beneath my own?'

Elizabeth felt herself growing more angry every moment; yet she tried to the utmost to speak with composure when she said –

'You are mistaken, Mr. Darcy, if you suppose that the mode of your declaration affected me in any other way, than as it spared the concern which I might have felt in refusing you, had you behaved in a more gentlemanlike manner.'

She saw him start at this, but he said nothing, and she continued –

'You could not have made me the offer of your hand in any possible way that would have tempted me to accept it.'

Again his astonishment was obvious; and he looked at her with an expression of mingled incredulity and mortification. She went on –

'From the very beginning – from the first moment, I may almost say – of my acquaintance with you, your manners, impressing me with the fullest belief of your arrogance, your conceit, and your selfish disdain of the feelings of others, were such as to form that groundwork of disapprobation on which succeeding events have built so immovable a dislike; and I had not known you a month before I felt that you were the last man in the world whom I could ever be prevailed on to marry.'

'You have said quite enough, madam. I perfectly comprehend your feelings, and have now only to be ashamed of what my own have been. Forgive me for having taken up so much of your time, and accept my best wishes for your health and happiness.'

And with these words he hastily left the room, and Elizabeth heard him the next moment open the front door and quit the house.

Next morning Elizabeth chances to meet Darcy again and he hands her a letter, in which he explains that he had thought Jane's regard for Bingley to be slight; that the Bennet family, anyway, were not suitable connections for one such as the Bingley's; and that Wickham, far from being ill-treated by

Darcy's family, had received every kindness and had repaid them by trying to elope with Darcy's sister, aged fifteen at the time. The letter ends: 'I will only add, God bless you.'

Once she has been able to admit to herself the truth of what Darcy has written, Elizabeth experiences a slight warming of feeling for him. She and Jane return to Meryton, and, against Elizabeth's advice, Mr Bennet allows Lydia to go with Mrs Foster, the young wife of the colonel commanding Wickham's regiment, to Brighton, where they are stationed. Elizabeth leaves again, this time with her Gardiner relations to Derbyshire, where she is shown over Darcy's house, Pemberley, by his housekeeper, and reflects ruefully that she might have been mistress of it, had she accepted him. The Bingleys and Darcy return while the visitors are there, and, somewhat to the general amazement, Darcy seems to put himself out to oblige the Gardiners. Elizabeth meets and likes Georgiana Darcy, but their acquaintance is cut short by a letter from Jane to say that Lydia has run off with Wickham, to where, no one knows. Elizabeth confides in Darcy, then leaves at once for Meryton.

Mr Bennet has already gone to London in search of the eloping pair, and Mr Gardiner joins him. The unhappy situation is made no easier by a characteristic letter from William Collins:

'MY DEAR SIR, –

'I feel myself called upon, by our relationship, and my situation in life, to condole with you on the grievous affliction you are now suffering under, of which we were yesterday informed by a letter from Hertfordshire. Be assured, my dear sir, that Mrs. Collins and myself sincerely sympathize with you and all your respectable family, in your present distress, which must be of the bitterest kind, because proceeding from a cause which no time can remove. No arguments shall be wanting on my part that can alleviate so severe a misfortune – or that may comfort you, under a circumstance that must be of all others most afflicting to a parent's mind. The death of your daughter would have been a blessing in comparison of this. And it is the more to be lamented, because there is reason to suppose as my dear Charlotte informs me, that this licentiousness of behaviour in your daughter has proceeded from a faulty degree of indulgence; though, at the same time, for the consolation of yourself and Mrs. Bennet, I am inclined to think that her own disposition must be naturally bad, or she could not be guilty of such an enormity, at so early an age. Howsoever that may be, you are grievously to be pitied; in which opinion I am not only joined by Mrs. Collins, but likewise by Lady Catherine and her daughter, to whom I have related the affair. They agree with me in apprehending that this false step in one daughter will be injurious to the fortunes of all the others; for who, as Lady Catherine herself condescendingly says, will connect themselves with such a family? And this consideration leads me moreover to reflect, with aug-mented satisfaction, on a certain event of last November; for had it been otherwise, I must have been involved in all your sorrow and disgrace. Let me advise you then, my dear sir, to console yourself as much as possible, to throw off your unworthy child from your affection for ever, and leave her to reap the fruits of her own heinous offence. – I am, dear sir, etc., etc.

Wickham has left behind a deal of debts and Lydia has only a small dowry to offer him: a marriage seems unlikely. Mr Bennet returns to Meryton in a cynically resigned frame of mind, while the rest of the family despair. Then a letter arrives from Mr Gardiner: he has traced Lydia and Wickham in London; she is safe with her aunt and uncle, and Wickham is going to marry her. Mrs Bennet's hysteria changes to rapture:

'My dear, dear Lydia!' she cried. 'This is delightful indeed! She will be married! I shall see her again! She will be married at sixteen! My good, kind brother! I knew how it would be. I knew he would manage every-thing! How I long to see her! and to see dear Wickham too! But the clothes, the wedding clothes! I will write to my sister Gardiner about them directly. Lizzy, my dear, run down to your father, and ask him how much he will give her. Stay, stay, I will go myself. Ring the bell, Kitty, for Hill. I will put on my things in a moment. My dear, dear Lydia! – How merry we shall be together when we meet!'

Mr Bennet is surprised to discover that his brother-in-law had needed to make no financial agreement with Wickham. The family decide to put the best face on things and receive the newly-weds, who are quite unrepentant. When Lydia reveals to

Elizabeth that Darcy had been at the wedding, Elizabeth writes
to her aunt Gardiner for an explanation and receives the reply
that since Darcy means to marry Elizabeth (as Mrs Gardiner had
surmised), he wished to give her sister his support.

The Bingleys arrive back at Netherfield with Darcy and Mrs
Bennet turns her attention from Lydia to Jane, now, surely, to
marry Bingley: she is not disappointed. Lady de Bourgh makes
an unexpected visit to demand of Elizabeth that she will never
marry Darcy, whom she wants for her own daughter. Elizabeth
is not overawed by the domineering old lady:

'If there is no other objection to my marrying your nephew, I shall
certainly not be kept from it by knowing that his mother and aunt
wished him to marry Miss de Bourgh. You both did as much as you
could, in planning the marriage; its completion depended on others. If
Mr. Darcy is neither by honour nor inclination confined to his cousin,
why is not he to make another choice? and if I am that choice, why may
I not accept him?'

'Because honour, decorum, prudence - nay, interest, forbid it. Yes,
Miss Bennet, interest; for do not expect to be noticed by his family or
friends if you wilfully act against the inclinations of all. You will be
censured, slighted, and despised by every one connected with him. Your
alliance will be a disgrace; your name will never even be mentioned by
any of us.'

'These are heavy misfortunes,' replied Elizabeth. 'But the wife of Mr.
Darcy must have such extraordinary sources of happiness necessarily
attached to her situation, that she could, upon the whole, have no cause
to repine.'

'Obstinate, headstrong girl! I am ashamed of you! Is this your gratitude for my attentions to you last spring? Is nothing due to me on that
score? Let us sit down. You are to understand, Miss Bennet, that I came
here with the determined resolution of carrying my purpose; nor will I
be dissuaded from it. I have not been used to submit to any person's
whims. I have not been in the habit of brooking disappointment.'

'*That* will make your ladyship's situation at present more pitiable; but
it will have no effect on *me*.'

'I will not be interrupted! Hear me in silence. My daughter and my
nephew are formed for each other. They are descended, on the maternal

side, from the same noble line; and on the fathers', from respectable, honourable, and ancient, though untitled families. Their fortune on both sides is splendid. They are destined for each other by the voice of every member of their respective houses; and what is to divide them? The up-start pretensions of a young woman without family, connexions, or fortune. Is this to be endured? But it must not, shall not be! If you were sensible of your own good, you would not wish to quit the sphere in which you have been brought up.'

'In marrying your nephew I should not consider myself as quitting that sphere. He is a gentleman; I am a gentleman's daughter; so far we are equal.'

'True. You *are* a gentleman's daughter. But who was your mother? Who are your uncles and aunts? Do not imagine me ignorant of their condition.'

'Whatever my connexions may be,' said Elizabeth, 'if your nephew does not object to them, they can be nothing to *you*.'

'Tell me, once for all, are you engaged to him?'

Though Elizabeth would not, for the mere purpose of obliging Lady Catherine, have answered this question, she could not but say, after a moment's deliberation, 'I am not.'

Lady Catherine seemed pleased.

'And will you promise me never to enter into such an engagement?'

'I will make no promise of the kind.'

Mr Collins adds his dissuasive efforts to Lady Catherine's, but with as little effect. Bingley brings Darcy to visit the Bennets and Elizabeth thanks the latter for looking after Lydia. He takes the opportunity to declare that his feelings for her are unchanged, and to propose once more, apologizing for his past selfishness an false pride, which he attributes to his upbringing, and telling Elizabeth that she has taught him the lesson humility that he needed. She responds favourably enough for Darcy to approach her father for her hand. Mr Bennet is astonished by her acceptance of so awesome a suitor, but her mother is overwhelmed with a different emotion:

Mrs. Bennet sat quite still, and unable to utter a syllable. Nor was it under many, many minutes, that she could comprehend what she heard, though not in general backward to credit what was for the advantage of her family, or that came in the shape of a lover to any of them. She began at length to recover, to fidget about in her chair, get up, sit down again, wonder, and bless herself.

'Good gracious! Lord bless me! only think! dear me! Mr. Darcy! Who would have thought it? And is it really true? Oh, my sweetest Lizzy! How rich and how great you will be! What pin-money, what jewels, what carriages you will have! Jane's is nothing to it – nothing at all. I am so pleased – so happy! Such a charming man! so handsome! so tall! Oh, my dear Lizzy! pray apologise for my having disliked him so much before. I hope he will overlook it. Dear, dear Lizzy! A house in town! Everything that is charming! Three daughters married! Ten thousand a year! Oh, Lord! what will become of me? I shall go distracted.'

MANSFIELD PARK

THIS longest of Jane Austen's novels, and to some of her admirers the finest, was begun early in 1811, some months before *Sense and Sensibility*. It was not completed, though, until the spring of 1814, by which time *Sense and Sensibility* had sold out its first edition, and *Pride and Prejudice* had already reached its second edition. Thus, she was working on *Mansfield Park* with the confidence that the kind of material she had chosen to use for her novels, and her style of writing them, was acceptable to the public.

Such confidence seems to have been lacking in her publisher, Thomas Egerton. He brought out the book at the end of May 1814, but ventured to charge no more for it than its much shorter predecessors and printed only a small number of copies. These sold out quite quickly, but even this did not bring conviction in its wake, for he produced no further edition. Like *Sense and Sensibility*, *Mansfield Park* was published by Egerton 'on commission', which meant that the author guaranteed him against loss and could re-dispose of the copyright as she chose when the edition had run out, so the decision to reprint or not to reprint was not his alone. In November 1814, Jane was writing to a relative: 'It is not settled yet whether I *do* hazard a 2ᵈ Edition. We are to see Egerton today, when it will probably be determined. – People are more ready to borrow & praise, than to buy – which I cannot wonder at; – but tho' I like praise as well as anybody, I like what Edward calls *Pewter* too.'

Even so, one assumes that if Egerton, the professional in the matter, had been less timorous and had quickly set about using the word-of-mouth engendered by the first edition to promote a second, she would have been glad to take the risk. In consequence, *Mansfield Park* remained out of print for more than a year while Jane wrote *Emma*, and its reappearance in 1816, with many corrections, was part of the 'package deal' offered by her new publisher, John Murray, in accepting the latest novel. It was first published in America by Carey and Lea, Philadelphia, in 1832.

. . . .

When Miss Maria Ward had the good fortune to marry Sir Thomas Bertram, Bart, MP, of Mansfield Park, Northampton-shire, it was supposed that her two sisters might do as well for themselves. But after six years one sister had found only a clergy-man, Mr Norris, incumbent of Mansfield, while the other had shocked the family, and cut herself from them, by marrying a lowly Lieutenant of Marines named Price.

Eleven years pass, and Mrs Price is at last forced to jettison her pride and resentment and turn to her sisters for help: her family is large, her income small, and her husband disabled and fond of the bottle. Preparing for the ninth lying-in, she writes to Lady Bertram asking if Sir Thomas might find a position for the eldest boy, aged ten. The letter results in help for the Price family and a healing of the breach between the sisters.

The following year Lady Bertram and Mrs Norris decide to take over the upbringing of another of the children, a nine-year-old girl. When Sir Thomas, thinking of his own children's interests, hesitates to agree, Mrs Norris urges him to consider:

'Do not let us be frightened from a good deed by a trifle. Give a girl an education, and introduce her properly into the world, and ten to one but she has the means of settling well, without farther expense to any body. A niece of our's, Sir Thomas, I may say, or, at least of *your's*, would not grow up in this neighbourhood without many advantages. I don't say she would be so handsome as her cousins. I dare say she would not; but she would be introduced into the society of this country under such very favourable circumstances as, in all human probability, would get her a creditable establishment. You are thinking of your sons – but do not you know that of all things upon earth *that* is the least likely to happen; brought up as they would be, always together like brothers and sisters? It is morally impossible. I never knew an instance of it. It is, in fact, the only sure way of providing against the connection. Suppose her a pretty girl, and seen by Tom or Edmund for the first time seven years hence, and

I dare say there would be mischief. The very idea of her having been suffered to grow up at a distance from us all in poverty and neglect, would be enough to make either of the dear, sweet-tempered boys in love with her. But breed her up with them from this time, and suppose her even to have the beauty of an angel, and she will never be more to either than a sister.'

Mrs Norris acts out of Christian charity only; tight-fisted and selfish, she has no intention of burdening her own house and her purse with a child when her rich brother-in-law can well afford to do so. Dignity and duty come first with Sir Thomas and his lady, and they agree that the child shall be raised and educated with their own two daughters. Little Fanny Price arrives and meets her cousins, Julia, aged twelve, Maria, aged thirteen, and their two older brothers, Edmund and Tom. Mrs Norris has impressed upon Fanny the honour being paid her, and the child is duly frightened and shy of Sir Thomas and the rest of the company. For some days she remains unhappy and homesick, her lack of education the scorn of her girl cousins:

Fanny could read, work, and write, but she had been taught nothing more; and as her cousins found her ignorant of many things with which they had been long familiar, they thought her prodigiously stupid, and for the first two or three weeks were continually bringing some fresh report of it into the drawing room. 'Dear mamma, only think, my cousin cannot put the map of Europe together – or my cousin cannot tell the principal rivers in Russia – or she never heard of Asia Minor – or she does not know the difference between water-colours and crayons! – How strange! – Did you ever hear anything so stupid?'

'My dear,' their considerate aunt would reply, 'it is very bad; but you must not expect every body to be as forward and quick at learning as yourself.'

'But, aunt, she is really so very ignorant! – Do you know, we asked her last night which way she would go to get to Ireland; and she said she should cross to the Isle of Wight. She thinks of nothing but the Isle of Wight, and she calls it *the Island*, as if there were no other island in the world. I am sure I should have been ashamed of myself, if I had not known better long before I was so old as she is. I cannot remember the time when I did not know a great deal that she has not the least notion of yet. How long ago it is, aunt, since we used to repeat the chronological order of the kings of England, with the dates of their accession, and most of the principal events of their reigns?'

'Yes,' added the other; 'and of the Roman emperors as low as Severus; besides a great deal of the Heathen Mythology, and all the Metals, Semi-Metals, Planets, and distinguished philosophers.'

'Very true, indeed, my dears, but you are blessed with wonderful memories, and your poor cousin has probably none at all. There is a vast deal of difference in memories, as well as in every thing else, and therefore you must make allowance for your cousin, and pity her deficiency.'

Edmund, the younger of the Bertram sons, finds her one morning sitting crying on the attic stairs. Learning how lonely she feels, he talks to her about her family and suggests that she write to her favourite brother, William. He helps her with the letter, enclosing a half-guinea for his cousin. This small encouragement helps Fanny to feel happier in her new surroundings, and, as her appearance and spirits improve everyone thinks better of her, though Mrs Norris never fails to remind Julia and Maria of their superior birth and intelligence.

During the years that follow, Tom develops into an extra-vagant young man about town, his sisters grow up into graceful, refined girls, and Edmund, with 'his strong good sense and uprightness of mind', is destined for holy orders. During all this time Fanny has not returned once to visit her family in Ports-mouth, though she has met William occasionally, and when he was to become a sailor he had been invited to spend a week at Mansfield Park before going to sea. Fanny's affections are divided between William and Edmund, who continues to encourage, praise and direct her.

Mr Norris dies when Fanny is fifteen, and his widow leaves the Parsonage to live in the village. The living had been intended to pass to Edmund, but Tom's reckless spending and heavy debts mean that for the moment Edmund must help to pay for his brother's excesses. The living is given instead to Dr Grant, a man in his middle forties with a wife fifteen years his junior. Tom's debts, together with recent losses on the family's West Indian estate, decide Sir Thomas to economize, and he suggests that Fanny should go to live with Mrs Norris. Fanny is upset by the proposed move, but her selfish aunt Norris pleads poor health and lack of room, so it does not eventuate. The Grants move into the Parsonage and provide Mrs Norris with an immediate reason for disliking them: Dr Grant enjoys his food, and his young wife, 'instead of contriving to gratify him at little expense', provides him with rich dishes and an expensive cook.

Sir Thomas and Tom leave for a year's visit to the family estates in Antigua, where Sir Thomas hopes a little serious work may curb his elder son's recklessness. The two Miss Bertrams are launched into society, while Fanny is given the duty of acting as companion to their mother, an indolent woman who cannot be bothered to attend balls or entertain company. Mrs Norris is happy to chaperone Maria and Julia in her place, since it involves no expense to herself. Fanny, aware of her lowly station, is quite content to spend the quiet evenings with Lady Bertram and enjoys hearing her cousins' lively accounts of the balls they attend. Her greatest pleasure is riding her old grey pony, but when it dies and her cousins cannot spare their horses for her use, she is forced to sit at home all day with one aunt, or walk 'beyond her strength at the instigation of the other':

Edmund was absent at this time, or the evil would have been earlier remedied. When he returned to understand how Fanny was situated, and perceive its ill effects, there seemed with him but one thing to be done, and that 'Fanny must have a horse,' was the resolute declaration with which he opposed whatever could be urged by the supineness of his mother, or the economy of his aunt, to make it appear unimportant. Mrs. Norris could not help thinking that some steady old thing might be found among the numbers belonging to the Park, that would do vastly well, or, that one might be borrowed of the steward, or that perhaps Dr. Grant might now and then lend them the poney he sent to the post. She could not but consider it as absolutely unnecessary, and even improper, that Fanny should have a regular lady's horse of her own in the style of her cousins. She was sure Sir Thomas never intended it: and she must say, that to be making such a purchase in his absence, and adding to the great expenses of his stable at a time when a large part of his income was unsettled, seemed to her very unjustifiable. 'Fanny must have a horse,' was Edmund's only reply. Mrs. Norris could not see it in the same light. Lady Bertram did; she entirely agreed with her son as to the necessity of it, and as to its being considered necessary by his father; – she only pleaded against there being any hurry, she only wanted him to wait till Sir Thomas's return, and then Sir Thomas might settle it all himself. He would be at home in September, and where would be the harm of only waiting till September?

He exchanges one of his own horses for a quiet mare for Fanny's use. Tom returns from the West Indies, leaving his father to finish his business there. Maria becomes engaged to a wealthy young man, Rushworth, but has to await her father's return at the end of the summer before marrying. It is now July, and Fanny has just turned eighteen, when Henry and Mary Crawford, the half-brother and sister of Mrs Grant, arrive in the village. After their mother's death the Crawfords had been brought up by an uncle, Admiral Crawford, and his wife; but when Mrs Crawford died and the Admiral installed his mistress in the house, Henry Crawford felt obliged to remove his sister elsewhere. He has brought her to live with Mrs Grant at the Parsonage, since she will enjoy more company here than at his own house in Norfolk. Mary Crawford is a wealthy young woman, with £20,000 of her own a year, and it is not long before Mrs Grant decides she will make an excellent wife for Tom Bertram. Mary has already met Tom in London, and she and her brother Henry agree to consider the match. Maria and Julia also favour a marriage between their brother and Mary, especially since Julia has rapidly fallen in love with Henry. Mary Crawford is a very proficient harpist, and when her instrument arrives at the Parsonage, Edmund, himself a keen player, becomes a frequent visitor:

A young woman, pretty, lively, with a harp as elegant as herself; and both placed near a window, cut down to the ground, and opening on a little lawn, surrounded by shrubs in the rich foliage of summer, was enough to catch any man's heart. The season, the scene, the air, were all favourable to tenderness and sentiment. Mrs. Grant and her tambour frame were not without their use; it was all in harmony; and as every thing will turn to account when love is once set going, even the sandwich tray, and Dr. Grant doing the honours of it, were worth looking at. Without studying the business, however, or knowing what he was about, Edmund was beginning, at the end of a week of such intercourse, to be a good deal in love; and to the credit of the lady it may be added, that without his being a man of the world or an elder brother, without any of the arts of flattery or the gaieties of small talk, he began to be agreeable to her. She felt it to be so, though she had not foreseen and could hardly understand it; for he was not pleasant by any common rule, he talked no nonsense, he paid no compliments, his opinions were unbending, his attentions tranquil and simple, There was a charm, perhaps, in his sincerity, his steadiness, his integrity, which Miss Crawford might be equal to feel, though not equal to discuss with herself. She did not think very much about it, however; he pleased her for the present; she liked to have him near her; it was enough.

Fanny misses Edmund's company, and is a little put out when he borrows her mare to teach Mary to ride. She watches unhappily as the pair exercise their horses and notes Edmund's attentions to his beautiful pupil. Edmund hurts her further by unwitting comparisons between Mary's horsemanship and her own. For the four following mornings Fanny is left behind while the Crawfords and Bertrams ride out over Mansfield common. She passes the time walking about the gardens in the hot sun, and as a result develops a bad headache. Edmund shows his concern and upbraids his mother for not showing greater care for Fanny. His desertion, and now his sympathy, upset Fanny further and she retires to bed in a bewildered state of mind.

Maria's suitor, Rushworth, arrives at Mansfield Park with his mother to arrange a visit to Sotherton, his fine Elizabethan house ten miles away. Lady Bertram characteristically does not wish to exert herself and expects Fanny to keep her company while the others are gone. Edmund offers to stay behind instead, but it is finally arranged that Mrs Grant shall stay with Lady Bertram, and the party leave for Sotherton. While they are examining the chapel and joking at Maria's and Rushworth's nearness to the altar, Henry Crawford hints to Maria that he is interested in her himself. Jealous of Rushworth and his elegant house, he spends the visit finding fault with everything. His sister Mary, having just learned that Edmund is to be a clergyman, hurriedly makes amends for some earlier indiscreet remarks about the lowliness of such a profession:

'So you are to be a clergyman, Mr. Bertram. This is rather a surprise to me.'

'Why should it surprise you? You must suppose me designed for some profession, and might perceive that I am neither a lawyer, nor a soldier, nor a sailor.'

'Very true; but, in short, it had not occurred to me. And you know there is generally an uncle or a grandfather to leave a fortune to the second son.'

'A very praiseworthy practice,' said Edmund, 'but not quite universal. I am one of the exceptions, and *being* one, must do something for myself.'

'But why are you to be a clergyman? I thought *that* was always the lot of the youngest, where there were many to choose before him.'

'Do you think the church itself never chosen, then?'

'*Never* is a black word. But yes, in the *never* of conversation, which means *not very often*, I do think it. For what is to be done in the church? Men love to distinguish themselves, and in either of the other lines distinction may be gained, but not in the church. A clergyman is nothing.'

'The *nothing* of conversation has its gradations, I hope, as well as the *never*. A clergyman cannot be high in state or fashion. He must not head mobs, or set the tone in dress. But I cannot call that situation nothing, which has the charge of all that is of the first importance to mankind, individually or collectively considered, temporally and eternally – which has the guardianship of religion and morals and consequently of the manners which result from their influence. No one here can call the *office* nothing. If the man who holds it is so, it is by the neglect of his duty, by foregoing its just importance, and stepping out of his place to appear what he ought not to appear.'

'*You* assign greater consequence to the clergyman than one has been used to hear given, or than I can quite comprehend. One does not see much of this influence and importance in society, and how can it be acquired where they are so seldom seen themselves? How can two sermons a week, even supposing them worth hearing, supposing the preacher to have the sense to prefer Blair's to his own, do all that you speak of – govern the conduct and fashion the manners of a large congregation for the rest of the week? One scarcely sees a clergyman out of his pulpit.'

'*You* are speaking of London, *I* am speaking of the nation at large.'

'The metropolis, I imagine, is a pretty fair sample of the rest.'

'Not, I should hope, of the proportion of virtue to vice throughout the kingdom. We do not look in great cities for our best morality. It is not there that respectable people of any denomination can do most good; and it certainly is not there that the influence of the clergy can be most felt. A fine preacher is followed and admired; but it is not in fine preaching only that a good clergyman will be useful in his parish and his neighbourhood, where the parish and neighbourhood are of a size capable of knowing his private character, and observing his general conduct, which in London can rarely be the case. The clergy are lost there in the crowds of their parishioners. They are known to the largest part only as preachers. And with regard to their influencing public manners, Miss Crawford must not misunderstand me, or suppose I mean to call them the arbiters of good breeding, the regulators of refinement and courtesy, the masters of the ceremonies of life. The *manners* I speak of might rather be called *conduct*, perhaps, the result of good principles; the effect, in short, of those doctrines which it is their duty to teach and recommend; and it will, I believe, be every where found, that as the clergy are, or are not what they ought to be, so are the rest of the nation.'

'Certainly,' said Fanny with gentle earnestness.

'There,' cried Miss Crawford, 'you have quite convinced Miss Price already.'

'I wish I could convince Miss Crawford too.'

'I do not think you ever will,' said she, with an arch smile; 'I am just as much surprised now as I was at first that you should intend to take orders. You really are fit for something better. Come do change, your mind. It is not too late. Go into the law.'

'Go into the law! with as much ease as I was told to go into this wilderness.'

'Now you are going to say something about law being the worst wilderness of the two, but I forestall you; remember I have forestalled you.'

'You need not hurry when the object is only to prevent my saying a bon-mot, for there is not the least wit in my nature. I am a very matter of fact, plain spoken being, and may blunder on the borders of a repartee for half an hour together without striking it out.'

Edmund and Mary walk away arm-in-arm, leaving Fanny to rest on a bench. She is shortly joined by Rushworth, Crawford and Maria, but when Rushworth goes to find a key, Crawford and Maria go off without him, and Fanny is distressed by the impropriety of Maria's conduct. Julia arrives, angrily demanding to know where everyone is. She has just escaped from Rushworth's 'horrible mother', and on learning that her sister and Crawford have wandered away by themselves, hurries after them. Rushworth returns with the key. Maria's obvious preference for Crawford's company upsets him, and he asks Fanny's opinion of his rival. Fearing to exacerbate the delicate situation, she says little. The afternoon's complications are resolved during dinner, and when the party leaves Sotherton Maria's affection is once more for Rushworth, and Crawford is paying all his attention to Julia.

The two sisters, however, remain secret rivals for Crawford's favour, and Maria shows little enthusiasm for her father's return from Antigua in November, when the plans for her marriage with Rushworth can go forward. Crawford leaves briefly for his Norfolk home, Everingham, and Tom Bertram arrives back at Mansfield Park after a few weeks of races and parties, bringing a friend, the Hon John Yates. Yates prides himself as something of an actor, and soon infects the entire household with plans for private theatricals. One of the rooms is to be turned into a theatre, by the estate carpenter, Christopher Jackson, and after some argument about parts and plays, they begin rehearsing for *Lovers' Vows*. Edmund, who has been out all morning, returns to find the house in an uproar, and is not too pleased by the choice of play or by the ladies taking part. Fanny is offered a small role, but declines and is consequently upbraided by Mrs Norris for ingratitude. Mary Crawford tries to comfort the distressed girl, but Fanny hurries away to the silence and privacy of her quarters, the former schoolroom. Edmund finds her there and asks her opinion as to whether or not he should take the role of 'Anhalt' in the play. He had been against performing at all, but since Tom has suggested bringing in another friend, Charles Maddox, of whom Edmund disapproves, he has been forced to change his mind. Fanny hesitates to give an answer: in the play 'Anhalt' has a love scene with 'Amelia', played by Mary Crawford. Unhappily, she finally agrees with Edmund that he must take the part.

Mrs Grant confides in Mary that she believes Julia to be in love with Crawford. Mary maintains that both the Bertram sisters are attached to her brother, but that things may change when Sir Thomas arrives home. Meanwhile, Crawford continues to pay flattering attention to both girls, and, to make matters worse for Julia, he has chosen Maria to play opposite him. The rehearsals take up several days and Edmund and Mary come to Fanny's room so that she can criticize their performance. It is a very painful experience for Fanny, but she hides her distress and assists them, though she feels that the scene is already played so naturally that little improvement is needed. Mrs Grant, playing the Cottager's Wife, has to give up the part to nurse her sick husband, and Fanny is prevailed upon by Edmund to take over the role. The dress rehearsal is just about to begin when Sir Thomas arrives at Mansfield Park. Everyone is thrown into confusion and rush out to greet him, Fanny holding back till last:

As she entered, her own name caught her ear. Sir Thomas was at that moment looking round him, and saying, 'But where is Fanny? Why do not I see my little Fanny?', and on perceiving her, came forward with a kindness which astonished and penetrated her, calling her his dear Fanny, kissing her affectionately, and observing with decided pleasure how much she was grown! Fanny knew not how to feel, nor where to look. She was quite oppressed. He had never been so kind, so *very* kind to her in his life. His manner seemed changed; his voice was quick from the

agitation of joy, and all that had been awful in his dignity seemed lost in
tenderness. He led her nearer the light and looked at her again – inquired
particularly after her health, and then correcting himself, observed that
he need *not* enquire, for her appearance spoke sufficiently on that point.
A fine blush having succeeded the previous paleness of her face, he was
justified in his belief of her equal improvement in health and beauty. He
inquired next after her family, especially William; and his kindness
altogether was such as made her reproach herself for loving him so little,
and thinking his return a misfortune; and when, on having courage to
lift her eyes to his face, she saw that he was grown thinner, and had the
burnt, fagged, worn look of fatigue and a hot climate, every tender
feeling was increased, and she was miserable in considering how much
unsuspected vexation was probably ready to burst on him.

When the excitement at his sudden arrival has finally died
down, Sir Thomas goes to his study, only to find that it, and the
adjoining billiard room, have been turned into the temporary
theatre. The Hon John Yates introduces himself and expands
upon his theatrical ambitions, while Sir Thomas ignores him to
study his intended son-in-law, Rushworth, of whom he approves. The following morning he admonishes Mrs Norris for
not having controlled his family better during his absence, since
his indolent wife relies entirely upon her for everything. Mrs
Norris counters by pointing out that it was she who encouraged
Rushworth's attentions towards Maria. All evidence of the theatre
is rapidly removed and the house restored to order. Yates takes the
hint that his presence is no longer desired and departs. Crawford
goes too, but only after intimating to Maria that she is his favourite.

The Mansfield Park household reverts to its previous quiet
existence. The Grants and Crawfords are no longer daily visitors,
and Fanny is delighted to find herself once again the object of
Edmund's quiet attention. Sir Thomas's approval of Rushworth is
short-lived when he visits Sotherton and discovers him to be 'an
inferior young man, as ignorant in business as in books, with
opinions in general unfixed, and without seeming much aware of
it himself'. Maria's cold indifference towards the young man

confirms her father's opinion that the match is unsuitable, but, when he tells her she may break off the engagement, Maria informs him that she wishes the marriage to go ahead. Maria and Rushworth are duly wed in November and Julia goes with them to Brighton, all rivalry between the two sisters now at an end.

Fanny's importance at Mansfield Park is increased by the girls' removal. She becomes a welcome guest at the Parsonage and is showered with belated attention from every quarter. Her qualities of good temper, cheerfulness and calmness seem suddenly apparent to everyone, and Mary Crawford claims her as her closest friend. Edmund calls at the Parsonage one day while Mary is playing her harp for Fanny, and learns Miss Crawford's ambition:

'A large income is the best recipe for happiness I ever heard of. It certainly may secure all the myrtle and turkey part of it.'

'You intend to be very rich,' said Edmund, with a look which, to Fanny's eye, had a great deal of serious meaning.

'To be sure. Do not you? Do not we all?'

'I cannot intend any thing which it must be so completely beyond my power to command. Miss Crawford may chuse her degree of wealth. She has only to fix on her number of thousands a year, and there can be no doubt of their coming. My intentions are only not to be poor.'

'By moderation and economy, and bringing down your wants to your income, and all that. I understand you – and a very proper plan it is for a person at your time of life, with such limited means and indifferent connections. What can *you* want but a decent maintenance? You have not much time before you; and your relations are in no situation to do any thing for you, or to mortify you by the contract of their own wealth and consequence. Be honest and poor, by all means – but I shall not envy you; I do not much think I shall even respect you. I have a much greater respect for those that are honest and rich.'

'Your degree of respect for honesty, rich or poor, is precisely what I have no manner of concern with. I do not mean to be poor. Poverty is exactly what I have determined against. Honesty, in the something between, in the middle state of worldly circumstances, is all that I am anxious for your not looking down on.'

'But I do look down upon it, if it might have been higher. I must look down upon any thing contented with obscurity when it might rise to distinction.'

'But how may it rise? How may my honesty at least rise to any distinction?'

This was not so very easy a question to answer, and occasioned an 'Oh!' of some length from the fair lady before she could add. 'You ought to be in parliament, or you should have gone into the army ten years ago.'

'*That* is not much to the purpose now; and as to my being in parliament, I believe I must wait till there is an especial assembly for the representation of younger sons who have little to live on. No, Miss Crawford,' he added, in a more serious tone, 'there *are* distinctions which I should be miserable if I thought myself without any chance – absolutely without chance or possibility of obtaining – but they are of a different character.'

Edmund and Fanny are invited to dine at the parsonage the following evening. Lady Bertram is surprised at such an invitation being extended to her poor relation, and her surprise is echoed by Mrs Norris when Sir Thomas allows Fanny to take the carriage. Edmund and Fanny arrive at the Parsonage to find that Crawford has preceded them. Crawford pays her excessive attention during dinner, and her unease is increased when she learns that Edmund is to take Holy Orders within a few weeks. The following morning, Mary Crawford hears from her brother that he means to make Fanny fall in love with him as a way of passing his time in Mansfield. But Fanny is not a young woman to be persuaded into loving someone against her better judgment, and, while she finds that her opinion of Crawford is improved by his attentions, her affections remain her own.

Her brother William writes to tell her that his ship has just anchored in Spithead and that he is coming to see her as soon as he lands. Sir Thomas is delighted to have his midshipman protégé as guest at Mansfield Park, and, though the visit is originally intended to last only a fortnight, the young man's conversation and charm are such that he is asked to remain as long as he can, and provided with a horse so that he may pursue his pastime of fox-hunting. Fanny and William are invited to join in a game of cards with the Bertrams, Crawfords and Grants, during which Henry Crawford relates how he has ridden past Thornton Lacey Parsonage, where Edmund will soon be living, and found it badly in need of repair. Crawford considers himself an expert renovator, and is soon discussing with Edmund possible alterations to the house. Sir Thomas observes Fanny's interest in the discussion and gains the impression that she and Crawford are mutually attracted. William wants to take his sister to a ball, so Sir Thomas decides to give one for them at Mansfield Park.

Edmund's mind is not only on his approaching ordination:

His duties would be established, but the wife who was to share, and animate, and reward those duties might yet be unattainable. He knew his own mind, but he was not always perfectly assured of knowing Miss Crawford's. There were points on which they did not quite agree, there were moments in which she did not seem propitious, and though trusting altogether to her affection, so far as to be resolved (almost resolved) on bringing it to a decision within a very short time, as soon as the variety of business before him were arranged, and he knew what he had to offer her he had many anxious feelings, many doubting hours as to the result. His conviction of her regard for him was sometimes very strong; he could look back on a long course of encouragement, and she was as perfect in disinterested attachment as in every thing else. But at other times doubt and alarm intermingled with his hopes, and when he thought of her acknowledged disinclination for privacy and retirement, her decided preference of a London life what could he expect but a determined rejection? unless it were an acceptance even more to be deprecated, demanding such sacrifices of situation and employment on his side as conscience must forbid.

The issue of all depended on one question. Did she love him well enough to forgo what had used to be essential points – did she love him well enough to make them no longer essential? And this question, which he was continually repeating to himself, though oftenest answered with a 'Yes', had sometimes its 'No.'

Miss Crawford was soon to leave Mansfield, and on this circumstance the 'no' and the 'yes' had been very recently in alternation. He had seen her eyes sparkle as she spoke of the dear friend's letter, which claimed a long visit from her in London, and of the kindness of Henry, in engaging to remain where he was till January, that he might convey her thither; he had heard her speak of the pleasure of such a journey with an animation which had 'no' in every tone. But this had occurred on the first day of its being settled, within the first hour of the burst of such enjoyment, when nothing but the friends she was to visit was before her. He had since heard her express herself differently – with other feelings – more checkered feelings; he had heard her tell Mrs. Grant that she should leave her with regret; that she began to believe neither the friends nor the pleasures she was going to were worth those she left behind; and that though she felt she must go, and knew she should enjoy herself when once away, she was already looking forward to being at Mansfield again. Was there not a 'yes' in all this?

The ball is the immediate preoccupation of the others. Fanny wishes to wear for it a pretty amber cross which William has brought back from Sicily for her, but she had nothing with which to fasten it, apart from a piece of ribbon. Mary presents her with a gold necklace, but Fanny regrets accepting it when she later learns it was given to Mary by her brother. She returns home and finds Edmund waiting for her. He makes her a present of a small gold chain to wear with her cross 'as a token of the love of one of your oldest friends'. Fanny tells him of the necklace Mary has given her, and he advises her to wear that for the ball and his own gift for commoner occasions, not wishing to cause any coolness between the two people he loves the most. His words make clear to Fanny that while he loves her as a sister, he means to marry Mary Crawford. But some days later Fanny and Edmund meet again and she finds the situation has altered:

'I come from Dr. Grant's,' said Edmund presently. 'You may guess my errand there, Fanny.' And he looked so conscious, that Fanny could think but of one errand, which turned her too sick for speech. – 'I wished to engage Miss Crawford for the two first dances,' was the explanation that followed, and brought Fanny to life again, enabling her, as she found she was expected to speak, to utter something like an inquiry as to the result.

'Yes,' he answered, 'she is engaged to me; but (with a smile that did not sit easy) she says it is to be the last time that she ever will dance with me. She is not serious, I think, I hope, I am sure she is not serious – but I would rather not hear it. She never has danced with a clergyman, she says, and she never *will*. For my own sake, I could wish there had been no ball just at – I mean not this very week, this very day – tomorrow I leave home.'

Fanny struggled for speech, and said, 'I am very sorry that any thing has occurred to distress you. This ought to be a day of pleasure. My uncle meant it so.'

'Oh! yes, yes, and it will be a day of pleasure. It will all end right. I'm only vexed for a moment. In fact, it is not that I consider the ball as ill-timed; – what does it signify? But, Fanny,' stopping her by taking her hand, and speaking low and seriously, 'you know what all this means. You see how it is; and could tell me, perhaps better than I could tell you, how and why I am vexed. Let me talk to you a little. You are a kind, kind listener. I have been pained by her manner this morning, and cannot get the better of it. I know her disposition to be as sweet and faultless as your own, but the influence of her former companions makes her seem, gives to her conversation, to her professed opinions, sometimes a tinge of wrong. She does not *think* evil, but she speaks it – speaks it in playfulness – and though I know it to be playfulness, it grieves me to the soul.'

'The effect of education,' said Fanny gently.

Edmund could not but agree to it. 'Yes, that uncle and aunt! They have injured the finest mind! – for sometimes, Fanny, I own to you, it does appear more than manner; it appears as if the mind itself was tainted.'

Fanny imagined this to be an appeal to her judgment, and therefore, after a moment's consideration, said, 'If you only want me as a listener, cousin, I will be as useful as I can; but I am not qualified for an adviser. Do not ask advice of *me*. I am not competent.'

'You are right, Fanny, to protest against such an office, but you need not be afraid. It is a subject on which I should never ask advice. It is the sort of subject on which it had better never be asked; and few I imagine do ask it but when they want to be influenced against their conscience. I only want to talk to you.'

'One thing more. Excuse the liberty – but take care *how* you talk to me. Do not tell me any thing now, which hereafter you may be sorry for. The time may come . . .'

The colour rushed into her cheeks as she spoke.

'Dearest Fanny!' cried Edmund, pressing her hand to his lips, with almost as much warmth as if it had been Miss Crawford's, 'you are all considerate thought! – But it is unnecessary here. The time will never come. No such time as you allude to will ever come. I begin to think it most improbable; the chances grow less and less. And even if it should – there will be nothing to be remembered by either you or me, that we need be afraid of, for I can never be ashamed of my own scruples; and if they are removed, it must be by changes that will only raise her character the more by the recollection of the faults she once had. You are the only being upon earth to whom I should say what I have said; but you have always known my opinion of her; you can bear me witness, Fanny, that I have never been blinded. How many a time have we talked over her little errors! You need not fear me. I have almost given up every serious idea of her; but I must be a blockhead indeed if, whatever befell me, I could think of your kindness and sympathy without the sincerest gratitude.'

Fanny decides to wear both the necklace and the chain for the ball. The evening is a great success, despite Crawford's constant attentions and Edmund's melancholy. William and Crawford leave Mansfield Park the following morning for London, followed shortly afterwards by Edmund. Mary begins to regret her coldness towards him and fears he might become attached to one of the daughters of Mr Owen, with whom he is staying in Peterborough. On his return, Crawford astonishes and delights his sister by declaring that he is truly in love with Fanny and means to marry her; he is certain that in her position she will not refuse him. He calls at Mansfield Park and informs Fanny that William has been made a lieutenant: in London, he had introduced William to his uncle, Admiral Crawford, who was so impressed by the young man's qualities that he has now secured his promotion in H.M. sloop *Thrush*. Delighted, Fanny thanks Crawford warmly: but when he begins to speak of his love for her and makes a proposal of marriage, her delight rapidly turns to dismay and she rushes from the room. Though beholden to him for his kindness to William, she cannot believe him to be serious about her, since she knows too well, from his behaviour towards Maria and Julia, what a superficially emotional man he is. He is invited to dine at Mansfield Park and hands Fanny a letter from Mary, who has obviously heard nothing of the refusal, congratulating Fanny on her engagement. She replies to it, disabusing Mary of her belief.

Sir Thomas visits Fanny's apartment, to find that, though there is snow on the ground outside, the girl has no fire in her room, an unnecessary indulgence in Mrs Norris's view. He tells Fanny that Crawford has called on him to ask for her hand, and invites her to go down to see her suitor. Since Sir Thomas is under the firm impression that Fanny has always welcomed Crawford's attentions, he is more than a little angry when she refuses to see him. She cannot bring herself to tell her uncle of Crawford's flirtatious conduct with Maria and Julia, and she is in tears as he leaves her to think the matter over. Crawford departs, promising Sir Thomas not to upset Fanny any further. Sir Thomas returns to Fanny to recommend that she compose herself by walking about the deserted shrubbery. When she goes back to her room she finds that a fire has been lighted in the grate.

Crawford continues to call at Mansfield Park and is expected by everyone to succeed in changing Fanny's mind. When Edmund returns he, too, takes Crawford's part, praising his suitability to an extent that makes Fanny suspect he is motivated by his own love for Mary Crawford, who has been hurt by Fanny's refusal of her brother. It is a great relief to her when the Crawfords depart for London.

William makes another visit to Mansfield and Sir Thomas decides that Fanny should return with him to visit their family in Portsmouth, thinking that her absence from Mansfield Park may make her change her mind about Crawford. After she has spent nine years 'in the abode of wealth and plenty', her father's poor house may reveal to her the value of a good income. Fanny is eager to go: growing up at Mansfield Park has been a largely painful experience, and she looks forward to the love and kindness her own family will show her. William, however, cautions her not to expect too much. When they reach Portsmouth, and he reintroduces her to the family, it becomes plain that his warning had not been unwarranted. The children are noisy and undisciplined; Mrs Price, though kind and well-meaning, has no idea how to keep her house in order; and Mr Price swears and reeks of spirits. Susan, aged fourteen, seems the most sensible of them all. William has to return to his ship and Fanny is left alone in this bedlam:

Such was the home which was to put Mansfield out of her head, and teach her to think of her cousin Edmund with moderated feelings. On the contrary, she could think of nothing but Mansfield, its beloved inmates, its happy ways. Every thing where she now was was in full contrast to it. The elegance, propriety, regularity, harmony – and perhaps, above all, the peace and tranquillity of Mansfield, were brought to her remembrance every hour of the day, by the prevalence of every thing opposite to them *here*.

The living in incessant noise was, to a frame and temper, delicate and nervous like Fanny's, an evil which no super-added elegance or harmony could have entirely atoned for. It was the greatest misery of all. At Mansfield, no sounds of contention, no raised voice, no abrupt bursts, no tread of violence, was ever heard; all proceeded in a regular course of cheerful orderliness; every body had their due importance; every body's feelings were consulted. If tenderness could be ever supposed wanting, good sense and good breeding supplied its place; and as to the little irritations, sometimes introduced by Aunt Norris, they were short, they were trifling, they were as a drop of water to the ocean, compared with the ceaseless tumult of her present abode. Here every body was noisy, every voice was loud (excepting, perhaps, her mother's, which resembled the soft monotony of Lady Bertram's, only worn into fretfulness). Whatever was wanted was halloo'd for, and the servants halloo'd out their excuses from the kitchen. The doors were in constant banging, the stairs were never at rest, nothing was done without a clatter, nobody sat still, and nobody could command attention when they spoke.

In a review of the two houses, as they appeared to her before the end of a week, Fanny was tempted to apply to them Dr. Johnson's celebrated judgment as to matrimony and celibacy, and say, that though Mansfield Park might have some pains, Portsmouth could have no pleasures.

Fanny receives a letter from Mary Crawford telling her that the

Rushworths are now settled in a house in Wimpole Street and that Julia is still with them. To pass the time Fanny instructs Susan, recognizing that the neglected girl could develop into an intelligent and charming young woman. She hears from Lady Bertram that Edmund has at last gone to London, and daily expects a letter informing her of his engagement to Mary Crawford.

Fanny has been in Portsmouth a month when Henry Crawford arrives unexpectedly. He puts himself out to win the esteem of Mr and Mrs Price, praising William and allowing Mr Price to take him on a tour of the dockyard. He tries once again to press Fanny into accepting him, but cannot speak freely, since Susan, 'all eyes and ears', is with her. To her horror, her father insists on Crawford's dining with them, but fortunately he has an engagement, and he leaves Portsmouth next day. A further letter arrives from Mary, who, to Fanny's relief, says nothing of a proposal from Edmund. But her happiness is short-lived when Edmund finally writes himself, declaring that though Mary is not without her faults, 'I cannot give her up ... She is the only woman in the world whom I could ever think of as a wife'.

A few days later a letter comes from Lady Bertram: Tom is dangerously ill with a fever and Edmund has come home to be with him. Further bulletins follow bearing increasingly bad news, but there is no invitation to Fanny to return to Mansfield. She is disgusted when Mary writes a jocular note to the effect that when Tom dies Edmund will become heir to the baronetcy. A new item of news supervenes: Maria Rushworth has run off with Henry Crawford. This is soon followed by word from Edmund that Julia has eloped to Scotland with the Hon John Yates. Sir Thomas is sending Edmund down to Portsmouth to fetch Fanny and Susan to Mansfield Park. He arrives next morning, looking ill and tired, and all except Susan pass a very gloomy journey to Northamptonshire. Mrs Norris blames Fanny for everything that has happened: if she had accepted Crawford, he could not have harmed Maria. Susan is another thorn to stick in her flesh, but Lady Bertram takes to the child and she settles happily into her new home. Fanny is worried by Edmund's continuing melancholy, and it is not until three days after her arrival that she learns its reason:

The opening was alarming. He had seen Miss Crawford. He had been invited to see her. He had received a note from Lady Stornaway to beg him to call; and regarding it as what was meant to be the last, last interview of friendship, and investing her with all the feelings of shame and wretchedness which Crawford's sister ought to have known, he had gone to her in such a state of mind, so softened, so devoted, as made it for a few moments impossible to Fanny's fears that it should be the last. But as he proceeded in his story, these fears were over. She had met him, he said, with a serious – certainly a serious – even an agitated air; but before he had been able to speak one intelligible sentence, she had introduced the subject in a manner which he owned had shocked him. 'I heard you were in town,' said she – 'I wanted to see you. Let us talk over this sad business. What can equal the folly of our two relations?' – 'I could not answer, but I believe my looks spoke. She felt reproved. Sometimes how quick to feel! With a graver look and voice she then added – "I do not mean to defend Harry at your sister's expence." So she began – but how she went on, Fanny, is not fit – is hardly fit to be repeated to you. I cannot recall all her words. I would not dwell upon them if I could. Their substance was great anger at the *folly* of each. She reprobated her brother's folly in being drawn on by a woman whom he had never cared for, to do what must lose him the woman he adored; but still more the folly of – poor Maria, in sacrificing such a situation, plunging into such difficulties, under the idea of being really loved by a man who had long ago made his indifference clear. Guess what I must have felt. To hear the woman whom – No harsher name than folly given! – So voluntarily, so freely, so coolly to canvass it! – No reluctance, no horror, no feminine – shall I say? no modest loathings! – This is what the world does. For where, Fanny, shall we find a woman whom nature had so richly endowed? – Spoilt, spoilt! – '

After a little reflection, he went on with a sort of desperate calmness – 'I will tell you every thing, and then have done for ever. She saw it only as folly, and that folly stamped only by exposure. The want of common discretion, of caution! – his going down to Richmond for the whole time of her being at Twickenham – her putting herself in the power of a servant; – it was the detection in short – Oh! Fanny, it was the detection, not the offence which she reprobated. It was the imprudence which had brought things to extremity, and obliged her brother to give up every dearer plan, in order to fly with her.'

He stopt – 'And what,' said Fanny (believing herself required to speak), 'what could you say?'

'Nothing, nothing to be understood. I was like a man stunned. She went on, began to talk of you; – yes, then she began to talk of you, regretting, as well she might, the loss of such a – There she spoke very rationally. But she always has done justice to you. "He has thrown away," said she, "such a woman as he will never see again. She would have fixed him, she would have made him happy for ever." – My dearest Fanny, I am giving you I hope more pleasure than pain by this retrospect of what might have been – but what never can be now. You do not wish me to be silent? – if you do, give me but a look, a word, and I have done.'

No look or word was given.

'Thank God!' said he. 'We were all disposed to wonder but it seems to have been the merciful appointment of Providence that the heart which knew no guile should not suffer. She spoke of you with high praise and warm affection; yet, even here, there was alloy, a dash of evil – for in the midst of it she could exclaim "Why, would not she have him? It is all her fault. Simple girl! – I shall never forgive her. Had she accepted him as she ought, they might now have been on the point of marriage, and Henry would have been too happy and too busy to want any other object. He would have taken no pains to be on terms with Mrs. Rushworth again. It would have all ended in a regular standing flirtation, in yearly meetings at Sotherton and Everingham." Could you have believed it possible? – But the charm is broken. My eyes are opened.'

Tom recovers and mends his ways. Julia and Yates are married, Rushworth divorces Maria, and Mrs Norris goes to take care of her in a house provided by Sir Thomas in a remote part of the country. Edmund at last realizes Fanny's quiet devotion to him, and all the pain he has caused her, and they are married. Susan takes her place at Mansfield Park:

In *her* usefulness, in Fanny's excellence, in William's continued good conduct, and rising fame, and in the general well-doing and success of the other members of the family, all assisting to advance each other, and doing credit to his countenance and aid, Sir Thomas saw repeated, and for ever repeated reason to rejoice in what he had done for them all, and acknowledge the advantages of early hardship and discipline, and the consciousness of being born to struggle and endure.

EMMA

THE publishing house of John Murray, founded in 1745, was already highly distinguished when encountered by Jane Austen in 1815 (only three years after its move to Albemarle Street, London, where the company still is today). Its eminence did not deter Jane from referring to the then head of the firm, John Murray II, in a letter to Cassandra, as 'a rogue of course, but a civil one'. He had praised the manuscript of *Emma* in terms which had both pleased and amused her, and had given substance to his admiration by offering £450 for the copyright of both it and *Mansfield Park*, whose second edition he was prepared to publish. *Emma* appeared in December 1815, though its title-page bore the date 1816.

The writing of *Emma* had been begun in January 1814; but it has been argued by more than one authority that its origins can be traced back many years to *The Watsons* (*q.v.*). The final version was completed in March 1815, and would have been published a few months earlier had there not been a delay in production, which the publisher blamed on the printer, and the printer on his paper-supplier. This postponement irked Jane particularly, for the novel was to bear a dedication to the Prince Regent, a situation brought about by the serious illness of her brother and adviser, Henry. His physician, Mr Haden, was acquainted with the Rev J. S. Clarke, librarian to the Prince Regent. 'Prinny' was already an admirer of Jane's works – though, of course, her identity was unknown – and when her carefully-guarded secret leaked from Henry to Haden and Clarke to the Prince, unsolicited permission to make the dedication was forthcoming.

Emma was the last of her novels to appear in Jane Austen's lifetime. It was the first to be published in the United States: in 1816 Harper and Brothers, New York, reprinted it from the London edition.

. . . .

Emma Woodhouse, aged almost twenty-one, is the younger daughter of an elderly, hypochondriacal widower; her sister, Isabella, is married to John Knightley and lives in London, sixteen miles from Hartfield, the Woodhouse home lying on the outskirts of the Surrey village of Highbury. A Miss Taylor has lived with the Woodhouse family for many years, first as governess and later as intimate friend of the independent, self-willed Emma. When Miss Taylor marries another widower, Mr Weston, and moves from Hartfield, Emma finds herself 'suffering from intellectual solitude' and wonders who might be suitable as a new confidante. Her father, being firmly opposed to the state of holy matrimony, is greatly upset by Miss Taylor's marriage:

'Poor Miss Taylor! – I wish she were here again. What a pity it is that Mr. Weston ever thought of her!'

'I cannot agree with you, papa; you know I cannot. Mr. Weston is such a good-humoured, pleasant, excellent man, that he thoroughly deserves a good wife; – and you would not have had Miss Taylor live with us for ever and bear all my odd humours, when she might have a house of her own?'

'A house of her own! – but where is the advantage of a house of her own? This is three times as large. – And you have never any odd humours, my dear.'

'How often we shall be going to see them and they coming to see us! – We shall be always meeting! *We* must begin, we must go and pay our wedding-visit very soon.'

'My dear, how am I to get so far? Randalls is such a distance, I could not walk half so far.'

'No, papa, nobody thought of your walking. We must go in the carriage, to be sure.'

'The carriage! But James will not like to put the horses to for such a little way; – and where are the poor horses to be while we are paying our visit?'

Mr Knightley, Isabella's brother-in-law, a bachelor in his mid-thirties, is a resident of Donwell Abbey, near Highbury, and a frequent visitor to Hartfield. Emma tells him how she arranged the Weston match. Though never herself intending to marry, she finds assisting others to do so 'the greatest amusement in the world', but her father complains of such unnatural meddling and Emma promises that when she has disposed of Mr Elton, High-bury's young clergyman, she will desist from such practices.

Mr Weston's first wife had been a Miss Churchill, who died three years after the marriage leaving a small son, Frank. Her brother and his wife, a rich but childless couple, had adopted the boy, and, when he came of age, gave him both their name and inheritance. Mr Weston has seen Frank regularly over the years and boasts about his fine young son to such an extent that the people of Highbury eagerly await the young man's first visit.

Among the frequent callers at Hartfield are a neighbour, Mrs Bates, her middle-aged daughter, and Mrs Goddard, mistress of a local boarding-school. One morning Mrs Goddard asks Emma if she might bring over a seventeen-year-old boarder, Harriet Smith. Emma agrees readily. She has been interested for some time in this beautiful girl, the natural daughter of a 'somebody' who had placed her at Mrs Goddard's school several years before. Harriet soon becomes a great favourite with Emma, who decides to make her her protegée; but she is alarmed to find that Harriet admires a young farmer, Robert Martin, with whose family she had recently spent two months. Emma sets out to prevent Harriet marrying this person of no consequence, whom they chance to meet while out walking. Emma is pleased to note that he looks 'as if he did not know what manner was', and impresses this upon Harriet:

'To be sure,' said Harriet, in a mortified voice, 'he – is not so genteel as real gentlemen.'

'I think, Harriet, since your acquaintance with us, you have been repeatedly in the company of some such very real gentlemen, that you must yourself be struck with the difference in Mr. Martin. At Hartfield you have had very good specimens of well-educated, well-bred men. I should be surprized if, after seeing them, you could be in company with Mr. Martin again without perceiving him to be a very inferior creature – and rather wondering at yourself for having ever thought him at all agreeable before. Do not you begin to feel that now? Were not you struck? I am sure you must have been struck by his awkward look and abrupt manner – and the uncouthness of a voice which I heard to be wholly unmodulated as I stood here.'

'Certainly, he is not like Mr. Knightley. He has not such a fine air and way of walking as Mr. Knightley. I see the difference plain enough. But Mr. Knightley is so very fine a man!'

'Mr. Knightley's air is so remarkably good, that it is not fair to compare Mr. Martin with *him*. You might not see one in a hundred with *gentleman* so plainly written as in Mr. Knightley. But he is not the only gentleman you have been lately used to. What say you to Mr. Weston and Mr. Elton? Compare Mr. Martin with either of *them*. Compare their manner of carrying themselves, of walking, of speaking, of being silent. You must see the difference.'

'Oh, yes – there is a great difference. But Mr. Weston is almost an old man. Mr. Weston must be between forty and fifty.'

'Which makes his good manners the more valuable. The older a person grows, Harriet, the more important it is that their manners should not be bad – the more glaring and disgusting any loudness, or coarseness, or awkwardness becomes. What is passable in youth is detestable in later age. Mr. Martin is now awkward and abrupt; what will he be at Mr. Weston's time of life?'

'There is no saying, indeed,' replied Harriet, rather solemnly.

'But there may be pretty good guessing. He will be a completely gross, vulgar farmer – totally inattentive to appearances, and thinking of nothing but profit and loss.'

'Will he, indeed, that will be very bad.'

Emma decides that Harriet will suit Mr Elton, the clergyman, a gentleman with sufficient income and a good home to offer, and a family not so high that objection to Harriet's doubtful birth might be raised. Mr Knightley does not approve of the friendship between Emma and Harriet, and remarks to Mrs Weston that 'they will neither to them do the other any good' since Emma is spoiled and Harriet naïve. Mr Elton, according to plan, duly admires Harriet and requests Emma to do a portrait of her. He attends during the sittings and takes the finished picture to London to choose a frame.

Harriet receives a letter from Robert Martin proposing

marriage, and asks Emma to advise her. By subtle tactics, Emma directs her friend to decline the offer. Mr Knightley calls at Hartfield and tells Emma that Robert Martin, of whom he approves highly, has visited him to ask whether he should offer marriage to Harriet Smith, and has been advised to do so unhesitatingly. Knightley is astonished to be told of Harriet's refusal, and is vexed with Emma for having interfered. He tells her that if she continues in leading Harriet to believe she will 'marry greatly', the girl will find herself a boarder at Mrs Goddard's for the rest of her life; besides, he thinks it highly unlikely that Mr Elton will marry Harriet. Emma respects his views, but the unease they leave her in disappears when Elton returns from London with the framed portrait of Harriet, and presents the girl with a 'charade':

To Miss –

CHARADE

My first displays the wealth and pomp of kings,
Lords of the earth! their luxury and ease.
Another view of man, my second brings,
Behold him there, the monarch of the seas!

But ah! united, what reverse we have!
Man's boasted power and freedom, all are flown:
Lord of the earth and sea, he bends a slave,
And woman, lovely woman, reigns alone.

Thy ready wit the word will soon supply,
May its approval beam in that soft eye!

She cast her eye over it, pondered, caught the meaning, read it through again to be quite certain, and quite mistress of the lines, and then passing it to Harriet, sat happily smiling, and saying to herself, while Harriet was puzzling over the paper in all the confusion of hope and dulness, 'Very well, Mr. Elton, very well, indeed. I have read worse charades. *Courtship* – a very good hint. I give you credit for it. This is

feeling your way. This is saying very plainly – 'Pray, Miss Smith, give
my leave to pay me addresses to you. Approve my charade and my
intentions in the same glance.'

Harriet is delighted, and copies it in her riddle-book. She goes
with her friend to visit a poor sick family in the village, and
learns Emma's reason for not marrying:

'I have none of the usual inducements of women to marry. Were I to
fall in love, indeed, it would be a different thing! but I never have been
in love; it is not my way, or my nature; and I do not think I ever shall.
And, without love, I am sure I should be a fool to change such a situation
as mine. Fortune I do not want; employment I do not want; consequence
I do not want. I believe few married women are half as much mistress of
their husband's house as I am of Hartfield; and never, never could I
expect to be so truly beloved and important, so always first and always
right in any man's eyes as I am in my father's.'

'But then, to be an old maid at last, like Miss Bates!'

'That is as formidable an image as you could present, Harriet; and if I
thought I should ever be like Miss Bates! so silly – so satisfied – so smiling – so prosing – so undistinguishing and unfastidious – and so apt to
tell every thing relative to every body about me, I would marry to-
morrow. But between *us*, I am convinced there never can be any like-
ness, except in being unmarried.'

'But still, you will be an old maid! and that's so dreadful!'

'Never mind, Harriet, I shall not be a poor old maid; and it is poverty
only which makes celibacy contemptible to a generous public! A single
woman, with a very narrow income, must be a ridiculous, disagreeable,
old maid! the proper sport of boys and girls; but a single woman, of
good fortune, is always respectable, and may be as sensible and pleasant
as anybody else. And the distinction is not quite so much against the
candour and common sense of the world as appears at first; for a very
narrow income has a tendency to contract the mind, and sour the
temper. Those who can barely live, and who live perforce in a very small,
and generally very inferior, society, may well be illiberal and cross.
This does not apply, however, to Miss Bates; she is only too good natured
and too silly to suit me; but, in general, she is very much to the taste of
everybody, though single and though poor. Poverty certainly has not
contracted her mind: I really believe, if she had only a shilling in the

world, she would be very likely to give away sixpence of it; and nobody is afraid of her: that is a great charm.'

'Dear me! but what shall you do? how shall you employ yourself when you grow old?'

'If I know myself, Harriet, mine is an active, busy mind, with a great many independent resources; and I do not perceive why I should be more in want of employment at forty or fifty than one-and-twenty. Woman's usual occupations of eye and hand and mind will be as open to me then, as they are now, or with no important variation. If I draw less, I shall read more; if I give up music, I shall take to carpet-work. And as for objects of interest, objects for the affections, which is in truth the great point of inferiority, the want of which is really the great evil to be avoided in *not* marrying, I shall be very well off, with all the children of a sister I love so much to care about. There will be enough of them, in all probability, to supply every sort of sensation that declining life can need. There will be enough for every hope and every fear; and though my attachment to none can equal that of a parent, it suits my ideas of comfort better than what is warmer and blinder.'

Harriet asks if Emma knows Miss Bates's niece, Jane Fairfax, and receives the short reply that Emma hears so much of Miss Fairfax that she is 'sick of the very name'. But Emma shows a more compassionate side to her nature in the presence of the humble family they have come to visit. On the way back they meet Mr Elton. Emma deliberately breaks her boot-lace, so that they must call at the vicarage for some string, and leaves Harriet alone in a room with Elton while she is repairing the damage.

The lovers were standing together at one of the windows. It had a most favourable aspect; and, for half a minute, Emma felt the glory of having schemed successfully. But it would not do; he had not come to the point. He had been most agreeable, most delightful; he had told Harriet that he had seen them go by, and had purposely followed them; other little gallantries and allusions had been dropt, but nothing serious.

'Cautious, very cautious,' thought Emma; 'he advances inch by inch, and will hazard nothing till he believes himself secure.'

Still, however, though every thing had not been accomplished by her ingenious device, she could not but flatter herself that it had been the occasion of much present enjoyment to both, and must be leading them forward to the great event.

John and Isabella Knightley and their children arrive to spend Christmas at Hartfield. The party is invited to dine at Randalls, the Westons' home. Harriet is included in the invitation, but develops a sore throat, and, since Emma does not wish Mr Elton to be at the dinner when he could be visiting Harriet, she persuades him that he, too, has caught a bad throat. Her scheme is foiled, however, when John Knightley offers the clergyman a seat in his carriage. John believes Mr Elton to be in love with Emma, and she is doubly amazed to find that, though news of Harriet is not good, Mr Elton in high spirits when they pick him up on their way to Randalls. At dinner he sits close to her, and she begins to suspect that John's observation might be correct.

Despite Emma's resolution never to marry, she is more than a little interested in Mr Weston's son, Frank Weston Churchill, and is pleased to learn that he intends visiting Highbury soon, for the first time. She knows that he is twenty-three and has been raised on his uncle's estate in Yorkshire, and, though she has never seen him, she has heard such pleasing reports of him that she feels he might well prove to her taste. Elton, however, is becoming more and more attentive as the evening passes, begging Emma not to visit Harriet in case she should catch her friend's 'disorder'. To Emma's dismay, she finds that she and Elton have to share a carriage alone on the drive back. She is further dismayed by his behaviour:

To restrain him as much as might be, by her own manners, she was immediately preparing to speak with exquisite calmness and gravity of the weather and the night; but scarcely had she begun, scarcely had they passed the sweep-gate and joined the other carriage, than she found her subject cut up – her hand seized – her attention demanded, and Mr. Elton actually making violent love to her: availing himself of the precious opportunity, declaring sentiments which must be already well known, hoping – fearing – adoring – ready to die if she refused him; but flattering himself that his ardent attachment and unequalled love and unexampled passion could not fail of having some effect, and in short, very much resolved on being seriously accepted as soon as possible. It really was so. Without scruple – without apology – without much apparent diffidence, Mr. Elton, the lover of Harriet, was professing himself *her* lover. She tried to stop him; but vainly; he would go on, and say it all. Angry as she was, the thought of the moment made her resolve to restrain herself when she did speak. She felt that half this folly must be drunkenness, and therefore could hope that it might belong only to the passing hour. Accordingly, with a mixture of the serious and the playful, which she hoped would best suit his half and half state, she replied,

'I am much astonished, Mr. Elton. This to *me!* you forget yourself – you take me for my friend – any message to Miss Smith I shall be happy to deliver; but no more of this to *me*, if you please.'

'Miss Smith! – message to Miss Smith! What could she possibly mean?' – And he repeated her words with such assurance of accent, such boastful pretence of amazement, that she could not help replying with quickness,

'Mr. Elton, this is the most extraordinary conduct! and I can account for it only in one way; you are not yourself, or you could not speak either to me, or of Harriet, in such a manner. Command yourself enough to say no more, and I will endeavour to forget it.'

But Mr. Elton had only drunk wine enough to elevate his spirits, not at all to confuse his intellects. Her perfectly knew his own meaning; and having warmly protested against her suspicion as most injurious, and slightly touched upon his respect for Miss Smith as her friend, – but acknowledging his wonder that Miss Smith should be mentioned at all, – he resumed the subject of his own passion, and was very urgent for a favourable answer.

As she thought less of his inebriety, she thought more of his inconstancy and presumption, and with fewer struggles for politeness, replied,

'It is impossible for me to doubt any longer. You have made yourself too clear. Mr. Elton, my astonishment is much beyond any thing I can express. After such behaviour, as I have witnessed during the last month, to Miss Smith – such attentions as I have been in the daily habit of observing – to be addressing me in this manner – this is an unsteadiness of character, indeed, which I had not supposed possible. Believe me, sir, I am far, very far, from gratified in being the object of such professions.'

'Good heaven!' cried Mr. Elton, 'what can be the meaning of this? – Miss Smith! – I never thought of Miss Smith in the whole course of my existence – never paid her any attentions, but as your friend; never cared whether she were dead or alive, but as your friend. If she has fancied otherwise, her own wishes have misled her, and I am very sorry – extremely sorry – But, Miss Smith, indeed! – Oh! Miss Woodhouse! who can think of Miss Smith, when Miss Woodhouse is near? No, upon my honour, there is no unsteadiness of character. I have thought only of you. I protest against having paid the smallest attention to any one else. Everything that I have said or done, for many weeks past, has been with the sole view of marking my adoration of yourself. You cannot really seriously doubt it. No' – (in an accent meant to be insinuating) – I am sure you have seen and understood me.'

It would be impossible to say what Emma felt on hearing this – which of all her unpleasant sensations was uppermost. She was too completely overpowered to be immediately able to reply; and two moments of silence being ample encouragement for Mr. Elton's sanguine state of mind, he tried to take her hand again, as he joyously exclaimed –

'Charming Miss Woodhouse! allow me to interpret this interesting silence. It confesses that you have long understood me.'

'No, sir,' cried Emma, 'it confesses no such thing. So far from having long understood you, I have been in a most complete error with respect to your views, till this moment. As to myself, I am very sorry that you should have been giving way to any feelings – Nothing could be farther from my wishes – your attachment to my friend Harriet – your pursuit of her, (pursuit, it appeared) gave me great pleasure, and I have been very earnestly wishing you success; but had I supposed that she were not your attraction to Hartfield, I should certainly have thought you judged ill in making your visits so frequent. Am I to believe that you have never sought to recommend yourself particularly to Miss Smith? – that you have never thought seriously of her?'

'Never, madam,' cried he, affronted in his turn; 'never, I assure you. *I* think seriously of Miss Smith! Miss Smith is a very good sort of girl; and I should be happy to see her respectably settled. I wish her extremely well; and, no doubt, there are men who might not object to – Every body has their level; but as for myself, I am not, I think, quite so much at a loss. I need not so totally despair of an equal alliance as to be addressing myself to Miss Smith! – No, madam, my visits to Hartfield have been for yourself only; and the encouragement I received' –

'Encouragement! I give you encouragement! – sir, you have been entirely mistaken in supposing it. I have seen you only as the admirer of my friend. In no other light could you have been more to me than a common acquaintance. I am exceedingly sorry; but it is well that the mistake ends where it does. Had the same behaviour continued, Miss Smith might have been led into a misconception of your views; not being aware, probably, any more than myself, of the very great inequality which you are so sensible of. But, as it is, the disappointment is single, and I trust, will not be lasting. I have no thoughts of matrimony at present.'

Angered at this rebuff, Elton is silent for the rest of the drive. At Hartfield that night, Emma sits miserably in her room, wishing she had heeded Knightley's warning. She feels most sorry for Harriet, and wonders whom else she might marry. The Knightleys leave Highbury after Christmas, and Mr Elton writes to Mr Woodhouse to inform him that he is leaving immediately to spend a few weeks in Bath. Emma is pleased to be rid of his embarrassing presence, especially since she has just informed Harriet of what has taken place and must divert the unhappy girl's attention: Elton's absence makes this easier. Frank Churchill postpones his visit to Highbury, and a discussion about him leads to a further disagreement between Emma and Mr Knightley:

'My idea of him is, that he can adapt his conversation to the taste of every body, and has the power as well as the wish of being universally agreeable. To you, he will talk of farming; to me, of drawing or music; and so on to every body, having that general information on all subjects which will enable him to follow the lead, or take the lead, just as propriety may require, and to speak extremely well on each; that is my idea of him.'

'And mine,' said Mr. Knightley warmly, 'is, that if he turn out any thing like it, he will be the most insufferable fellow breathing! What! at three-and-twenty to be the king of his company – the great man – the practised politician, who is to read every body's character, and make every body's talents conduce to the display of his own superiority; to be dispensing his flatteries around, that he may make all appear like fools compared with himself! My dear Emma, your own good sense could not endure such a puppy when it came to the point.'

'I will say no more about him,' cried Emma, 'you turn every thing to evil. We are both prejudiced; you against, I for him; and we have no chance of agreeing till he is really here.'

'Prejudiced! I am not prejudiced.'

Emma and Harriet call on deaf old Mrs Bates and her daughter who, as usual, talk of nothing but Jane Fairfax. Jane is an orphan and has been brought up in the family of Colonel Campbell, a friend of her deceased father. The Campbells are going to their country seat in Ireland and Jane is coming to stay in Highbury during their absence, to recover from a severe cold. Emma is displeased by the prospect of three months in the company of this beautiful and accomplished young woman; but the compassionate side of her nature gets the better of jealousy once Jane arrives, and she decides to take the ailing orphaned girl under her wing. But Jane soon proves to be aloof and reserved, and angers Emma by her reticence about a recent meeting with Frank Churchill in Weymouth. Miss Bates and Jane call one day at Hartfield to thank Mr Weston for the gift of a leg of pork. They also have news of Mr Elton's coming marriage to a Miss Hawkins, whom he has met in Bath. After their departure, Harriet Smith arrives with news of her own: she has met Robert Martin and his sister Elizabeth and has been treated very courteously by them. Emma is relieved that this meeting should have taken Harriet's mind off Elton's marriage, but she cautions her friend about renewing her association with Robert Martin.

The long-awaited day comes at last: Frank Churchill arrives in the district and promptly calls at Hartfield with his father. Emma finds him quite as handsome and interesting as she had expected. His conversation is equally pleasing, and Mr Weston observes the two young people together with obvious interest. Emma is a little put out to learn that Frank intends calling on Jane Fairfax and her relatives, and when Mrs Weston and Emma accompany him on a conducted tour of Highbury next day, which takes them past the Bates's cottage, Emma inquires if he has called on Jane. He replies that he has, and that he had found her looking very ill. He had met Jane frequently while in Weymouth, and adds how well she plays the piano.

Emma returns from the walk confirmed in her good opinion of Frank Churchill; but her admiration for his qualities is soon shaken when she hears that he has gone all the way to London, sixteen miles, simply to have his hair cut. She considers this the act of a coxcomb, but is mollified to learn from Mr Weston how much his son admires her. Mr Knightley is the only resident of the village who does not think highly of Frank, dismissing him as a 'trifling, silly fellow'.

Another Highbury family, the Coles, have gradually worked their way up the social ladder. Emma regards them as upstarts, so she is indignant to hear that they intend inviting everyone to a *soirée*. She decides in advance to decline their invitation, and is subsequently vexed when none arrives. Such is her chagrin that, when a belated invitation does come, she accepts it readily. Attending the *soirée*, she overhears Mrs Cole relating how a large pianoforté has mysteriously arrived at the Bates's cottage for Jane Fairfax's use. No one seems to know who has sent it, but Jane believes it has come as a gift from Colonel Campbell. Frank Churchill is greatly amused at the idea of so large an instrument in so small a dwelling. He considers that Colonel Campbell's newly-married daughter and son-in-law, Mr and Mrs Dixon, may be responsible for the present. Mrs Dixon had been Jane Fairfax's friend, and it is Frank's belief that Mr Dixon, having committed himself to the one, had then fallen in love with the other: after all, he and Jane Fairfax were known to be fond of music, while his wife was not; and he had once saved Jane from being dashed overboard during a water-party.

Frank pays Emma noticeable attention all evening, and delights her by his charm towards Harriet and his unflattering remarks about Jane Fairfax's hairstyle. Emma hears from Mrs Weston that Mr Knightley has offered the use of his carriage to Miss Bates and Jane, and she suspects a match in the offing. Emma is appalled at the idea; Knightley must never marry; his home, Donwell Abbey, must pass to his nephew Henry, the six-year-old son of John and Isabella. But Mrs Weston persists in her belief:

'Imprudent, if you please – but not mad. Excepting inequality of fortune, and perhaps a little disparity of age, I can see nothing unsuitable.'

'But Mr. Knightley does not want to marry. I am sure he has not the least idea of it. Do not put it into his head. Why should he marry? – He is as happy as possible by himself with his farm, and his sheep, and his library, and all the parish to manage; and he is extremely fond of his brother's children. He has no occasion to marry, either to fill up his time or his heart.'

'My dear Emma, as long as he thinks so, it is so; but if he really loves Jane Fairfax – '

'Nonsense! He does not care about Jane Fairfax. In the way of love, I am sure he does not. He would do any good to her, or her family; but – '

'Well,' said Mrs. Weston, laughing, 'perhaps the greatest good he could do them would be to give Jane such a respectable home.'

When Emma sings for the company later in the evening, Frank joins her in a duet and later partners Jane Fairfax; the latter's musical superiority is very evident. After Emma has spoken to Knightley about the mysterious pianoforté, she is confident that he had nothing to do with the gift, but is surprised when, a little later, he becomes very angry with Frank for urging Jane to sing too much.

Harriet calls at Hartfield next day and tells Emma that Robert Martin is thought likely to marry one of the Cox girls, members of another Highbury family. While shopping, Emma is persuaded by Mrs Weston to go with her to the Bates's cottage to hear Jane play. They find Frank Churchill wedging a leg of the pianoforté to steady it. He tries once more to discover from Jane who sent her the instrument, but she can only conjecture that it was Colonel Campbell, especially as the pianoforté was accompanied by a set of Irish melodies. While Jane is playing, Knightley arrives, but, on finding Frank present, departs immediately.

Frank proposes to hold a ball at the Crown Inn. This causes great excitement in Highbury, with only Knightley remaining indifferent. But a letter arrives from Frank's uncle urging him to return immediately to Yorkshire, and the evening has to be postponed. Frank takes his leave of Emma:

'Of all horrid things, leave-taking is the worst.'

'But you will come again,' said Emma. 'This will not be your only visit to Randalls.'

'Ah! – (shaking his head) – the uncertainty of when I may be able to return! – I shall try for it with a zeal! – It will be the object of all my thoughts and cares! – and if my uncle and aunt go to town this spring – but I am afraid – they did not stir last spring – I am afraid it is a custom gone for ever.'

'Our poor ball must be quite given up.'

'Ah! that ball! – why did we wait for any thing? why not seize the pleasure at once? – How often is happiness destroyed by preparation, foolish preparation! – You told us it would be so – Oh! Miss Woodhouse, why are you always so right?'

'Indeed, I am very sorry to be right in this instance. I would much rather have been merry than wise.'

'If I can come again, we are still to have our ball. My father depends on it. Do not forget your engagement.'

Emma looked graciously.

'Such a fortnight as it has been!' he continued; 'every day more precious and more delightful than the day before! – every day making me less fit to bear any other place. Happy those, who can remain at Highbury!'

'As you do us such ample justice now,' said Emma, laughing, 'I will venture to ask, whether you did not come a little doubtingly at first? Do not we rather surpass your expectations? I am sure we do. I am sure you did not much expect to like us. You would not have been so long in coming if you had had a pleasant idea of Highbury.'

He laughed rather consciously; and though denying the sentiment, Emma was convinced that it had been so.

'And you must be off this very morning?'

'Yes; my father is to join me here: we shall walk back together, and I must be off immediately. I am almost afraid that every moment will bring him.'

'Not five minutes to spare even for your friends Miss Fairfax and Miss Bates? How unlucky! Miss Bates's powerful, argumentative mind might have strengthened yours.'

'Yes – I *have* called there; passing the door, I thought it better. It was a right thing to do. I went in for three minutes, and was detained by Miss Bates's being absent. She was out; and I felt it impossible not to wait till she came in. She is a woman that one may, that one *must* laugh at; but that one would not wish to slight. It was better to pay my visit, then' –

He hesitated, got up, walked to a window.

'In short,' said he, 'perhaps, Miss Woodhouse – I think you can hardly be quite without suspicion' –

He looked at her, as if wanting to read her thoughts. She hardly knew what to say. It seemed like the forerunner of something absolutely serious, which she did not wish. Forcing herself to speak, therefore, in the hope of putting it by, she calmly said,

'You are quite in the right; it was most natural to pay your visit, then' –

He was silent. She believed he was looking at her; probably reflecting on what she had said, and trying to understand the manner. She heard him sigh. It was natural for him to feel that he had *cause* to sigh. He could not believe her to be encouraging him. A few awkward moments passed, and he sat down again; and in a more determined manner said,

'It was something to feel that all the rest of my time might be given to Hartfield. My regard for Hartfield is most warm' –

He stopt again, rose again, and seemed quite embarrassed. He was more in love with her than Emma had supposed; and who can say how it might have ended, if his father had not made his appearance? Mr. Woodhouse soon followed; and the necessity of exertion made him composed.

A very few minutes more, however, completed the present trial. Mr. Weston, always alert when business was to be done, and as incapable of procrastinating any evil that was inevitable, as of foreseeing any that was doubtful, said, 'It was time to go;' and the young man, though he might and did sigh, could not but agree, and rise to take leave.

'I shall hear about you all,' said he; 'that is my chief consolation. I shall hear of every thing that is going on among you. I have engaged Mrs. Weston to correspond with me. She has been so kind as to promise it. Oh, the blessing of a female correspondent, when one is really interested in the absent! – she will tell me everything. In her letters I shall be at dear Highbury again.'. .

A very friendly shake of the hand, a very earnest 'Good bye,' closed the speech, and the door had soon shut out Frank Churchill.

By now Emma is confident that Frank loves her a great deal,

and has to admit to herself that she is not entirely indifferent towards him. Since such affection is against her inclination, however, she decides to divert his attentions towards Harriet. Mr Elton returns to Highbury with his bride, and Emma and Harriet are forced to pay the customary wedding-visit to the vicarage. The visit is returned, and Emma is extremely indignant when the voluble Mrs Elton compares Hartfield unfavourably with her sister's home, Maple Grove. She further offends Emma by a patronizing offer to introduce her into Bath society. Emma makes her dislike of this 'insufferable woman' plain, and gradually the ill-feeling is returned and Mrs Elton becomes cold and distant towards Emma, whilst taking a great fancy to Jane Fairfax. Jane is invited frequently to the vicarage and is to be seen out with the Eltons every day. Emma is amazed that the quiet, refined girl can bear the constant company of so superficial a woman. Jane receives an invitation from the Campbells to join them in Ireland, but she declines. Knightley assures Emma that she is not remaining in Highbury because of him; he has no intention of marrying Jane since 'she has not the open temper which a man would wish for in a wife'.

Annoyed by Mrs Elton's unceasing criticism of the rustic hospitality of Highbury, Emma decides to give a dinner for the Eltons at Hartfield. John Knightley arrives to bring his two older sons for a visit, and shows great concern for Jane Fairfax's health: she has been out to post letters in the rain. Mr Weston shows Emma a letter from Frank saying he is returning to Highbury with his aunt, who is in poor health and needs a change of air. On his arrival he calls immediately at Hartfield, but for the next ten days is required to stay at his aunt's side at Randalls. However, fresh plans to hold a ball at the Crown Inn are made, and the long-awaited evening arrives at last, with Emma wondering whether Frank will show further proof of his love for her. Her immediate regret, though, is that Mr Knightley is not amongst the dancers:

There he was, among the standers-by, where he ought not to be; he ought to be dancing, – not classing himself with the husbands, and fathers, and whist-players, who were pretending to feel an interest in the dance till their rubbers were made up, – so young as he looked! – He could not have appeared to greater advantage perhaps any where, than where he had placed himself. His tall, firm, upright figure, among the bulky forms and stooping shoulders of the elderly men, was such as Emma felt must draw every body's eyes; and, excepting her own partner, there was not one among the whole row of young men who could be compared with him. – He moved a few steps nearer, and those few steps were enough to prove in how gentlemanlike a manner, with what natural grace, he must have danced, would he but take the trouble. – Whenever she caught his eye, she forced him to smile; but in general he was looking grave. She wished he could love a ball-room better, and could like Frank Churchill better.

He does dance, however; when Elton displays great rudeness by refusing to dance with Harriet, Knightley rescues her and leads her out on to the floor. Later he offers an affectionate invitation to Emma to dance with him.

Next morning Emma strolls about the Hartfield lawns congratulating herself on the outcome of the evening: Harriet's infatuation for Elton is cured, Frank Churchill is not *too* much in love with her, and Knightley is being sensible. Her reveries are interrupted, however, by the unexpected arrival of Frank, with Harriet leaning on his arm, obviously in a state of shock. She and Miss Bickerton, a fellow boarder at Mrs Goddard's, while taking a walk, have been importuned for money by some gipsies. Miss Bickerton had made her escape up a bank and over a hedge, but Harriet had been unable to follow. Fortunately, Frank had appeared providentially on the scene and had driven the gipsies away.

After such a romantic rescue, Emma is convinced that Frank and Harriet are a perfect match. Harriet conducts a touching little ritual when she destroys the contents of a Tunbridge Ware box marked 'Most Precious Treasures', containing a piece of sticking plaster once used to bind Elton's finger, and a pencil stub of his. After burning these relics she declares she will emulate Emma and never marry, but Emma persuades her of Frank Churchill's interest.

A continuous round of social occasions begins in June. Knightley's distrust of Frank deepens and he begins to see a certain amount of double-dealing behind the gay superficiality: Frank, he is certain, is playing some game with Jane Fairfax. He questions Emma about the degree of intimacy between the pair and is assured that there is no attachment whatsoever.

Knightley invites a party to Donwell Abbey, famed for its strawberries. It is a very hot day and the guests sit in the gardens eating fruit.

Strawberries, and only strawberries, could now be thought or spoken of. – 'The best fruit in England – every body's favourite – always wholesome. – These the finest beds and finest sorts. – Delightful to gather for one's self – the only way of really enjoying them. – Morning decidedly the best time – never tired – every sort good – hautboy infinitely superior – no comparison – the others hardly eatable – hautboys very scarce – Chili preferred – white wood finest flavour of all – price of strawberries in London – abundance about Bristol – Maple Grove – cultivation – beds when to be renewed – gardeners thinking exactly different – no general rule – gardeners never to be put out of their way – delicious fruit – only too rich to be eaten much of – inferior to cherries – currants more refreshing – only objections to gathering strawberries the stooping – glaring sun – tired to death – could bear it no longer – must go and sit in the shade.'

Such, for half an hour, was the conversation.

Mrs Elton has been seeking a suitable position for Jane and has heard that a situation is vacant in the home of a friend of her sister Mrs Suckling at Maple Grove. How Jane can tolerate such patronizing behaviour amazes Emma. Frank Churchill has not yet arrived, which gives rise to some speculation. Jane leaves the party early, begging Emma to make excuses for her, and walks home alone. She has been not gone a quarter of an hour when Frank arrives in a temper. One of his aunt's bad turns has delayed him, and he is complaining of having had to make his way to Knightley's in such heat. He speaks of removing his aunt to 'Swisserland'.

A picnic has been planned for the following day on Box Hill.

The weather is fine again and the whole party goes along. After a somewhat dull beginning which makes Emma wish she had not come, Frank begins to pay her excessive attention, drawing everyone's notice to his gaiety:

'I say nothing of which I am ashamed,' replied he, with lively impudence. 'I saw you first in February. Let every body on the Hill hear me if they can. Let my accent swell to Mickleham on one side, and Dorking on the other. I saw you first in February.' And then whispering – 'Our companions are excessively stupid. What shall we do to rouse them? Any nonsense will serve. They *shall* talk. Ladies and gentlemen, I am ordered by Miss Woodhouse (who, wherever she is, presides) to say, that she desires to know what you are all thinking of.'

Some laughed, and answered good-humouredly. Miss Bates said a great deal; Mrs. Elton swelled at the idea of Miss Woodhouse's presiding; Mr. Knightley's answer was the most distinct.

'Is Miss Woodhouse sure that she would like to hear what we are all thinking of?'

'Oh! no, no' – cried Emma, laughing as carelessly as she could. 'Upon no account in the world. It is the very last thing I would stand the brunt of just now. Let me hear any thing rather than what you are all thinking of. I will not say quite all. There are one or two, perhaps, (glancing at Mr. Weston and Harriet) 'whose thoughts I might not be afraid of knowing.'

'It is a sort of thing,' cried Mrs. Elton emphatically, 'which *I* should not have thought myself privileged to inquire into. Though, perhaps, as the *Chaperon* of the party – *I* never was in any circle – exploring parties – young ladies – married women – '

Her mutterings were chiefly to her husband; and he murmured, in reply,

'Very true, my love, very true. Exactly so, indeed – quite unheard of – but some ladies say any thing. Better pass it off as a joke. Every body knows what is due to *you*.'

'It will not do,' whispered Frank to Emma, 'they are most of them affronted. I will attack them with more address. Ladies and gentlemen – I am ordered by Miss Woodhouse to say, that she waives her right of knowing exactly what you may all be thinking of, and only requires something very entertaining from each of you, in a general way. Here are seven of you, besides myself (who, she is pleased to say, am very entertaining already) and she only demands from each of you, either one thing very clever, be it prose or verse, original or repeated – or two things moderately clever – or three things very dully indeed, – and she engages to laugh heartily at them all.'

'Oh! very well,' exclaimed Miss Bates, 'then I need not be uneasy. "Three things very dully indeed." That will just do for me, you know. I shall be sure to say three dull things as soon as ever I open my mouth, shan't I?' – (looking round with the most good-humoured dependence on every body's assent) – 'Do not you all think I shall?'

Emma could not resist.

'Ah! ma'am, but there may be a difficulty. Pardon me – but you will be limited as to number – only three at once.'

Miss Bates, deceived by the mock ceremony of her manner, did not immediately catch her meaning; but, when it burst on her, it could not anger, though a slight blush showed that it could pain her.

'Ah! – well – to be sure. Yes. I see what she means (turning to Mr. Knightley) 'and I will try to hold my tongue. I must make myself very disagreeable, or she would not have said such a thing to an old friend.'

As the party is dispersing, Knightley takes Emma sternly to task for being so rude to Miss Bates, whose position and prospects are so much below her own. She is so mortified by his low opinion of her behaviour that she determines to apologize to her victim next day, but the latter seems to have forgotten the incident and is as garrulous as ever in her concern over a headache Jane Fairfax has developed. It seems that Jane has decided to accept the position Mrs Elton has found for her at Maple Grove: she is leaving Highbury within a fortnight. On arriving back at Hartfield Emma finds Harriet and Knightley waiting. The latter, who is about to leave for London to spend a few days with John and Isabella, is impressed that Emma has humbled herself to apologize to Miss Bates, and, as he goes, takes her hand and seems for a moment about to kiss it.

The following day news is brought from Randalls that Frank's aunt, Mrs Churchill, has died. This means that there need be no opposition to his marriage with Harriet. Jane Fairfax continues to suffer from severe headaches; Emma grows concerned and makes up potions for her. Ten days after Mrs Churchill's death,

Mrs Weston takes Emma to Randalls. Something of great importance is obviously about to be revealed:

'Have you indeed no idea?' said Mrs. Weston in a trembling voice.
'Cannot you, my dear Emma – cannot you form a guess as to what you
are to hear?'

'So far as that it relates to Mr. Frank Churchill, I do guess.'

'You are right. It does relate to him, and I will tell you directly,'
(resuming her work, and seeming resolved against looking up). 'He has
been here, this very morning, on a most extraordinary errand. It is
impossible to express our surprise. He came to speak to his father on a
subject, – to announce an attachment –'

She stopped to breathe. Emma thought first of herself, and then of
Harriet.

'More than an attachment, indeed,' resumed Mrs. Wetson; 'an engagement – a positive engagement. What will you say, Emma – what will
anybody say, when it is known that Frank Churchill and Miss Fairfax are
engaged; – nay, that they have been long engaged!'

Emma even jumped with surprise; – and, horror-struck, exclaimed,

'Jane Fairfax! – Good God! You are not serious? You do not mean it?'

'You may well be amazed,' returned Mrs. Weston, still averting her
eyes, and talking on with eagerness, that Emma might have time to
recover – 'you may well be amazed. But it is even so. There has been a
solemn engagement between them ever since October – formed at
Weymouth, and kept a secret from everybody. Not a creature knowing
it but themselves – neither the Campbells, nor her family, nor his. – It is
so wonderful, that though perfectly convinced of the fact, it is yet almost
incredible to myself. I can hardly believe it. – I thought I knew him.'

Emma scarcely heard what was said. – Her mind was divided between
two ideas – her own former conversations with him about Miss Fairfax;
and poor Harriet; – and for some time she could only exclaim, and require confirmation, repeated confirmation.

'Well,' said she at last, trying to recover herself; 'this is a circumstance
which I must think of at least half a day, before I can at all comprehend it.
What! – engaged to her all the winter – before either of them came to
Highbury?'

'Engaged since October – secretly engaged, – It has hurt me, Emma,
very much. It has hurt his father equally. *Some part* of his conduct we
cannot excuse.'

Emma pondered a moment, and then replied, 'I will not pretend *not* to understand you; and to give you all the relief in my power, be assured that no such effect has followed his attentions to me as you are apprehensive of.'

Mrs. Weston looked up, afraid to believe; but Emma's countenance was as steady as her words.

'That you may have less difficulty in believing this boast, of my present perfect indifference,' she continued, 'I will farther tell you, that there was a period in the early part of our acquaintance when I did like him, when I was very much disposed to be attached to him – nay, was attached – and how it came to cease is perhaps the wonder. Fortunately, however, it did cease. I have really for some time past, for at least three months, cared nothing about him. You may believe me, Mrs. Weston. This is the simple truth.'

The marriage is to take place soon. Emma is greatly concerned about Harriet's reaction to the news: she recalls Knightley telling her that she had been 'no friend to Harriet Smith' and realizes how her interference has blighted the girl's happiness. Harriet, however, is found to be not in the least upset; her affections have now been transferred to Knightley. Emma is so annoyed to learn this, and that Knightley returns Harriet's regard, that she is glad to be rid of the girl and remarks 'Oh God! that I had never seen her!'

She spends the rest of the day and most of the night examining her conscience and realizes where her persistent interference in other people's lives has led them all. Knightley calls next day, while this melancholy mood is still at its height, and escorts Emma for a walk. He is inclined to sympathize with her for the loss of Frank, but she sets him right:

'I have very little to say for my own conduct. – I was tempted by his attentions, and allowed myself to appear pleased. – An old story, probably – a common case – and no more than has happened to hundreds of my sex before; and yet it may not be the more excusable in one who sets up as I do for Understanding. Many circumstances assisted the temptation. He was the son of Mr. Weston – he was continually here – I always found him very pleasant – and, in short, for (with a sigh) let me swell out the causes ever so ingeniously, they all centre in this at last – my vanity was flattered, and I allowed his attentions. Latterly, however – for some time, indeed – I have had no idea of their meaning any thing. – I thought them a habit, a trick, nothing that called for seriousness on my side. He has imposed on me, but he has not injured me. I have never been attached to him. And now I can tolerably comprehend his behaviour. He never wished to attach me. It was merely a blind to conceal his real situation with another. – It was his object to blind all about him; and no one, I am sure, could be more effectually blinded than myself – except that I was *not* blinded – that it was my good fortune – that, in short, I was somehow or other safe from him.'

She had hoped for an answer here – for a few words to say that her conduct was at least intelligible; but he was silent; and, as far as she could judge, deep in thought. At last, and tolerably in his usual tone, he said,

'I have never had a high opinion of Frank Churchill. – I can suppose, however, that I may have under rated him. My acquaintance with him has been but trifling. – And even if I have not under rated him hitherto, he may yet turn out well. – With such a woman he has a chance. – I have no motive for wishing him ill – and for her sake, whose happiness will be involved in his good character and conduct, I shall certainly wish him well.'

'I have no doubt of their being happy together,' said Emma; 'I believe them to be very mutually and very sincerely attached.'

'He is a most fortunate man!' returned Mr. Knightley, with energy. 'So early in life – at three and twenty – a period when, if a man chooses a wife, he generally chooses ill. At three and twenty to have drawn such a prize! – What years of felicity that man, in all human calculation, has before him! Assured of the love of such a woman – the disinterested love, for Jane Fairfax's character vouches for her disinterestedness; every thing in his favour, – equality of situation – I mean, as far as regards society, and all the habits and manners that are important; equality in every point but one – and that one, since the purity of her heart is not to be doubted, such as must increase his felicity, for it will be his to bestow the only advantages she wants. – A man would always wish to give a woman a better home than the one he takes her from; and he who can do it, where there is no doubt of *her* regard, must, I think, be the happiest of mortals. – Frank Churchill is, indeed, the favourite of fortune. Every thing turns out for his good. – He meets with a young woman at a watering-place, gains her affection, cannot even weary her by negligent treatment – and had he and all his family sought round the world for a perfect wife for him, they could not have found her superior. – His aunt is in the way. – His aunt dies. – He has only to speak. – His friends are eager to promote his happiness. – He has used every body ill – and they are all delighted to forgive him. He is a fortunate man indeed!'

'You speak as if you envied him.'

'And I do envy him, Emma. In one respect he is the object of my envy.'

Emma could say no more. They seemed to be within half a sentence of Harriet, and her immediate feeling was to avert the subject, if possible. She made her plan; she would speak of something totally different – the children in Brunswick Square; and she only waited for breath to begin, when Mr. Knightley startled her, by saying,

'You will not ask me what is the point of envy. – You are determined, I see, to have no curiosity. – You are wise – but *I* cannot be wise. Emma, I must tell what you will not ask, though I may wish it unsaid the next moment.'

'Oh! then, don't speak it, don't speak it,' she eagerly cried. 'Take a little time, consider, do not commit yourself.'

'Thank you,' said he, in an accent of deep mortification, and not another syllable followed.

Emma could not bear to give him pain. He was wishing to confide in her – perhaps to consult her; cost her what it would, she would listen. She might assist his resolution, or reconcile him to it; she might give just praise to Harriet, or, by representing to him his own in-dependence, relieve him from that state of indecision which must be more intolerable than any alternative to such a mind as his. They had reached the house.

'You are going in, I suppose?' said he.

'No' – replied Emma – quite confirmed by the depressed manner in which he still spoke – 'I should like to take another turn. Mr. Perry is not gone.' And, after proceeding a few steps, she added – 'I stopped you ungraciously just now, Mr. Knightley, and I am afraid, gave you pain. – But if you have any wish to speak openly to me as a friend, or to ask my opinion of any thing that you may have in contemplation – as a friend, indeed, you may command me. – I will hear whatever you like. I will tell you exactly what I think.'

'As a friend!' – repeated Mr. Knightley. – 'Emma, that I fear, is a word – No, I have no wish. – Stay, yes, why should I hesitate? I have gone too far already for concealment. – Emma, I accept your offer – Extraordinary as it may seem, I accept it, and refer myself to you as a friend. – Tell me, then, have I no chance of ever succeeding?'

He stopped in his earnestness to look the question, and the expression of his eyes overpowered her.

'My dearest Emma,' said he, 'for dearest you will always be, whatever the event of this hour's conversation, my dearest, most beloved Emma – tell me at once. Say "No," if it is to be said.' – She could really say nothing. 'You are silent,' he cried, with great animation; 'absolutely silent! at present I ask no more.'

Emma was almost ready to sink under the agitation of this moment. The dread of being awakened from the happiest dream, was perhaps the most prominent feeling.

Emma's happiness would be complete were it not for two people – her father and Harriet. Mr Woodhouse is sure to be very upset at his daughter entering the dreaded state of holy matrimony, and Harriet will believe Emma has cheated her by stealing Knightley's affection. She decides that it would be best if the girl could have her mind diverted by going to stay with Isabella in London for a few weeks, thus hearing of Emma's engagement to Knightley in a letter. Mrs Weston forwards Emma a letter she has received from Frank explaining the circumstances of his secret engagement to Jane Fairfax. It seems that he was the mysterious donor of the pianoforté. Emma shows the letter to Knightley and while he still considers Frank to have faults, he admits that the letter shows his character in a better light.

Emma and Knightley now have to decide what to do about Mr Woodhouse. Since she cannot leave her father alone at Hartfield, and he would certainly refuse to live at Donwell Abbey, Knightley must move in with them after the wedding. Harriet proves tactful enough to develop a toothache, so that she must go to London to have it treated while staying with Isabella. Mrs Weston has a baby, and Emma waits until after her lying-in before telling her about her engagement. When the news is broken to Mr Woodhouse he takes it very badly, but is gradually won round by Knightley, Emma and Mrs Weston. As the time draws near for Harriet's return from London, Knightley has a grave disclosure to make to Emma:

'I am very much afraid, my dear Emma, that you will not smile when you hear it.'

'Indeed! but why so? – I can hardly imagine that any thing which pleases or amuses you should not please and amuse me too.'

'There is one subject,' he replied, 'I hope but one, on which we do not think alike.' He paused a moment, again smiling, with his eyes fixed on her face. 'Does nothing occur to you? – Do not you recollect? – Harriet Smith.'

Her cheeks flushed at the name, and she felt afraid of something, though she knew not what.

'Have you heard from her yourself this morning?' cried he. 'You have, I believe, and know the whole.'

'No, I have not; I know nothing; pray tell me.'

'You are prepared for the worst, I see – and very bad it is. Harriet Smith marries Robert Martin.'

Emma gave a start, which did not seem like being prepared – and her eyes, in eager gaze, said, 'No, this is impossible!' but her lips were closed.

'It is so, indeed,' continued Mr. Knightley; 'I have it from Robert Martin himself. He left me not half an hour ago.'

She was still looking at him with the most speaking amazement.

'You like it, my Emma, as little as I feared – I wish our opinions were the same. But in time they will be. Time, you may be sure, will make one or the other of us think differently; and in the meanwhile, we need not talk much on the subject.'

'You mistake me, you quite mistake me,' she replied, exerting herself. 'It is not that such a circumstance would now make me unhappy, but I cannot believe it. It seems an impossibility! – You cannot mean to say that Harriet Smith has accepted Robert Martin. You cannot mean that he has even proposed to her again – yet. You only mean that he intends it.'

'I mean that he has done it,' answered Mr. Knightley with smiling but determined decision, 'and been accepted.'

Knightley had sent Robert Martin to town on business with his brother, and during the visit the friendship between Harriet and

Robert was renewed. Really, Emma is delighted at last that her
friend has made a suitable match. Harriet and Robert are married
in September; Emma and Knightley follow them to church in
October.

NORTHANGER ABBEY

Northanger Abbey has the curious distinction of being the first of Jane Austen's novels to have been accepted for publication and the last, simultaneously with *Persuasion*, to appear. She wrote it in its first form in 1797-8 as a two-volume novel entitled *Susan*, but did not make her final revisions until 1803, after which she gave the manuscript to her brother Henry, who, using his 'man of business', Mr Seymour, as intermediary, offered it to a publisher, Richard Crosby. Crosby accepted it for £10, announced it as a forthcoming publication – and then did nothing more.

Not until 1809 did Jane attempt to put any pressure upon Crosby to proceed. Using the name 'Mrs Ashton Dennis', she wrote tartly to ask why he had not published it, and whether he had carelessly lost the manuscript, in which event she would provide a copy. She concluded: 'Should no notice be taken of this address, I shall feel myself at liberty to secure the publication of my work, by applying elsewhere.' These tactics did not work on Crosby, who replied that he had never guaranteed publication and would take proceedings if she, or anyone else, should produce the work. Alternatively, she might have it back by repaying the £10. Another nine years elapsed before she took up this offer and retrieved her manuscript. But it seems that she never revised it thoroughly, and it did not see publication until the year after her death, when John Murray brought it out simultaneously with *Persuasion*, under the title *Northanger Abbey*.

It is ironic to think that the dilatory Crosby sat for thirteen years on a novel whose true authorship he cannot have known, and, indeed, probably envied the publishers of *Sense and Sensibility*, *Pride and Prejudice*, *Mansfield Park* and *Emma*, all of which appeared during that period.

First American publication of *Northanger Abbey* was in 1833 by Carey and Lea, Philadelphia.

. . . .

Catherine Morland, aged seventeen, is the eldest daughter of a clergyman's large family, living at Fullerton in Wiltshire. She is introduced to Bath society by a middle-aged couple, Mr and Mrs Allen, with whom she lodges, but her first ball proves a disappointment. At the second, she is introduced to Henry Tilney, a young clergyman, who partners her. They indulge in literary badinage:

'I see what you think of me,' said he gravely – 'I shall make but a poor figure in your journal to-morrow.'

'My journal!'

'Yes, I know exactly what you will say: Friday, went to the Lower Rooms; wore my sprigged muslin robe with blue trimmings – plain black shoes – appeared to much advantage; but was strangely harassed by a queer, half-witted man, who would make me dance with him, and distressed me by his nonsense.'

'Indeed I shall say no such thing.'

'Shall I tell you what you ought to say?'

'If you please.'

'I danced with a very agreeable young man, introduced by Mr. King; had a great deal of conversation with him – seems a most extraordinary genius – hope I may know more of him. *That*, madam, is what *I* wish you to say.'

'But, perhaps, I keep no journal.'

'Perhaps you are not sitting in this room, and I am not sitting by you. These are points in which a doubt is equally possible. Not keep a journal! How are your absent cousins to understand the tenour of your life in Bath without one? How are the civilities and compliments of every day to be related, as they ought to be, unless noted down every evening in a journal? How are your various dresses to be remembered, and the particular state of your complexion, and curl of your hair to be described in all their diversities, without having constant recourse to a journal? – My dear madam, I am not so ignorant of young ladies' ways as you wish to believe me: it is this delightful habit of journalizing which largely contributes to form the easy style of writing for which ladies are so generally celebrated. Every body allows that the talent of writing agreeable letters is peculiarly female. Nature may have done something, but I am sure it must be essentially assisted by the practice of keeping a journal.'

'I have sometimes thought,' said Catherine, doubtingly, 'whether ladies *do* write so much better letters than gentlemen! That is – I should not think the superiority was always on our side.'

'As far as I have had opportunity of judging, it appears to me that the usual style of letter-writing among women is faultless, except in three particulars.'

'And what are they?'

'A general deficiency of subject, a total inattention to stops, and a very frequent ignorance of grammar.'

'Upon my word! I need not have been afraid of disclaiming the compliment! You do not think too highly of us in that way.'

'I should not more lay it down as a general rule that women write better letters than men, than that they sing better duets, or draw better landscapes. In every power, of which taste is the foundation, excellence is pretty fairly divided between the sexes.'

The next day Catherine hopes to see Mr Tilney again, but he does not appear. Instead, the Allens and she chance to meet Mrs Thorpe, who is an old schoolfriend of Mrs Allen and the widowed mother of three sons and three daughters. They learn that John Thorpe and James Morland are at Oxford together and that James had spent a week with the Thorpes during the last Christmas vacation. Catherine quickly forms a strong friendship with the eldest Thorpe girl, Isabella:

They called each other by their Christian name, were always arm in arm when they walked, pinned up each other's train for the dance, and were not to be divided in the set; and if a rainy morning deprived them of other enjoyments, they were still resolute in meeting in defiance of wet and dirt, and shut themselves up, to read novels together. Yes, novels; – for I will not adopt that ungenerous and impolitic custom so common with novel writers, of degrading by their contemptuous censure the very performances, to the number of which they are themselves adding – joining with their greatest enemies in bestowing the harshest epithets on such works, and scarcely ever permitting them to be read by their own heroine, who, if she accidentally take up a novel, is sure to turn over its insipid pages with disgust. Alas! if the heroine of one novel be not patronized by the heroine of another, from whom can she expect protection and regard? I cannot approve of it. Let us leave it to the Reviewers to abuse such effusions of fancy at their leisure, and over every new novel to talk in threadbare strains of the trash with which the press now groans. Let us not desert one another; we are an injured body. Although our productions have afforded more extensive and unaffected pleasure than those of any other literary corporation in the world, no species of composition has been so much decried. From pride, ignorance, or fashion, our foes are almost as many as our readers. And while the abilities of the nine-hundredth abridger of the History of England, or of the man who collects and publishes in a volume some dozen lines of Milton, Pope, and Prior, with a paper from the Spectator, and a chapter from Sterne, are eulogized by a thousand pens, – there seems almost a general wish of decrying the capacity and undervaluing the labour of the novelist, and of slighting the performances which have only genius, wit, and taste to recommend them. 'I am no novel reader – I seldom look into novels – Do not imagine that *I* often read novels – It is really very well for a novel.' – Such is the common cant. – 'And what are you reading, Miss –?' 'Oh! it is only a novel!' replies the young lady; while she lays down her book with affected indifference, or momentary shame. – 'It is only Cecilia, or Camilla, or Belinda;' or, in short, only some work in which the greatest powers of the mind are displayed, in which the most thorough knowledge of human nature, the happiest delineation of its varieties, the liveliest effusions of wit and humour are conveyed to the world in the best chosen language. Now, had the same young lady been engaged with a volume of the Spectator, instead of such a work, how proudly would she have produced the book, and told its name; though the chances must be against her being occupied by any part of that voluminous publication, of which either the matter or manner would not disgust a young person of taste: the substance of its papers so often consisting in the statement of improbable circumstances, unnatural characters, and topics of conversation, which no longer concern any one living; and their language, too, frequently so coarse as to give no very favourable idea of the age that could endure it.

John Thorpe and James Morland arrive in Bath in John's open carriage and encounter the two girls in the street. Thorpe, a swaggering, tactless braggart, boasts about his fearless driving and insists that Catherine accompany him the following morning. Against her will, she agrees. James Morland and Isabella renew a flirtation begun at their earlier meeting. That same evening all four attend a ball at the assembly rooms. Catherine engages to dance with John Thorpe for the evening, and is consequently mortified to find that Henry Tilney and his sister, Eleanor, are at the ball too, and she has to refuse Henry's invitation to dance. However, she makes a friend of his sister.

The following morning Catherine takes her promised drive with John Thorpe, and he questions her keenly about the Allens, especially concerning Mr Allen's wealth, health, drinking habits, and the closeness of the relationship between the Allens and herself. On their return they hear from Isabella and James that they have met the Tilneys and have learned that the grandfather was a wealthy man who left a fortune to his daughter, now dead.

At a further ball, Henry Tilney partners Catherine, to the annoyance of the persistent John Thorpe, and introduces her to his father, General Tilney. She arranges to walk out with Henry and Eleanor next morning, but the weather is wet and they do not arrive to meet her. By the afternoon she is still hopeful, but John, James and Isabella call to invite her to drive with them to visit Blaize Castle, and, when she hesitates, John tells her he has seen the Tilneys driving out of Bath. Resignedly, she goes with the trio. They have only driven a short way before Catherine sees Henry and Eleanor walking towards her lodgings. She asks John to stop:

'Stop, stop, Mr. Thorpe,' she impatiently cried, 'it is Miss Tilney; it is indeed. – How could you tell me they were gone? – Stop, stop, I will get out this moment and go to them.' But to what purpose did she speak? – Thorpe only lashed his horse into a brisker trot; the Tilneys, who had soon ceased to look after her, were in a moment out of sight round the corner of Laura-place, and in another moment she was herself whisked into the Market–place. Still, however, and during the length of another street, she intreated him to stop. 'Pray, pray stop, Mr. Thorpe. – I cannot go on. – I will not go on. – I must go back to Miss Tilney.' But Mr. Thorpe only laughed, smacked his whip, encouraged his horse, made odd noises, and drove on; and Catherine, angry and vexed as she was, having no power of getting away, was obliged to give up the point and submit. Her reproaches, however, were not spared. 'How could you deceive me so, Mr. Thorpe? – How could you say, that you saw them driving up the

Lansdown-road? – I would not have had it happen so for the world. – They must think it so strange: so rude of me! to go by them, too, without saying a word! You do not know how vexed I am. – I shall have no pleasure at Clifton, nor in any thing else. I had rather, ten thousand times rather get out now, and walk back to them. How could you say, that you saw them driving out in a phaeton?' Thorpe defended himself very stoutly, declared he had never seen two men so much alike in his life, and would hardly give up the point of its having been Tilney himself.

The visit to the castle is an unhappy one for Catherine, and the next day, when she calls at the Tilneys' to explain her apparent rudeness, she is told Miss Tilney is not at home. Soon afterwards she sees Eleanor leaving the house and supposes that her discourtesy of yesterday is being repaid. At the theatre that evening Catherine meets Henry Tilney and manages to explain what had happened: he assures her, on his own and his sister's behalf, that there is no resentment towards her. During their talk she notices Thorpe in close conversation with General Tilney.

The next time Isabella, James and John try to persuade Catherine to break an arrangement to walk out with Henry and Eleanor she adamantly refuses to drive with them. Isabella accuses her of liking Eleanor more than herself, and even her mild brother James reproaches her. Catherine visits the Tilneys' again and almost forces them to hear her explanation. The air is cleared and Catherine returns gaily to her lodgings, where she finds that Mr and Mrs Allen have something to say on the subject of young people gadding about in carriages together:

'These schemes are not at all the thing. Young men and women driving about the country in open carriages! Now and then it is very well; but going to inns and public places together! It is not right; and I wonder Mrs. Thorpe should allow it. I am glad you do not think of going; I am sure Mrs. Morland would not be pleased. Mrs. Allen, are not you of my way of thinking? Do not you think these kind of projects objectionable?'

'Yes, very much so indeed. Open carriages are nasty things. A clean gown is not five minutes wear in them. You are splashed getting in and getting out; and the wind takes your hair and your bonnet in every direction. I hate an open carriage myself.'

'I know you do; but that is not the question. Do not you think it has an odd appearance, if young ladies are frequently driven about in them by young men, to whom they are not even related?'

'Yes, my dear, a very odd appearance indeed. I cannot bear to see it.'

'Dear madam,' cried Catherine, 'then why did not you tell me so before? I am sure if I had known it to be improper, I would not have gone with Mr. Thorpe at all; but I always hoped you would tell me, if you thought I was doing wrong.'

'And so I should, my dear, you may depend on it; for as I told Mrs. Morland at parting, I would always do the best for you in my power. But one must not be over particular. Young people *will* be young people, as your good mother says herself. You know I wanted you, when we first came, not to buy that sprigged muslin, but you would. Young people do not like to be always thwarted.'

The Tilneys call for Catherine next morning and they walk agreeably together round Beechen Cliff. Their talk is first of Gothic literature:

'I never look at it,' said Catherine, as they walked along the side of the river, 'without thinking of the south of France.'

'You have been abroad then?' said Henry, a little surprised.

'Oh! no, I only mean what I have read about. It always puts me in mind of the country that Emily and her father travelled through in the "Mysteries of Udolpho." But you never read novels, I dare say?'

'Why not?'

'Because they are not clever enough for you – gentlemen read better books.'

'The person, be it gentleman or lady, who has not pleasure in a good novel, must be intolerably stupid. I have read all Mrs. Radcliffe's works, and most of them with great pleasure. The Mysteries of Udolpho, when I had once begun it, I could not lay down again; – I remember finishing it in two days – my hair standing on end the whole time.'

The conversation shifts to history and art, and Catherine realizes that the Tilneys are far more clever than she, and is ashamed to display her ignorance:

She knew nothing of drawing – nothing of taste: – and she listened to them with an attention which brought her little profit, for they talked in phrases which conveyed scarcely any idea to her. The little which she could understand however appeared to contradict the very few notions she had entertained on the matter before. It seemed as if a good view were no longer to be taken from the top of an high hill, and that a clear blue sky was no longer a proof of a fine day. She was heartily ashamed of her ignorance. A misplaced shame. Where people wish to attach, they should always be ignorant. To come with a well–informed mind, is to come with an inability of administering to the vanity of others, which a sensible person would always wish to avoid. A woman especially, if she have the misfortune of knowing any thing, should conceal it as well as she can.

The advantages of natural folly in a beautiful girl have been already set forth by the capital pen of a sister author; – and to her treatment of the subject I will only add in justice to men, that though to the larger and more trifling part of the sex, imbecility in females is a great enhancement of their personal charms, there is a portion of them too reasonable and too well informed themselves to desire any thing more in woman than ignorance. But Catherine did not know her own advantages – did not know that a good-looking girl, with an affectionate heart and a very ignorant mind, cannot fail of attracting a clever young man, unless circumstances are particularly untoward. In the present instance, she confessed and lamented her want of knowledge; declared that she would give any thing in the world to be able to draw; and a lecture on the picturesque immediately followed, in which his instructions were so clear that she soon began to see beauty in every thing admired by him, and her attention was so earnest, that he became perfectly satisfied of her having a great deal of natural taste. He talked of fore-grounds, distances, and second distances – side-screens and perspectives – lights and shades; – and Catherine was so hopeful a scholar, that when they gained the top of Beechen Cliff, she voluntarily rejected the whole city of Bath, as unworthy to make part of a landscape.

Isabella Thorpe and James Morland become engaged and James departs for Fullerton to see his father. John Thorpe also leaves, after making overtures to Catherine, which she politely refuses to acknowledge. At a further ball, Henry and Eleanor's elder brother, Captain Frederick Tilney, are introduced. A letter arrives from James saying that his father has arranged for him to receive a living of £400 a year when he is of age, plus an estate of equal value, but that he and Isabella must wait a few years before they marry. This annoys Isabella and disillusions the Thorpes about the financial prospects of a union with the Morlands. The newly-engaged girl begins to flirt openly with Captain Tilney and this conduct worries Catherine:

It seemed to her that Captain Tilney was falling in love with Isabella, and Isabella unconsciously encouraging him; unconsciously it must be, for Isabella's attachment to James was as certain and well acknowledged as her engagement. To doubt her truth or good intentions was impossible; and yet, during the whole of their conversation her manner had been odd. She wished Isabella had talked more like her usual self, and not so much about money; and had not looked so well pleased at the sight of Captain Tilney. How strange that she should not perceive his admiration! Catherine longed to give her a hint of it, to put her on her guard, and prevent all the pain which her too lively behaviour might otherwise create both for him and her brother.

Eleanor Tilney invites Catherine to return with her and her brother to their home, Northanger Abbey in Gloucestershire. Isabella is jealous and tells Catherine that she has received a letter from her brother John urging her to use her influence on Catherine in his interest. Catherine protests that she has done nothing to encourage John's affection and makes it plain that she has no designs upon him.

On the journey to Northanger, Henry Tilney, playing upon Catherine's fondness for Gothic novels, ribs her about the Abbey, implanting expectations of mystery and horror in her mind:

He smiled, and said, 'You have formed a very favourable idea of the abbey.'

'To be sure I have. Is not it a fine old place, just like what one reads about?'

'And are you prepared to encounter all the horrors that a building such as "what one reads about" may produce? – Have you a stout heart? – Nerves fit for sliding panels and tapestry?'

'Oh! yes – I do not think I should be easily frightened, because there would be so many people in the house – and besides, it has never been uninhabited and left deserted for years, and then the family come back to it unawares, without giving any notice, as generally happens.'

'No, certainly. – We shall not have to explore our way into a hall dimly lighted by the expiring embers of a wood fire – nor be obliged to spread out beds on the floor of a room without windows, doors, or furniture. But you must be aware that when a young lady is (by whatever means) introduced into a dwelling of this kind, she is always lodged apart from the rest of the family. While they snugly repair to their own end of the house, she is formally conducted by Dorothy the ancient housekeeper up a different staircase, and along many gloomy passages, into an apartment never used since some cousin or kin died in it about twenty years before. Can you stand such a ceremony as this? Will not your mind misgive you, when you find yourself in this gloomy chamber – too lofty and extensive for you, with only the feeble rays of a single lamp to take in its size – its walls hung with tapestry exhibiting figures as large as life, and the bed, of dark green stuff or purple velvet, presenting even a funereal appearance. Will not your heart sink within you?'

'Oh! but this will not happen to me, I am sure.'

'How fearfully will you examine the furniture of your apartment! – And what will you discern? – Not tables, toilettes, wardrobes, or drawers, but on one side perhaps the remains of a broken lute, on the other a ponderous chest which no efforts can open, and over the fireplace the portrait of some handsome warrior, whose features will so incomprehensibly strike you, that you will not be able to withdraw your eyes from it. Dorothy meanwhile, no less struck by your appearance, gazes on you in great agitation, and drops a few unintelligible hints. To raise your spirits, moreover, she gives you reason to suppose that the part of the abbey you inhabit is undoubtedly haunted, and informs you that you will not have a single domestic within call. With this parting cordial she curtseys off – you listen to the sound of her receding footsteps as long as the last echo can reach you – and when, with fainting spirits, you attempt to fasten your door, you discover, with increased alarm, that it has no lock.'

'Oh! Mr. Tilney, how frightful! – This is just like a book! – But it cannot really happen to me. I am sure your housekeeper is not really Dorothy. – Well, what then?'

'Nothing further to alarm perhaps may occur the first night. After surmounting your *unconquerable* horror of the bed, you will retire to rest, and get a few hours' unquiet slumber. But on the second, or at farthest the *third* night after your arrival, you will probably have a violent storm. Peals of thunder so loud as to seem to shake the edifice to its foundation will roll round the neighbouring mountains – and during the frightful gusts of wind which accompany it, you will probably think you discern (for your lamp is not extinguished) one part of the hanging more violently agitated than the rest. Unable of course to repress your curiosity in so favourable a moment for indulging it, you will instantly arise, and throwing your dressing-gown around you, proceed to examine this mystery. After a very short search, you will discover a division in the tapestry so artfully constructed as to defy the minutest inspection, and on opening it a door will immediately appear, which door being only secured by massy bars and a padlock, you will, after a few efforts, succeed in opening, – and, with your lamp in your hand, will pass through it into a small vaulted room.'

'No, indeed; I should be too much frightened to do any such thing.'

'What! not when Dorothy has given you to understand that there is a secret subterraneous communication between your apartment and the chapel of St. Anthony, scarcely two miles off – could you shrink from so simple an adventure? No, no, you will proceed into this small vaulted room, and through this into several others, without perceiving any thing very remarkable in either. In one perhaps there may be a dagger, in another a few drops of blood, and in a third the remains of some instrument of torture; but there being nothing in all this out of the common way, and your lamp being nearly exhausted, you will return towards your own apartment. In repassing through the small vaulted room, however, your eyes will be attracted towards a large, old-fashioned cabinet of ebony and gold, which, though narrowly examining the furniture before, you had passed unnoticed. Impelled by an irresistible presentiment, you will eagerly advance to it, unlock its folding doors, and search into every drawer; – but for some time without discovering any thing of importance – perhaps nothing but a considerable hoard of diamonds. At last, however, by touching a secret spring, an inner compartment will open – a roll of paper appears: – you seize it – it contains many sheets of manuscript – you hasten with the precious treasure into your own chamber, but scarcely have you been able to decipher "Oh! thou – whomsoever thou mayst be, into whose hands these memoirs of the wretched Matilda may fall" – when your lamp suddenly expires in the socket, and leaves you in total darkness.'

'Oh! no, no – do not say so. Well, go on.'

The discovery that Northanger Abbey is quite a comfortable modernized place comes as an anti-climax to this. But that night a storm rises. Alone at last in her room, Catherine hears the wind and rain rattling her windows. She sees a mysterious-looking cabinet, which she manages to open. One drawer contains a rolled manuscript, exactly as Henry had foretold; and, as he had also said it would, her candle goes out, leaving her to creep into bed and lie there in the darkness waiting for the door to crash open and the bed-curtains to be whisked aside. Nothing of the sort happens, and she falls fast asleep.

Next morning Catherine examines the 'manuscript' and finds it is only an inventory of linen. All seems normal that day, but Catherine's novel-fired imagination is ready to seize on any suitable fuel, to the extent of beginning to suspect that General Tilney may have murdered his wife, who had died suddenly nine years earlier. She confides her suspicions to Henry, when he finds her examining the late Mrs Tilney's room. He dismisses them for what they are worth, leaving her feeling ashamed and silly.

Catherine has been at Northanger almost a fortnight when a letter arrives from her brother James at Oxford, telling her that his engagement to Isabella Thorpe is broken and that Isabella intends to become engaged to Captain Tilney. She confides in Henry and Eleanor, who assure her that it is more unlikely that their brother is in earnest about Isabella: he is too honourable to disrupt an engagement, and, in any case, Isabella has no fortune or social position. Another letter soon arrives, this time from Isabella, saying that she abhors Captain Tilney and is worried by James's long absence, and urging Catherine to write to him on her behalf. Catherine realizes what a superficial person Isabella is, and ignores the request.

Another fortnight passes. General Tilney leaves for a visit to London. So far, he has treated Catherine very civilly, and when they visit Henry's parsonage at Woodston, some twenty miles away, implies that he wishes her for a daughter-in-law. But when he returns from London he is in a very different frame of mind, ordering Catherine to leave the house next morning and telling Eleanor she is not to write to her. Mystified and upset, Eleanor lends Catherine the money to return home to Fullerton. Catherine finds little comfort from her placid, unimaginative mother, who instead upbraids her for letting the grandeur of the Northanger surroundings turn her head.

Henry Tilney arrives at Fullerton. On the pretext of getting Catherine to show him to the Allens' house, a quarter of a mile away, so that he might pay his respects, he reveals to Catherine what has happened. The General had been led by John Thorpe to believe that she was heiress to a considerable fortune, and had accordingly welcomed her as a prospective daughter-in-law. During his London visit he had met Thorpe again, who, embittered by the ending of the engagement between his sister Isabella and James Morland, and by Catherine's refusal of his own advances, had told the General that she was of no consequence whatsoever, and the General, furious with himself and everyone else, had rushed back to Northanger Abbey to dismiss Catherine from his sight.

Henry, however, had condemned his father's action hotly, and, almost to spite him, had determined to ask Catherine to marry him, for which purpose he has arrived in Fullerton. She is willing enough, and so are her parents, but they insist that the General must give his permission too. Fortunately, Eleanor marries a viscount that summer; the General is able to convince himself that Catherine is well connected after all, is reconciled with his son, and gives his permission for the marriage.

PERSUASION

THE last 'complete' novel Jane Austen wrote was *Persuasion*, begun at some time in 1815, and finished, so far as it ever was, in July 1816. In March 1817, she was writing of it as 'a something ready for Publication, which may perhaps appear about a twelvemonth hence'; but these are conflicting terms, for had it been ready for publication she would presumably have let it go forward; while the reference to 'a twelvemonth hence', in an age when it took very few weeks to get a book produced, implies that it was not ready in the fullest sense, but still needed the meticulous polishing to which she had habitually subjected her work. This twelvemonth estimate, and the fact that she was dead within a third of that time, may well suggest that the *Persuasion* we read today never quite reached the state that would have satisfied its author completely. Its very title was most probably supplied, in the absence of any provided by her, by Henry, her brother, who arranged for John Murray to publish the book simultaneously with *Northanger Abbey*, in 1818. First American publication was in 1832 by Carey and Lea, Philadelphia.

Attempts have been made to read significance into the autumnal atmosphere of *Persuasion*, in that it was written as Jane's health declined towards death. Certainly, it is the most wistfully melancholy of the novels, and I detect in that letter of March 1817, to Edward Knight's eldest daughter, Fanny, at Godmersham, a note of despondency: 'Do not be surprised at finding Uncle Henry acquainted with my having another ready for publication. I could not say No when he asked me, but he knows nothing more of it. – You will not like it, so you need not be impatient. You may *perhaps* like the Heroine, as she is almost too good for me. –' But, if there is any validity in the symbolism of this evocation of autumn, then the almost farcical *Sanditon* (*q.v.*),

her last fragment of work, must have been a truly remarkable
flickering of the dying flame.

. . . .

Sir Walter Elliot of Kellynch Hall, Somerset, is a widower with
three adult daughters: Elizabeth, aged twenty-nine, Anne, aged
twenty-seven, and Mary. He considers Elizabeth and Anne plain
old maids who will never marry, especially since the younger
sister, Mary is already married to Charles Musgrove of Uppercross nearby and has two small sons.

Since their mother's death thirteen years earlier, the girls have
been brought up under the care of Lady Russell, an old friend,
whose favourite is Anne. Some years ago it had been hoped to
arrange a marriage between Elizabeth and William Walter Elliot,
a cousin and, since Sir Walter had no sons, heir to the baronetcy.
But William Elliot preferred to marry elsewhere and in 1814, the
year the story opens, he has been a widower for six months.

Kellynch Hall and estates are proving expensive to maintain
and Sir Walter is advised by Lady Russell and his agent, John
Shepherd, to lease the hall and take apartments in Bath or London. Lady Russell is additionally eager that Elizabeth should be
removed from what she feels is the bad influence of Mrs Penelope
Clay, Shepherd's daughter. But Anne does not wish to go either
to Bath or London, so it is arranged for her to stay for two months
at Uppercross Cottage with Mary, her perpetually ailing sister,
after which she will stay with Lady Russell at Kellynch Lodge,
before visiting her father and sister. Sir Walter and Elizabeth
depart for Bath with the insidious Mrs Clay who, despite Anne's
warning to her sister that the ageing woman may have designs on
Sir Walter, has managed to get herself taken along as companion.

The tenants of Kellynch Hall are Admiral and Mrs Croft, and
they remind Anne of an unhappy incident years before, when
she was nineteen: she had been unofficially engaged to Mrs
Croft's brother, Captain Frederick Wentworth. Her father and
Lady Russell had talked her out of the understanding, but Anne
has never forgotten her former love.

While at Uppercross Cottage she pays a visit with Mary to Uppercross House, where Charles Musgrove's parents and two sisters, Henrietta and Louisa, live. Anne has to listen to the grievances of the family, who consider her to be practical and sensible and much more to their taste than Mary. The likeable new tenants of Kellynch Hall call on Mary, and Anne is dismayed to learn that Captain Wentworth will soon be staying with them.

Charles Musgrove had had a brother, Richard, who had died two years before. He had been in the Navy, and Wentworth had been his captain, so it is natural that Wentworth should visit the Musgrove family on his arrival. The meeting takes place at Uppercross House. Anne is invited, but is prevented from being present when one of the small Musgrove boys falls and dislocates his collar-bone: she stays behind to nurse him. But the encounter with Wentworth is not long postponed. The following morning he comes to Uppercross Cottage with Charles and briefly sees Anne: the meeting is cool but civil. Later, Anne is distressed by Mary's report that Wentworth had remarked how very much changed he had found Anne. It is a release of a kind: there can be no hope of a renewal of their love since he finds her so un-attractive and still resents her rejection of him. Anne learns that he intends to marry any pleasing young woman, preferably Henrietta or Louisa Musgrove, but certainly not herself.

All the same, Wentworth and Anne often find themselves in one another's company at the Musgroves'. Inevitably, she reflects ruefully how he once behaved towards her and is made miserable by his present studied politeness. At a dinner at Uppercross House, the Musgrove girls and their cousins, the Hayters, pay the captain flattering attention, while Mrs Musgrove mournfully talks of 'poor Dick', her dead son:

'Poor dear fellow!' continued Mrs. Musgrove; 'he was grown so steady, and such an excellent correspondent, while he was under your care! Ah! it would have been a happy thing, if he had never left you. I assure you, Captain Wentworth, we are very sorry he ever left you.'

There was a momentary expression in Captain Wentworth's face at this speech, a certain glance of his bright eye, and curl of his handsome mouth, which convinced Anne, that instead of sharing in Mrs. Musgrove's kind wishes, as to her son, he had probably been at some pains to get rid of him; but it was too transient an indulgence of self-amusement to be detected by any who understood him less than herself; in another moment he was perfectly collected and serious; and almost instantly afterwards coming up to the sofa, on which she and Mrs. Musgrove were sitting, took a place by the latter, and entered into conversation with her, in a low voice, about her son, doing it with so much sympathy and natural grace, as shewed the kindest consideration for all that was real and unabsurd in the parent's feelings.

They were actually on the same sofa, for Mrs. Musgrove had most readily made room for him; – they were divided only by Mrs. Musgrove. It was no insignificant barrier, indeed. Mrs. Musgrove was of a comfortable substantial size, infinitely more fitted by nature to express good cheer and good humour, than tenderness and sentiment; and while the agitations of Anne's slender form, and pensive face, may be considered as very completely screened, Captain Wentworth should be allowed some credit for the self-command with which he attended to her large fat sighings over the destiny of a son, whom alive nobody had cared for.

Personal size and mental sorrow have certainly no necessary proportions. A large bulky figure has as good a right to be in deep affliction, as the most graceful set of limbs in the world. But, fair or not fair, there are unbecoming conjunctions, which reason will patronize in vain, – which taste cannot tolerate, – which ridicule will seize.

By the end of the evening Anne is very unhappy. Wentworth's 'cold politeness and ceremonious grace were worse than any thing'. He is a permanent guest at Kellynch, and finds the people of Uppercross so much to his taste that he is soon calling there every day. But the general admiration for him is not shared by Charles Hayter, the eldest of the cousins, a young clergyman who has been paying court to Henrietta Musgrove. He has returned after a brief absence to find that Henrietta's head has been turned by Wentworth. Wentworth himself seems to favour Henrietta and Louisa equally. Mary Musgrove and her husband discuss his affections with Anne. Mary is not in favour of a match between Henrietta and Charles Hayter, but Charles Musgrove speaks up for his cousin as a better choice for her than Wentworth, who would be more suited to Louisa.

Wentworth comes to Uppercross Cottage one morning and finds Anne alone. She is flustered, and their conversation is confined to little Charles Musgrove's accident. Charles Hayter joins them and sits silently reading a newspaper. Then little Walter Musgrove comes in and starts tugging at Anne. Charles Hayter orders the child to stop but is ignored. To Anne's surprise, it is Wentworth who releases her from the clinging arms:

Her sensations on the discovery made her perfectly speechless. She could not even thank him. She could only hang over little Charles, with most disordered feelings. His kindness in stepping forward to her relief – the manner – the silence in which it had passed – the little particulars of the circumstance – with the conviction soon forced on her by the noise he was studiously making with the child, that he meant to avoid hearing her thanks, and rather sought to testify that her conversation was the last of his wants, produced such a confusion of varying, but very painful agitation, as she could not recover from, till enabled by the entrance of Mary and the Miss Musgroves to make over her little patient to their cares, and leave the room. She could not stay. It might have been an opportunity of watching the loves and jealousies of the four; they were now all together, but she could stay for none of it. It was evident that Charles Hayter was not well inclined towards Captain Wentworth. She had a strong impression of his having said, in a vext tone of voice, after Captain Wentworth's interference, 'You ought to have minded *me*, Walter; I told you not to teaze your aunt;' and could comprehend his regretting that Captain Wentworth should do what he ought to have done himself. But neither Charles Hayter's feelings, nor any body's feelings, could interest her, till she had a little better arranged her own. She was ashamed of herself, quite ashamed of being so nervous, so overcome by such a trifle; but so it was; and it required a long application of solitude and reflection to recover her.

One fine November morning the Musgrove girls and Mary and Anne take a walk with Charles Musgrove and Captain Wentworth. They approach Winthrop, the Hayters' house, and Charles and Henrietta go down to greet their relatives. While they are away Anne, unobserved, overhears a conversation between Louisa and Wentworth, during which Louisa tells him of her family's wish that their brother Charles had married Anne, as he had wished, instead of Mary:

The sounds were retreating, and Anne distinguished no more. Her own emotions still kept her fixed. She had much to recover from, before she could move. The listener's proverbial fate was not absolutely hers; she had heard no evil of herself, – but she had heard a great deal of very painful import. She saw how her own character was considered by Captain Wentworth; and there had been just that degree of feeling and curiosity about her in his manner, which must give her extreme agitation.

Charles Musgrove and Henrietta return with Charles Hayter: Henrietta and Hayter have obviously solved their emotional problems and are happy again. Now it seems clear that Louisa will be the one to marry Captain Wentworth, and, consequently, Mary and Charles Musgrove are out of temper with each other as they all walk back towards Uppercross. Admiral and Mrs Croft drive up in their gig and offer a lift to any one of the ladies who is particularly fatigued. All decline except Anne, who does not speak. To her surprise, Wentworth speaks to Mrs Croft and then once more becomes the man of action on her behalf:

Anne was still in the lane; and though instinctively beginning to decline, she was not allowed to proceed. The admiral's kind urgency came in support of his wife's; they would not be refused; they compressed themselves into the smallest possible space to leave her a corner, and Captain Wentworth, without saying a word, turned to her, and quietly obliged her to be assisted into the carriage.

Yes, – he had done it. She was in the carriage, and felt that he had placed her there, that his will and his hands had done it, that she owed it to his perception of her fatigue, and his resolution to give her rest. She was very much affected by the view of his disposition towards her which all these things made apparent. This little circumstance seemed the completion of all that had gone before. She understood him. He could not forgive her, – but he could not be unfeeling. Though condemning her for the past, and considering it with high and unjust resentment, though perfectly careless of her, and though becoming attached to another, still he could not see her suffer, without the desire of giving her relief. It was a remainder of former sentiment; it was an impulse of pure, though unacknowledged friendship; it was a proof of his own warm and amiable heart, which she could not contemplate without emotions so compounded of pleasure and pain, that she knew not which prevailed.

On the drive home, Mrs Croft confides that she considers neither of the Musgrove girls a suitable match for her brother Wentworth.

A friend of Wentworth's, Captain Harville, has settled with his family not far away at Lyme Regis for the winter, and Charles, Mary, Henrietta and Louisa Musgrove, Anne and Wentworth, go to visit him. The Harvilles have another guest living with them, Captain James Benwick, who had been engaged to Harville's sister until her death, which he is still mourning, the previous summer. Anne talks to him at dinner and finds him a shy young man of considerable literary taste, with an especial fondness for the kind of dismal verse which reflects his own state of mind. She advises him to broaden his reading with works calculated to fortify the spirit.

Next morning Anne and Henrietta go down to walk by the sea before breakfast. Louisa and Wentworth meet them and as they stroll back to their inn together they pass a stranger in mourning who looks admiringly at Anne. Wentworth notices the glance. Back at the inn, Anne almost runs into this same man in a passage; and during breakfast the whole party sees him leave in a carriage. Wentworth learns from a waiter that the gentleman is their widowed cousin William Walter Elliot, heir to their father's title. He is on his way to Bath.

After breakfast the Harvilles and Captain Benwick call for the party and they all set off for a walk. Harville talks to Anne about his sister's death and Benwick's grief, and thanks her for her kindness to the young man. It is a windy day and they decide to take the less-exposed way by the sea wall, Captain and Mrs Harville leaving them as they pass their house. The rest go down the few steep steps to the lower walk, except Louisa, who is accustomed to being 'jumped' from stiles by Wentworth on their walks. Now she insists, against his advice, on jumping from the wall into his arms. The sensation pleases Louisa so much that she runs back up the steps, jumps again before he is quite ready, and knocks herself unconscious.

Louisa is carried back to the Harvilles' house, where a surgeon, fetched by Benwick, examines her. She is uninjured except for concussion, with good prospects of recovery. It is arranged that Mary and Charles Musgrove stay behind to nurse her, while Henrietta, Wentworth and Anne return to Uppercross with the bad news. Wentworth's obvious distress and self-reproach for the accident move Anne. After delivering the girls safely to Uppercross he returns to Lyme, where Mrs Harville, Charles and Mary nurse Louisa slowly back to health. Charles Hayter takes it upon himself to travel daily to Lyme for news of her progress.

It is time for Anne to end her visit to Uppercross and go to stay with Lady Russell at Kellynch Lodge. The Musgroves beg her to stay, but she wishes for some peace after all the upsets of the past weeks. Lady Russell finds her looking much better for her brief holiday and the sea air. Both are embarrassed at the certain prospect of Wentworth visiting his sister, Mrs Croft, at the hall. Lady Russell hears Anne's news, and her belief that Wentworth and Louisa are firmly attached, with 'angry pleasure' and 'pleased contempt, that the man who at twenty-three had seemed to understand something of the value of an Anne Elliot should, eight years afterwards, be charmed by a Louisa Musgrove.'

Lady Russell and Anne call on Admiral and Mrs Croft and are relieved to hear that Wentworth intends remaining in Lyme. Charles and Mary Musgrove, now back at Uppercross, drive over to see Anne, and Mary tells her that Captain Benwick had been most disconcerted to learn that Anne did not live at Uppercross where he might see her. He evidently admires Anne a great deal and seems to be recovering from his melancholia.

Anne and Lady Russell now leave for Bath to join Sir Walter Elliot and Anne's elder sister, Elizabeth. At their lodgings in Camden Place, Sir Walter and Elizabeth do nothing but talk of the social delights of Bath, and Anne marvels that the master of

Kellynch Hall can feel so proud of these humbler surroundings. She learns that William Elliot has been in Bath a fortnight, has been forgiven for not marrying Elizabeth so many years ago, and is a constant caller:

They had not a fault to find in him. He had explained away all the appearance of neglect on his own side. It had originated in misapprehension entirely. He had never had an idea of throwing himself off; he had feared that he was thrown off, but knew not why; and delicacy had kept him silent. Upon the hint of having spoken disrespectfully or carelessly of the family, and the family honours, he was quite indignant. He, who had ever boasted of being an Elliot, and whose feelings, as to connection, were only too strict to suit the unfeudal tone of the present day! He was astonished, indeed! But his character and general conduct must refute it. He could refer Sir Walter to all who knew him; and, certainly, the pains he had been taking on this, the first opportunity of reconciliation, to be restored to the footing of a relation and heir-presumptive, was a strong proof of his opinions on the subject.

The circumstances of his marriage too were found to admit of much extenuation. This was an article not to be entered on by himself; but a very intimate friend of his, a Colonel Wallis, a highly respectable man, perfectly the gentleman, (and not an ill-looking man, Sir Walter added) who was living in very good style in Marlborough Buildings, and had, at his own particular request, been admitted to their acquaintance through Mr. Elliot, had mentioned one or two things relative to the marriage, which made a material difference in the discredit of it.

Colonel Wallis had known Mr. Elliot long, had been well acquainted also with his wife, had perfectly understood the whole story. She was certainly not a woman of family, but well educated, accomplished, rich, and excessively in love with his friend. There had been the charm. She had sought him. Without that attraction, not all her money would have tempted Elliot, and Sir Walter was, moreover, assured of her having been a very fine woman. Here was a great deal to soften the business. A very fine woman, with a large fortune, in love with him! Sir Walter seemed to admit it as complete apology, and though Elizabeth could not see the circumstance in quite so favourable a light, she allowed it be a great extenuation.

It would seem that Mr Elliot is hoping to marry Elizabeth after all, as a second wife. Her friend Mrs Clay is all in favour of the match, and, when Elliot pays a visit that evening, Anne likes him. However, during the days that follow she believes her father to be in love with Mrs Clay, and her dislike for this woman runs apace with her growing admiration for William Elliot. His least agreeable feature in her eyes is his inclination to share the interest of her father and sister in Sir Walter's high connections. Two such personages, the Dowager Viscountess Dalrymple and her daughter, the Hon Miss Carteret, cousins of the Elliot family, arrive in Bath. Sir Walter assiduously seeks them out and Anne is ashamed to find herself associated with such superficial, uncultivated people. William Elliot gently chides her, with the assurance that 'Good company requires only birth, education and manners, and with regard to education is not very nice'.

Anne is better pleased to renew the acquaintance of an older schoolfriend, Mrs Smith, formerly Miss Hamilton, an impoverished widow who has come to Bath to recover from rheumatic fever which has left her crippled. Her lodgings are poor, and Sir Walter is not pleased that his daughter should spend time with the widow of one of the five thousand Mr Smiths, whose names are to be encountered everywhere, when his noble relations wish her to attend on them. But Elliot seems touched by her concern for her friend, and now appears more attracted to Anne than to Elizabeth. Lady Russell encourages Anne to favour Elliot, pointing out that their union would in time translate Anne to her late mother's title and position as mistress of Kellynch. The appeal of this prospect momentarily stirs Anne, until she realizes that Elliot would not suit her.

Anne receives a letter from Mary containing the surprising news that Louisa, who is now almost recovered in Lyme, is to marry Captain Benwick. Anne wonders about Wentworth's reaction to the engagement, since he had seemed to favour Louisa so much himself, and questions Admiral Croft, who is in Bath on a visit with his wife; he assures her that Wentworth has shown no resentment.

Wentworth himself has arrived in Bath, and he and Anne meet

by accident in a shop. He asks politely after Uppercross and the
Musgroves, and offers her his umbrella since it is raining; but
Elliot arrives and escorts her away. Anne and Wentworth see
each other again next morning, when she is out walking with
Lady Russell. The latter still disapproves of him and pretends
not to have noticed him:

'You will wonder,' said she, 'what has been fixing my eye so long; but
I was looking after some window-curtains, which Lady Alicia and Mrs.
Frankland were telling me of last night. They described the drawing-
room window-curtains of one of the houses on this side of the way, and
this part of the street, as being the handsomest and best hung of any in
Bath, but could not recollect the exact number, and I have been trying
to find out which it could be; but I confess I can see no curtains here-
abouts that answer their description.'

Sir Walter Elliot, Anne, Elizabeth and Mrs Clay, accompanied
by the Dalrymples, attend a social evening at the assembly rooms.
Wentworth appears and talks to Anne about the engagement of
Benwick and Louisa. It is clear that he genuinely wishes them
well; and it is also clear that his regard for Anne is growing.
Later that evening he appears jealous of Elliot's attentions to
Anne and leaves the gathering. Next morning Anne goes to tell
her friend Mrs Smith about these developments. Mrs Smith had
believed Anne to be fond of Mr Elliot, but when enlightened, she
admits her relief. She has bitter knowledge of his true character,
and spares Anne none of it:

'I think you ought to be made acquainted with Mr. Elliot's real
character. Though I fully believe that, at present, you have not the
smallest intention of accepting him, there is no saying what may happen.
You might, some time or other, be differently affected towards him.
Hear the truth, therefore, now, while you are unprejudiced. Mr. Elliot is
a man without heart or conscience; a designing, wary, cold-blooded
being, who thinks only of himself; who, for his own interest or ease,
would be guilty of any cruelty, or any treachery, that could be per-
petrated without risk of his general character. He has no feeling for
others. Those whom he has been the chief cause of leading into ruin, he

can neglect and desert without the smallest compunction. He is totally beyond the reach of any sentiment of justice or compassion. Oh! he is black at heart, hollow and black!'

Anne's astonished air, and exclamation of wonder, made her pause, and in a calmer manner she added,

'My expressions startle you. You must allow for an injured, angry woman. But I will try to command myself. I will not abuse him. I will only tell you what I have found him. Facts shall speak. He was the intimate friend of my dear husband, who trusted and loved him, and thought him as good as himself. The intimacy had been formed before our marriage. I found them most intimate friends; and I, too, became excessively pleased with Mr. Elliot, and entertained the highest opinion of him. At nineteen, you know, one does not think very seriously, but Mr. Elliot appeared to be quite as good as others, and much more agreeable than most others, and we were almost always together. We were principally in town, living in very good style. He was then the inferior in circumstances, he was then the poor one; he had chambers in the Temple, and it was as much as he could do to support the appearance of a gentleman. He had always a home with us whenever he chose it; he was always welcome; he was like a brother. My poor Charles, who had the finest, most generous spirit in the world, would have divided his last farthing with him; and I know that his purse was open to him; I know that he often assisted him.'

'This must have been about that very period of Mr. Elliot's life,' said Anne, 'which has always excited my particular curiosity. It must have been about the same time that he became known to my father and sister. I never knew him myself, I only heard of him, but there was a something in his conduct then with regard to my father and sister, and afterwards in the circumstances of his marriage, which I never could quite reconcile with present times. It seemed to announce a different sort of man.'

'I know it all, I know it all,' cried Mrs. Smith. 'He had been introduced to Sir Walter and your sister before I was acquainted with him, but I heard him speak of them for ever. I know he was invited and encouraged, and I know he did not choose to go. I can satisfy you, perhaps, on points which you would little expect; and as to his marriage, I knew all about it at the time. I was privy to all the fors and againsts, I was the friend to whom he confided his hopes and plans, and though I did not know his wife previously, (her inferior situation in society, indeed, rendered that impossible) yet I knew her all her life afterwards, or, at least, till within the last two years of her life, and can answer any question you wish to put.'

'Nay,' said Anne, 'I have no particular enquiry to make about her. I have always understood they were not a happy couple. But I should like to know why, at that time of his life, he should slight my father's acquaintance as he did. My father was certainly disposed to take very kind and proper notice of him. Why did Mr. Elliot draw back?'

'Mr. Elliot,' replied Mrs. Smith, 'at that period of his life, had one object in view – to make his fortune, and by a rather quicker process than the law. He was determined to make it by marriage. He was determined, at least, not to mar it by an imprudent marriage; and I know it was his belief, (whether justly or not, of course I cannot decide) that your father and sister, in their civilities and invitations, were designing a match between the heir and the young lady; and it was impossible that such a match should have answered his ideas of wealth and independance. That was his motive for drawing back, I can assure you. He told me the whole story. He had no concealments with me.'

She adds that Elliot had brought about the Smiths' ruin by encouraging their natural extravagance. Anne returns to the Camden Place lodgings to tell Lady Russell what she has learned, and is heartily relieved to hear that Elliot is on his way from Bath to visit friends in the country. She now recognizes Mrs Clay's hypocrisy in championing him, and the deception she is practising on Sir Walter and Elizabeth.

Mary and Charles Musgrove arrive with Mrs Musgrove, Henrietta and Captain Harville. Anne learns that Charles Hayter has been promised a good living only twenty-five miles from Uppercross and that he and Henrietta are to marry soon after Louisa. Visiting the Musgroves, Anne finds Wentworth among the company, but his manner is disturbingly distant. Mary calls Anne's attention to Mrs Clay, talking to Elliot in the street below. Anne is astonished, since Elliot should by this time be well away from Bath, and later confronts Mrs Clay, who, however, has a ready explanation:

'Oh dear! very true. Only think, Miss Elliot, to my great surprise I met with Mr. Elliot in Bath-street! I was never more astonished. He turned back and walked with me to the Pump-yard. He had been prevented setting off for Thornberry, but I really forget by what – for I was in a hurry, and could not much attend, and I can only answer for his being determined not to be delayed in his return. He wanted to know how early he might be admitted to-morrow. He was full of 'to-morrow;' and it is very evident that I have been full of it too ever since I entered the house, and learnt the extension of your play, and all that had happened, or my seeing him could never have gone so entirely out of my head.'

Next day Anne again visits the Musgroves. Harville and Wentworth are writing letters. The former tells Anne of his displeasure that Benwick should become engaged again so soon after his first fiancée's death. She gives him a quiet lesson in the difference between the sexes where constancy of affection is concerned:

'We certainly do not forget you, so soon as you forget us. It is, perhaps, our fate rather than our merit. We cannot help ourselves. We live at home, quiet, confined, and our feelings prey upon us. You are forced on exertion. You have always a profession, pursuits, business of some sort or other, to take you back into the world immediately, and continual occupation and change soon weaken impressions.'

'Granting your assertion that the world does all this so soon for me, (which, however, I do not think I shall grant) it does not apply to Benwick. He has not been forced upon any exertion. The peace turned him on shore at the very moment, and he has been living with us, in our little family-circle, ever since.'

'True,' said Anne, 'very true; I did not recollect; but what shall we say now, Captain Harville? If the change be not from outward circumstances, it must be from within; it must be nature, man's nature, which has done the business for Captain Benwick.'

'No, no, it is not man's nature. I will not allow it to be more man's nature than woman's to be inconstant and forget those they do love, or have loved. I believe the reverse. I believe in a true analogy between our bodily frames and our mental; and that as our bodies are the strongest, so are our feelings; capable of bearing most rough usage, and riding out the heaviest weather.'

'Your feelings may be the strongest,' replied Anne, 'but the same spirit of analogy will authorise me to assert that ours are the most tender. Man is more robust than woman, but he is not longer-lived; which exactly explains my view of the nature of their attachments. Nay, it would be too hard upon you, if it were otherwise. You have difficulties, and privations, and dangers enough to struggle with. You are always labouring and toiling, exposed to every risk and hardship. Your home, country, friends, all quitted. Neither time, nor health, nor life, to be called your own. It would be too hard, indeed' (with a faltering voice) 'if woman's feelings were to be added to all this.'

'We shall never agree upon this question' – Captain Harville was beginning to say, when a slight noise called their attention to Captain Wentworth's hitherto perfectly quiet division of the room. It was nothing more than that his pen had fallen down, but Anne was startled at finding him nearer than she had supposed, and half inclined to suspect that the pen had only fallen, because he had been occupied by them, striving to catch sounds, which yet she did not think he could have caught.

'Have you finished your letter?' said Captain Harville.

'Not quite, a few lines more. I shall have done in five minutes.'

'There is no hurry on my side. I am only ready whenever you are. – I am in very good anchorage here,' (smiling at Anne) 'well supplied, and want for nothing. – No hurry for a signal at all. – Well, Miss Elliot,' (lowering his voice) 'as I was saying, we shall never agree I suppose upon this point. No man and woman would, probably. But let me observe that all histories are against you, all stories, prose and verse. If I had such a memory as Benwick, I could bring you fifty quotations in a moment on my side the argument, and I do not think I ever opened a book in my life which had not something to say upon woman's inconstancy. Songs and proverbs, all talk of woman's fickleness. But perhaps you will say, these were all written by men.'

'Perhaps I shall. – Yes, yes, if you please, no reference to examples in books. Men have had every advantage of us in telling their own story. Education has been theirs in so much higher a degree; the pen has been in their hands. I will not allow books to prove any thing.'

'But how shall we prove any thing?'

'We never shall. We never can expect to prove any thing upon such a point. It is a difference of opinion which does not admit of proof. We each begin probably with a little bias towards our own sex, and upon that bias build every circumstance in favour of it which has occurred within our own circle; many of which circumstances (perhaps those very cases which strike us the most) may be precisely such as cannot be brought forward without betraying a confidence, or in some respect saying what should not be said.'

'Ah!' cried Captain Harville, in a tone of strong feeling, 'if I could but make you comprehend what a man suffers when he takes a last look at his wife and children, and watches the boat that he has sent them off in, as long as it is in sight, and then turns away and says, "God knows whether we ever meet again!" And then, if I could convey to you the glow of his soul when he does see them again; when, coming back after a twelve-months' absence perhaps, and obliged to put into another port, he calculates how soon it be possible to get them there, pretending to deceive himself, and saying, "They cannot be here till such a day," but all the while hoping for them twelve hours sooner, and seeing them arrive at last, as if Heaven had given them wings, by many hours sooner still! If I could explain to you all this, and all that a man can bear and do, and glories to do for the sake of these treasures of his existence! I speak, you know, only of such men as have hearts!' pressing his own with emotion.

'Oh!' cried Anne eagerly, 'I hope I do justice to all that is felt by you, and by those who resemble you. God forbid that I should undervalue the warm and faithful feelings of any of my fellow-creatures! I should deserve utter contempt if I dared to suppose that true attachment and constancy were known only by woman. No, I believe you capable of every thing great and good in your married lives. I believe you equal to every important exertion, and to every domestic forbearance, so long as – if I may be allowed the expression, so long as you have an object. I mean, while the woman you love lives, and lives for you. All the privilege I claim for my own sex (it is not a very enviable one, you need not covet it) is that of loving longest, when existence or when hope is gone.'

The men leave the room, but moments later Wentworth hurries back and gives Anne a letter before departing rapidly again. She reads: 'You pierce my soul. I am half agony, half hope. Tell me not that I am too late, that such precious feelings are gone for ever. I offer myself to you again with a heart even more your own that when you almost broke it eight years ago.'

Before Anne can recover her wits the Musgroves are back again and she has to pretend indisposition to get away from them. Charles offers to escort her to her lodgings but they meet Wentworth and Charles hands her over to him. On the way to

Camden Place, Wentworth tells Anne of his emotional struggles, the social entanglements, his jealousy, his remorse, his disfavour in the eyes of Lady Russell and his mistrust of Elliot.

Sir Walter and Elizabeth have no objection to Anne and Wentworth becoming engaged, and even Lady Russell admits she had been wrong about his qualities and intentions. Elliot leaves Bath and is last heard of living with Mrs Clay in London. Wentworth helps Mrs Smith to recover her late husband's property in the West Indies. Anne contentedly assumes her position as the wife of a sailor who loves her tenderly and truly, but who may be taken from her yet again, should war resume.

SANDITON

THE last prose work Jane Austen started to write, in the year of her death, remains her equivalent of Dickens's *The Mystery of Edwin Drood*, in the sense of the novel begun, with characters of recognizable traits already on stage and their relationships established; yet with no certain idea of the author's intended conclusion. I have suggested in the introduction to *Persuasion* that if that work, as has been propounded, was written under the influence of approaching death, *Sanditon*, which immediately followed it, presents a distinct contrast. It is very bright, and amusing, and, perhaps because the predominant figure in the completed portion is a property developer, seems to relate particularly to our own times. Certainly, there is nothing of the shadow of death over it, and there is just enough information about the characters and probable plot development to afford scholars plenty of scope for speculation. The passing reference above to Dickens may perhaps be justified on other grounds: like his *Drood*, Sanditon represents an entirely new direction for Jane (though *Drood* may be considered as Dickens's most mature writing, while *Sanditon* can hardly be so described). But, *Sanditon* departs further in style from the influence of eighteenth-century traditions, and, in its pace and the more down-to-earth materialism of Mr Palmer and the hypochondria of his brothers and sisters, it is moving towards that of Dickens. Dickens was already alive when Jane Austen died, and *Sketches by Boz* and the first parts of *Pickwick Papers* were published less than two decades later.

Sanditon was given its title by her family; she herself had thought of calling it *The Brothers*. It was first published in 1925 by the Clarendon Press, Oxford.

. . . .

A Gentleman & Lady travelling from Tunbridge towards that part of the Sussex Coast which lies between Hastings & E. Bourne, being induced by Business to quit the high road, & attempt a very rough Lane, were overturned in toiling up it's long ascent half rock, half sand.

The driver of the unfortunate vehicle never had wanted to take this route, but the gentleman had insisted. The lane dwindles to an uneven track, and, almost inevitably, the carriage pitches on to its side. Luckily, it has been moving so slowly that its occupants are only slightly bruised and shaken, but on alighting the gentleman chances to sprain an ankle.

He bears the injury cheerfully enough, though, and confidently asks the little group of men, who come hurrying from a nearby hayfield, that the local surgeon be fetched. The farmer, Mr Heywood, assures him that there is no such thing as a surgeon in the area. The gentleman is incredulous: he has come all this way especially to interview the surgeon of Willingden. Is not this Willingden? It is. Then there must be a surgeon – and the gentleman produces newspaper advertisements placed by the surgeon of Willingden to the effect that his partnership is being dissolved and he is seeking a new post. The misunderstanding is soon revealed: there is another Willingden, seven miles away, 'quite down in the Weald. And *we* Sir – (speaking rather proudly) are not in the Weald.'

Thus Thomas Parker of Trafalgar House, Sanditon, and his wife Mary make the acquaintance of the Heywood family; for ladies are soon on the spot and the Parkers are conducted to the farmhouse for refreshment and some homely remedies for the injured ankle. Their stay there proves longer than anticipated: both the carriage and Mr Parker's ankle are damaged quite badly. It is two complete weeks before it is possible for the journey to be resumed, by which time the Parkers and the Heywoods have come to know and respect one another.

The Heywoods have heard of Sanditon, which is on the coast not very far away, but have never been there. As contented countryfolk, with a large family, they have neither the means nor the incentive ever to go far from home. Thomas Parker, though, knows all about Sanditon, and will sing its virtues at the slightest encouragement:

'Such a place as Sanditon Sir, I may say was wanted, was called for. – Nature had marked it out – had spoken in most intelligible Characters – The finest, purest Sea Breeze on the Coast – acknowledged to be so – Excellent Bathing – fine hard sand – Deep Water 10 yards from the Shore – no Mud – no Weeds – no slimey rocks – Never was there a place more palpably designed by Nature for the resort of the Invalid – the very Spot which Thousands seemed in need of. – The most desirable distance from London! One complete, measured mile nearer than East Bourne. Only conceive Sir, the advantage of saving a whole Mile, in a long Journey.'

He is more than an enthusiast: he is a developer and an entrepreneur, set upon transforming Sanditon from an unpretentious village into a small, fashionable bathing resort. He is succeeding well; but elderly and infirm people feel more secure about visiting seaside resorts if they can be sure of any necessary medical attention. Sanditon at present has no doctor, which is why Mr Parker has brought his wife on this abortive journey to try to secure one.

The simple care administered by the Heywoods proves all the treatment Mr Parker himself needs, however, and at length the couple are fit to leave. Mr Parker presses the family to take advantage of some reciprocal hospitality at Sanditon, which he can guarantee will benefit even them:

Sanditon was a second Wife & 4 Children to him – hardly less Dear – & certainly more engrossing. – He could talk of it for ever. – It had indeed the highest claims; – not only those of Birthplace, Property, and Home, – it was his Mine, his Lottery, his Speculation & his Hobby Horse; his Occupation his Hope & his Futurity . . . He held it indeed as certain, that no person could be really well, no person, (however upheld for the present by fortuitous aids of exercise & spirits in a semblance of Health) could be really in a state of secure & permanent Health without spending at least 6 weeks by the Sea every year. – The Sea air & Sea Bathing together were nearly infallible, one or the other of them being a match for every Disorder, of the Stomach, the Lungs or the Blood; They were anti-spasmodic, anti-pulmonary, anti-sceptic, anti-bilious & anti-rheumatic. Nobody could catch cold by the Sea, Nobody wanted

appetite by the Sea, Nobody wanted Spirits, Nobody wanted Strength. –
They were healing, softing, relaxing – fortifying & bracing – seemingly
just as was wanted – sometimes one, sometimes the other. – If the Sea
breeze failed, the Sea-Bath was the certain corrective; – & where Bathing
disagreed, the Sea Breeze alone was evidently designed by Nature for the
cure.

Mr and Mrs Heywood are not to be persuaded; but while they
prefer to stay at home themselves, they are broadminded enough
to wish their children to go out into the world, and readily agree
to one of their daughters travelling back to Sanditon with Mr
and Mrs Parker. Charlotte is the chosen one. She is twenty-two,
the eldest of the girls and the one who has been most helpful to
the Parkers and got to know them best. She takes an affectionate
farewell of her family; Mr Heywood makes Mr Parker the parting promise that he will send anyone to Sanditon who might
happen to ask his advice about a holiday resort, and, though he
will never go there himself, will undertake never to spend even
as little as five shillings at its rival, Brinshore.

The journey begins. Mr Parker talks all the way to Charlotte
about the delights awaiting her; but, as they pass through a
sheltered dip within two miles of the sea, she indicates a pleasant,
medium-sized house, well set amongst garden, orchard and
meadows, and asks to whom it belongs. Mr Parker is pleased at
her discernment: it is the house his forefathers had owned, where
he himself had been born, and where his wife and he had lived
until their new home in Sanditon had been ready two years ago,
It is now lived in by his chief tenant, Mr Hillier. 'It was always a
very comfortable house,' Mrs Parker remarks wistfully, watching
it recede, 'And such a nice garden – such an excellent garden.'
Her husband has no use for such sentiments:

'Yes, my Love, but *that* we may be said to carry with us. – *It* supplies
us, as before, with all the fruit & vegetables we want; & we have in fact
all the comfort of an excellent Kitchen Garden, without the constant
Eyesore of its formalities; or the yearly nuisance of its decaying vege-
tation. – Who can endure a Cabbage Bed in October?' 'Oh! dear – yes. –

We are quite as well off for Gardenstuff as ever we were – for if it is for-
got to be brought at any time, we can always buy what we want at
Sanditon-House. – The Gardiner there, is glad enough to supply us. –
But it was a nice place for the Children to run about in. So shady in
Summer!' 'My dear, we shall have shade enough on the Hill & more
than enough in the course of a very few years; – The Growth of my
Plantations is a general astonishment. In the mean while we have the
Canvas Awning, which gives us the most complete comfort within
doors – & you can get a Parasol at Whitby's for little Mary at any time, or
a large Bonnet at Jebb's – and as for the Boys, I must say I would rather
them run about in the Sunshine than not. I am sure we agree my dear, in
wishing our Boys to be as hardy as possible.' – 'Yes indeed, I am sure we
do – & I will get Mary a little Parasol, which will make her as proud as
can be. How Grave she will walk about with it, and fancy herself quite
a little Woman. – Oh! I have not the smallest doubt of our being a great
deal better off where we are now. If we any of us want to bathe, we have
not a quarter of a mile to go. – But you know, (still looking back) one
loves to look at an old friend, at a place where one has been happy. –
The Hilliers did not seem to feel the Storms last Winter at all. – I remember seeing Mrs. Hillier after one of those dreadful Nights, when *we* had
been literally rocked in our bed, and she did not seem at all aware of the
Wind being anything more than common.' 'Yes, yes – that's likely
enough. *We* have all the Grandeur of the Storm, with less real danger,
because the Wind meeting with nothing to oppose or confine it around
our House, simply rages & passes on – while down in this Gutter –
nothing is known of the state of the Air, below the Tops of the Trees –
and the Inhabitants may be taken totally unawares, by one of those
dreadful Currents which do more mischief in a Valley, when they *do*
arise than an open Country ever experiences in the heaviest Gale.

They leave the house behind and pass through the old village
from which the resort of Sanditon takes its name:

The Village contained little more than Cottages, but the Spirit of the
day had been caught, as Mr. P. observed with delight to Charlotte, &
two or three of the best of them were smartened up with a white Curtain
& "Lodgings to let" – , and farther on, in the little Green Court of an
old Farm House, two Females in elegant white were actually to be seen
with their books & camp stools – and in turning the corner of the

Baker's shop, the sound of a Harp might be heard through the upper Casement. – Such sights & sounds were highly Blissful to Mr. P. – Not that he had any personal concern in the success of the Village itself; for considering it as too remote from the Beach, he had done nothing there – but it was a most valuable proof of the increasing fashion of the place altogether. If the *Village* could attract, the Hill might be nearly full. – He anticipated an amazing Season. – At the same time last year, (late in July) there had not been a single Lodger in the Village! – nor did he remember any during the whole Summer, excepting one family of children who came from London for sea air after the hooping Cough, and whose Mother would not let them be nearer the shore for fear of their tumbling in. – 'Civilization, Civilization indeed! – cried Mr. P. –, delighted. – Look my dear Mary – Look at William Heeley's windows. – Blue Shoes, & nankin Boots! – Who would have expected such a sight at a Shoemaker's in old Sanditon! – This is new within the Month. There was no blue Shoe when we passed this way a month ago. – Glorious indeed! – Well, I think I *have* done something in my Day.

The horses labour up a steep hill, and Sanditon 'proper' begins. Mr Parker is as excited as a boy, noting every detail, every change. He frowns a little at the number of 'Lodgings to Let' bills in the windows, and at the comparatively small number of carriages and strollers about at a time of day when visitors should be 'returning from their Airings to dinner', but quickly reassures himself that many are doubtless on the Sands and the Terrace.

Trafalgar House itself is reached. (Mr Parker has remarked to Charlotte that he almost wishes he had called it Waterloo, to be more in keeping with the times, though the latter name is in reserve for a little crescent he has in mind to have built.) There is a joyous reunion with the four little Parkers; and, at journey's end Charlotte finds herself in her apartment in the elegant new house, 'standing at her ample Venetian window, & looking over the miscellaneous foreground of unfinished Buildings, waving Linen & tops of Houses, to the Sea, dancing & sparkling in Sunshine & Freshness.'

As they await dinner that evening, Mr Parker deplores the failure of his gadabout younger brother, Sidney, in writing to him after hearing of the accident at Willingden. But there are brief condolences from Susan, Diana and Arthur, his sisters and youngest brother, a sickly trio preoccupied with their own ailments, whom he has tried in vain to persuade to come to Sanditon. Diana speaks for them:

'As for getting to Sanditon myself, it is quite an Impossibility. I greive to say that I dare not attempt it, but my feelings tell me too plainly that in my present state, the Sea air would probably be the death of me. – And neither of my dear Companions will leave me, or I would promote their going down to you for a fortnight. But in truth, I doubt whether Susan's nerves would be equal to the effort. She has been suffering much from the Headache and Six Leaches a day for 10 days together relieved her so little that we thought it right to change our measures – and being convinced on examination that much of the Evil lay in her Gum, I persuaded her to attack the disorder there. She has accordingly had 3 Teeth drawn, & is decidedly better, but her Nerves are a good deal deranged. She can only speak in a whisper – and fainted away twice this morning on poor Arthur's trying to suppress a cough. He, I am happy to say is tolerably well – tho' more languid than I like – & I fear for his Liver.'

However they have done their best for Sanditon by arranging for two large families, 'one a rich West Indian from Surry, the other, a most respectable Girls Boarding School, or Academy, from Camberwell', to come there.

After dinner Mr Parker cannot wait to whisk the ladies off for a walk round the deserted town and a visit to the library, presided over by Mrs Whitby, whom they find 'reading one of her own Novels, for want of Employment'. He is disappointed by the List of Subscribers which is undistinguished and shorter than he had hoped, although it is headed by the local *grande dame*, Lady Denham, a twice-widowed vigorous woman of seventy, who lives at Sanditon House with a young 'poor cousin', Miss Clara Brereton, a sweet, pretty girl who has found growing favour in the eyes of Lady Denham and Sanditon folk in general. Taking a turn on the cliff, the Trafalgar House party meets these very ladies. Charlotte recognizes Lady Denham's forthright, shrewd but amiable, qualities, and finds that Mr Parker has underestimated considerably Miss Brereton's attributes: she is as beautiful as any fictional heroine.

Lady Denham proves to be as keen for Sanditon to prosper as is Mr Parker, but his notion of introducing a surgeon shocks her:

'Here have I lived 70 good years in the world & never took Physic above twice – and never saw the face of a Doctor in all my Life, on my *own* account. – And I verily believe if my poor dear Sir Harry had never seen one neither, he would have been alive now. – Ten fees, one after another, did the Man take who sent *him* out of the World. – I beseech you Mr. Parker, no Doctors here.'

Visitors call at Trafalgar House next day. Among them are Sir Edward Denham, Bart, nephew of Lady Denham's last husband, and his sister Esther. Miss Denham strikes Charlotte as rather proud and discontented, but she finds Sir Edward fine-looking and noticeably attentive to herself. A morning stroll on the Terrace being *de rigueur* for the better folk of Sanditon, the Trafalgar House and Sanditon House people soon encounter each other again, whereupon Sir Edward at once places himself beside Charlotte and proceeds to wax poetic about the grandeur of the elements:

She could not but think him a Man of Feeling – till he began to stagger her by the number of his Quotations, & the bewilderment of some of his sentences. – 'Do you remember, said he, Scott's beautiful Lines on the Sea? – Oh! what a description they convey! – They are never out of my Thoughts when I walk here. – That Man who can read them unmoved must have the nerves of an Assassin! – Heaven defend me from meeting such a Man un-armed.' – 'What description do you mean? – said Charlotte. I remember none at this moment, of the Sea, in either of Scott's Poems.' – 'Do you not indeed? – Nor can I exactly recall the beginning at this moment – But – you cannot have forgotten his description of Woman. –

"Oh! Woman in our Hours of Ease – "

Delicious! Delicious! – Had he written nothing more, he would have been Immortal. And then again, that unequalled, unrivalled address to Parental affection –

> "Some feelings are to Mortals given
> With less of Earth in them than Heaven" etc.

But while we are on the subject of Poetry, what think you Miss H. of Burns Lines to his Mary? – Oh! there is Pathos to madden one! – if ever there was a Man who *felt*, it was Burns. – Montgomery has all the Fire of Poetry, Wordsworth has the true soul of it – Campbell in his pleasures of Hope has touched the extreme of our Sensations – "Like Angel's visits, few & far between." Can you conceive any thing more subduing, more melting, more fraught with the deep Sublime than that Line? – But Burns – I confess my sence of his Pre-eminence Miss H. – If Scott *has* a fault, it is the want of Passion. – Tender, Elegant, Descriptive – but *Tame*. – The Man who cannot do justice to the attributes of Woman is my contempt. – Sometimes indeed a flash of feeling seems to irradiate him – as in the Lines we were speaking of – "Oh! Woman in our hours of Ease" –. But Burns is always on fire. – His Soul was the Altar in which lovely Woman sat enshrined, his Spirit truly breathed the immortal Incence which is her Due.' 'I have read several of Burn's Poems with great delight, said Charlotte as soon as she had time to speak, but I am not poetic enough to separate a Man's Poetry entirely from his Character; – & poor Burns's known Irregularities, greatly interrupt my enjoyment of his Lines. – I have difficulty in depending on the *Truth* of his Feelings as a Lover. I have not faith in the *sincerity* of the affections of a Man of his Description. He felt & he wrote & he forgot.' 'Oh! no no – exclaimed Sir Edward in an extasy. He was all ardour & Truth! – His Genius & his Susceptibilities might lead him into some Aberrations – But who is perfect? – it were Hyper-criticism, it were Pseudo-philosophy to expect from the soul of high toned Genius, the grovellings of a common mind. The Coruscations of Talent, elicited by impassioned feeling in the breast of Man, are perhaps incompatible with some of the prosaic Decencies of Life; – nor can you, loveliest Miss Heywood – speaking with an air of deep sentiment) – nor can any Woman be a fair Judge of what a Man may be propelled to say, write or do, by the sovereign impulses of illimitable Ardour.' This was very fine; – but if Charlotte understood it at all, not very moral – & being moreover by no means pleased with his extraordinary stile of compliment, she gravely answered 'I really know nothing of the matter. – This is a charming day. The Wind I fancy must be Southerly.'

Lady Denham has observed Sir Edward's eagerness to monopolize Charlotte. She makes a point of lingering behind with the girl after the others have walked on, and gives her to understand that, while her nephew is handsome and much addicted to paying compliments to young ladies, he will need to marry an heiress. Charlotte surprises and mollifies her by agreeing. Lady Denham continues that Edward's sister, too, must marry well. Charlotte's initial amusement changes to suppressed indignation at the old lady's autocracy.

Lady Denham and Charlotte are rejoined by the others. Sir Edward immediately resumes his flow of compliments and erudite display. But she now knows what he is about:

Clara saw through him, & had not the least intention of being seduced – but she bore with him patiently enough to confirm the sort of attachment which her personal Charms had raised. – A greater degree of discouragement indeed would have not affected Sir Edward –. He was armed against the highest pitch of Disdain and Aversion. – If she could not be won by affection, he must carry her off. He knew his Business. – Already had he had many Musings on the Subject. If he *were* constrained so to act, he must naturally wish to strike out something new, to exceed those who had gone before him – and he felt a strong curiosity to ascertain whether the Neighbourhood of Tombuctoo might not afford some solitary House adapted for Clara's reception; – but the Expence alas! of Measures in that masterly style was ill-suited to his Purse, & Prudence obliged him to prefer the quietest sort of ruin & disgrace for the object of his Affections, to the more renowned. –

Returning to Trafalgar House one day soon afterwards, Charlotte reaches the door at the same time as another lady, who has overtaken her briskly from behind. She is astonished to learn that this is the ailing Miss Diana Parker, come to tell her brother that she, her brother Arthur and sister Susan, at great risk to what remains of their constitutions, have struggled to Sanditon for a stay in lodgings:

'Susan has born it wonderfully. She had not a wink of sleep either the night before we set out, or last night at Chichester, and as this is not so common with her as with *me*, I have had a thousand fears for her – but she had kept up wonderfully. – had no Hysterics of consequence till we came within sight of poor old Sanditon – and the attack was not very violent – nearly over by the time we reached your Hotel – so that we got her out of the Carriage extremely well, with only Mr. Woodcock's assistance & – when I left her she was directing the Disposal of the Luggage, & helping old Sam uncord the Trunks.'

The three invalids are soon comfortably settled in a terraced house, where, a week after their arrival, the Parkers and Charlotte take tea with them. Charlotte finds them anything but the enfeebled sufferers they regard themselves. But, despite constant talk of symptoms, they seem interested in helping Thomas Parker to find families who can be persuaded to come to Sanditon. Arthur Parker, in particular, fascinates Charlotte. Far from being the puny creature of her imagination, he is a big, red-faced young man, whose preoccupation, besides his health, is his stomach:

He took his own Cocoa from the Tray, – which seemed provided with almost as many Teapots &c as there were persons in company, Miss P. drinking one sort of Herb-Tea & Miss Diana another, & turning completely to the Fire, sat coddling and cooking it to his own satisfaction & toasting some Slices of Bread, brought up ready-prepared in the Toast rack – and till it was all done, she heard nothing of his voice but the murmuring of a few broken sentences of self-approbation & success. – When his Toils were over however, he moved back his Chair into as gallant a Line as ever, & proved that he had not been working only for himself, by his earnest invitation to her to take both Cocoa & Toast. – She was already helped to Tea – which surprised him – so totally self-engrossed he had been. – 'I thought I should have been in time, said he, but cocoa takes a great deal of Boiling.' – 'I am much obliged to you, replied Charlotte – but I *prefer* Tea.' 'Then I will help myself, said he. – A large Dish of rather weak Cocoa every evening, agrees with me better than anything.' It struck her however, as he poured out this rather weak Cocoa, that it came forth in a very fine, dark coloured stream – and at the same moment, his Sisters both crying out – 'Oh! Arthur, you get your

Cocoa stronger & stronger every Evening' –, with Arthur's somewhat conscious reply of '*Tis* rather stronger than it should be tonight' – convinced her that Arthur was by no means so fond of being starved as they could desire, or as he felt proper himself. – He was certainly very happy to turn the conversation on dry Toast, & hear no more of his sisters. – 'I hope you will eat some of this Toast, said he, I reckon myself a very good Toaster; I never burn my Toasts – I never put them too near the Fire at first – & yet, you see, there is not a Corner but what is well browned. – I hope you like dry Toast.' – 'With a reasonable quantity of Butter spread over it, very much – said Charlotte – but not otherwise. –' 'No more do I – said he exceedingly pleased – We think quite alike there. – So far from dry Toast being wholesome, *I* think it a very bad thing for the Stomach. Without a little butter to soften it, it hurts the Coats of the Stomach. I am sure it does. – I will have the pleasure of spreading some for you directly – & afterwards I will spread some for myself. – Very bad indeed for the Coats of the Stomach – but there is no convincing *some* people. – It irritates & acts like a nutmeg grater. –' He could not get command of the Butter however, without a struggle; His Sisters accusing him of eating a great deal too much, & declaring he was not to be trusted; – and he maintaining that he only eat enough to secure the Coats of his Stomach; – & besides, he only wanted it now for Miss Heywood. – Such a plea must prevail, he got the butter & spread away for her with an accuracy of Judgement which at least delighted himself; but when her Toast was done, & he took his own in hand, Charlotte could hardly contain herself as she saw him watching his sisters, while he scrupulously scraped off almost as much butter as he put on, & then seize an odd moment for adding a great dab just before it went into his Mouth. – Certainly, Mr. Arthur P.'s enjoyments in Invalidism were very different from his sisters – by no means so spiritualized. – A good deal of Earthy Dross hung about him. Charlotte could not but suspect him of adopting that line of Life, principally for the indulgence of an indolent Temper & – to be determined on having no Disorders but such as called for warm rooms & good Nourishment.

Unfortunately, the well-intended efforts of the invalid Parkers to procure business for Sanditon result in a misunderstanding. The two large families – the West Indians and the young ladies from Camberwell – prove, on arrival, to be one and the same party, so that Thomas Parker's expectations are halved.

Charlotte has been in Sanditon ten days and still has not seen Sanditon House, Lady Denham's home. Mrs Parker resolves to take her there one morning and they set off on foot. They see a sporty-looking carriage coming smartly along the road, and Mary Parker is delighted to recognize its driver as her brother-in-law, Sidney, who is at the reins, with his servant as passenger. He tells them he has come over from Eastbourne for a few days and will stay in a Sanditon hotel. Arrangements to meet later are made and he drives on, leaving Charlotte with an agreeable impression of his looks and fashionable air.

The two ladies enter the grounds of Sanditon House. Almost at once Charlotte catches a glimpse over a line of palings of 'something White & Womanish in the field on the other side'. Pausing, she is able to observe that it is Miss Clara Brereton, 'seated, apparently very composedly – & Sir Edward Denham by her side. – They were sitting so near each other & appeared so closely engaged in gentle conversation, that Charlotte instantly felt she had nothing to do but to step back again & say not a word. – Privacy was certainly their object.'